James W. Bennett's

uncompromising, challenging books for teens have earned him recognition as one of the nation's leading (and most provocative) novelists for young adults.

His fiction has been used as a curriculum choice at the Jr. High, Sr. High and community college levels.

His 1996 novel, *The Squared Circle*, was named the year's finest by the English Journal and other publications. It was also chosen as one of the 25 best YAs during the past quarter century.

Bennett has served as guest author at **Miami Book Fair International**, featured speaker at **ALAN** and **NCTE**, and as **Writer in Residence** (a program he established) for secondary schools in Illinois. He has also been director for the **Blooming Grove Writers' Conference**.

Books by James W. Bennett

Loopey
to
Beau

A Troubled Author's
Journey with Dogs

JAMES BENNETT

PAGE PUBLISHING, INC.
New York, NY

First originally published by Page Publishing, Inc. 2018

ISBN 978-1-64214-034-7 (Paperback)
ISBN 978-1-64214-035-4 (Digital)

Printed in the United States of America

"To my wife, Judith, who has stood by me through it all."

Author's Note

All the events in this memoir are true, reported precisely as they happened in time, space, and location. I have changed a few names in cases where people are depicted in a negative or mildly negative manner. All other names are real.

Never pass by an animal in need.

—PETA

Loopey

OVER A PERIOD of many years, I'd had, and would have again, experiences involving injured dogs or dogs at risk, in addition to lost neighborhood creatures or those slipping away from their owners. Sometimes I was able to help, other times not. There were happy endings and sad ones.

I don't know how it came about, when I was a child, that I developed a strong affection for dogs and a nearly consuming compassion for those of them that suffered.

That childhood love and compassion would turn out to be a lifetime consumption. I never put my life on the line for any organization, but I have been an animal rights advocate most of my adult life.

My wife, Judie, and I have supported the Humane Society at the local and national level, as well as the ASPCA and PETA. In addition to donating more money than we could afford, I have spent big chunks of time volunteering in various capacities at local shelters. Most of the volunteer work has involved delivering supplies, cleaning crates/cages and/or walking dogs.

As a newspaper journalist, I have written more columns on dogs than my editor appreciates (but tolerates), urged readers to avoid puppy mills, report suspected pet neglect and/or abuse, buy only cage-free eggs, and support organizations that work to alleviate animal suffering wherever it is found.

If I had what I call the "proper" motivation and strength of character, I would be a strict vegetarian, if not a committed vegan. I often avoid eating flesh, but not so often as to make it a way of life.

Sometimes the burger or Kentucky Fried Chicken is the easy way out. Like most people with noble intentions, I find my moral compass gets stuck in place from time to time.

My childhood predisposition to love and seek relief for at-risk dogs, was pretty much my own. I guess it's how I am wired. My parents were very responsible people; they never abused or neglected the dogs that shared in our family life, but neither did they ever seem emotionally drawn to them.

I can't recall any childhood mentor (scoutmaster, teacher, a parent, or a friend) who modeled a love of dogs or an exceptional commitment to their welfare. What I do know is that I can trace my love for these creatures at least as far back as 1950, when I was eight. Even then, I felt concern as well as anxiety if I spotted a stray dog wandering in the rain or running near traffic.

I remember waking up more than once in the middle of the night if I heard a thunderstorm, wondering anxiously if we had accidentally left the family dog outside. I can also remember actually getting out of bed to go downstairs and check.

It was unusual behavior for a child so young, and I would often recall it during therapy years later as one harbinger of a long and often disabling mental illness.

Over all the years, when my sister and I were still youngsters, our family usually had a dog as a pet, and after I was married, my wife, son, and I brought six canines into the family fold. Each was unique. I wish I could say each was also the narrator of a happy story, but that wasn't the case. Some suffered too much and died too soon or got lost and never found their way home. Others suffered but survived. Some brought me a stern measure of guilt. The constant was my love—as well as my wife's—and compassion for all six.

I will say I never attempted to train a dog in any way except for housebreaking. I've never *crated* a dog for this or any other purpose. I've never been a hunter, so I never needed a hunting dog. I've never trained a dog for any competitive event of any kind. I've never attempted to teach one of my canine buddies any tricks. I've never had more than one dog at a time.

I've always let my dogs come to me, bringing what their natures and temperaments inclined them to be. And then found a way to thoroughly enjoy what they brought to our relationship. They were all pets that enriched my life by their love and companionship. Each was unique and uniquely endearing. My attachment to each one was deep and abiding. I will remember with joy (and some sorrow) each one of them until the day I die.

THE FIRST family dog I can remember was named Loopey. He was a midsize Border Collie mix, with standard black-and-white border Collie markings. My memories of him are piecemeal at best, most of them occurring about 1950, when I was a very young child. I don't remember how my parents got him or why or where he'd come from. I don't remember how long he'd been part of the family. Maybe Mom and Dad got him for me, thinking a young boy needed a canine partner growing up, but I don't know.

Loopey (as I remember him) was never a house pet. He ate and slept inside but otherwise spent most of his time outdoors. It was common for dog owners in Monticello to allow their dogs to wander around town, but they always found their way back home in time for supper. That was Loopey's lifestyle, but like most dogs, he spent a good deal of time in his own yard. I can remember how he charged enthusiastically to greet us when we came home.

Unfortunately, he also charged enthusiastically after cars that passed along the street. There were no busy streets in Monticello, but Main Street had more traffic than others. Loopey couldn't seem to resist running after them, barking at a rear wheel, then pulling up after twenty yards or so before jogging back into the front yard.

If my dad happened to be home at the time and caught him in the act, he would often whack him with a rolled-up newspaper. Then Loopey would skulk his way back to the porch; I felt a case of nerves every time the dog took a whacking like that, but Dad said it was important to break him of the habit. Apparently several locals had complained to Dad, and he found it embarrassing, especially since he was pastor of the largest church in town.

Sometimes, in the middle of the night when we had thunderstorms, I woke up with a case of nerves; I was afraid Loopey might have been left outside. Now, looking back some sixty-five years, I (along with professional therapists) have come to understand that these nerve moments might have been early warning signs of the emotional difficulties that would come later in life.

One day when I came home from school, my mother told me she needed to talk to me. This seemed ominous. She told me my dad had taken Loopey to live on a farm owned by one of the church parishioners. She told me Loopey's car chasing was just too dangerous, so country living was probably best for him.

I remember feeling numb. I didn't know what to say. If this was my first encounter with grief and loss, it was a mild case. I don't think I shed any tears, because I hadn't known Loopey long enough or well enough; we had never *bonded*. Later on, I wondered if my parents had really told me the truth. *Maybe he got hit by one of those cars and died,* I remember thinking. *Maybe they'd had him put to sleep because of the car chasing.* Maybe they'd just told me the farm story to shield me from sorrow. But I never asked them about those possibilities; maybe I just wanted to believe the farm story, which was very likely the truth anyway.

Until one has loved an animal, a part
of one's soul remains unawakened.
                                        —Anatole France

Dog Day Afternoon

ONE DAY IN THE SUMMER of 1975, I was sitting in the shade of the large maple tree in the yard behind our stone house. I was trying to read a *New York Times* review of a new movie called *Jaws*. I say "trying" because at that time, my concentration was so poor I could rarely finish even a single newspaper article. I was just too sick.

The mailman surprised me when he came around the corner of the house. "I couldn't get a response at your front door," he said. "I've got a package somebody has to sign for."

"Okay," I said. My wife and our little boy had gone to town. He handed me the package, which didn't weigh much, and I signed for it. As he was turning to leave, he asked me, "What's the story on those two dogs in your stairwell there?"

"Dogs?" I didn't know anything about dogs in the stairwell.

"They look in pretty bad shape," he said then started on his way back.

The ever-present knot in my stomach tightened significantly as I got up to look; my pulse began to race. Two mangy dogs, dirty gray in color, had found their way to our small stone house. Actually, such huge chunks of their coats were missing it was hard to guess what color these dogs actually were or might have been earlier. "Mangy" in this case was not derogatory. These dogs clearly had the disease and in an advanced stage.

The two sorry dogs found me severely compromised, too lost and disoriented to make sound decisions about much of anything, least of all when faced with difficult situations.

13

It was still fairly early in the morning, no more than an hour or so after breakfast, which I had been mostly unable to eat. I had weighed myself and was down to 120 pounds. A sixty-pound weight loss over the past eighteen months.

The dogs were huddled together at the bottom of an outside stairway that led to an exterior basement door of our house. Long and lean like greyhounds or whippets, so emaciated they were scarcely more than skeletons, they trembled and stared up at me with those mournful, glazed eyes often found in dogs whose suffering is so acute they have given up.

They didn't bark or whine, didn't make any noise at all. They just huddled together in what they seemed to hope was a safe port in whatever storm of life they had endured. Maybe just a safe place to curl up and hope for the blessing of death.

They were sick for sure. I had worked enough in animal shelters and conversed with enough veterinarians to recognize the presence of mange when I saw it—sections of missing coat with exposed areas of pink skin featuring plenty of open ulcers. Their rib cages were so prominent I couldn't begin to guess when they might last have eaten. I didn't doubt they were severely dehydrated as well.

Their extraordinary suffering was obvious. I tried with no success to imagine what kind of terrifying events or narratives made up their history or what brutal pathway they had followed to somehow find their way to our house. My urge to do something useful for them was strong, but I had no idea what that might be.

I stared for a long time. Then Judie and Jason pulled into the driveway. Once she was inside the house, I followed and told her about them. Our toddler, Jason, was chewing on an animal cracker.

"We should take them to the vet," she said immediately. "We should take them to Jacob."

I knew she was right, but I was afraid to try and pick them up to put them in the car; sick and afraid, they might lash out. I didn't want two desperate dogs tearing my arms apart. Fear—it was my constant companion.

I shared this fear with Judie, and she said it made sense. "I don't want you trying that either," she said. "It's too dangerous." Even though she spoke sincerely and was probably right, I didn't feel much better; the knot in my stomach held firm.

Even after more than fourteen months, Nanook's old food and water bowls were still in the cupboard beneath the kitchen sink. I might have tried to feed and water the dogs; that might have been a responsible, if minimal gesture. But reminded of Nanook's disappearance, I felt the sting once more of her loss. It was a loss I still felt keenly; I found myself in tears, thinking of her rather than the two miserable creatures next to our basement door. Just like fear, distraction was also a part of the new and dysfunctional me.

Those days I was volunteering weekends at the Orange County Humane Society, so I called Earl, the OCHS board chairman, to see what he would say. "You'd better take them to the vet," he said. "Either that or call animal control."

I tried the animal control number, but the officer there told me they only assisted with animals inside the city limits of Middletown. When I asked him if there was a county animal control officer, he said no.

I tried Earl again to ask him if he could come and pick the dogs up, but he said he couldn't; he would be out of town for a couple of days. When he asked me why I didn't just do it myself, I was too ashamed to tell him. I mumbled something irrelevant and hung up.

I drove to town to get a few groceries we needed, hoping when I returned the dogs would be gone, maybe to the woods to live out their final days—or hours—in peace. But such was not the case; the dogs were still there.

In a panic, with my stomach turned inside out, I did what people with anxiety/depressive disorders often resorted to: a terribly wrong decision based on the urgent need to "resolve" or "finalize." Difficulties magnified to crisis condition simply couldn't be allowed to fester or play themselves out. "Sleeping on it" was not an option.

I decided to ask Slive to shoot the dogs, to put them out of their misery.

Slive the farmer lived in the A-frame in the woods. There was a modest-sized meadow behind our home that led to the barn, some two hundred yards away. Beyond that, a wooded area that partially hid the huge meadow where the cows grazed. Our landlord's property included hundreds—if not thousands—of acres of woods.

I didn't own a gun, have never owned one in my life. But I knew Slive was a deer hunter and would probably have plenty of firepower to give these two miserable dogs eternal rest. It seemed like a radical idea, one that Judie tried to talk me out of. But I was driven to conclude and had exhausted the strategies I could think of. I just wanted this whole thing over with and wasn't capable of rational decision-making.

On shaky legs, I went to Slive's house. He was watching some soap opera on TV. "Sure," he said matter-of-fact when I made the proposal. He reacted with about the same level of unperturbed emotion he'd shown a couple months earlier when I asked his help removing a very large stone from my vegetable garden.

"I saw them in the barn early this morning. They were curled up in the hay. They were a mess. I kicked their sorry ass out. I sure as hell don't need no sick dogs in the barn." Saying this, he stood up to get his rifle.

So they had been in the barn first, I thought. *It probably seemed like a safe haven.* "They're very sick," I said.

Slive was a young man in his thirties whom I had always regarded as simpleminded, if not in fact unfeeling, based on the heartless way he had dealt with his own dog at an earlier time.

He had his rifle now. At that moment I realized that these executions were actually going to take place and quickly. It knotted my stomach all the more.

We veered off the path worn bare by the cattle where they moved to and from the barn and headed toward our house.

The small meadow we crossed had iron horseshoe stakes some one hundred yards south of Landlord Victor's large house. It crossed my mind Victor or his wife might be watching from a window what we were doing and raise hell about it.

"We can tie them to this horseshoe stake," said Slive.

"We can?"

"Hell yes, I can't just shoot 'em down your basement stairway."

I guess it made some sense to him, but I didn't understand why. Hoping against hope that the dogs would be gone this time, I led Slive to the top of those stairs. But they were still there.

I got Nanook's old leash, while Judie implored me not to do this, but I simply wasn't myself, whatever that was. Outside, I crept slowly down the steps, watching the dogs stir. Closer, I could see how truly sick they were. *At least their suffering would be over*, I kept telling myself over and over, longing to cling to some sliver of positive in the face of this out-of-control urgency.

Neither one of them growled or snapped as I slipped the collar over their necks. Slive stood at the top of the stairs. "Jesus Christ, just look at 'em," he exclaimed. "We'll put these poor bastards out of their misery quick enough."

Both dogs were docile enough as I led them to the closer of the two stakes. Slive tied the first one up with some clothesline he had thought to bring along. Then I went to the other one and put him on the leash. I found myself mumbling soothing words of comfort all the while, as if I were leading them to the pleasure of a dog park rather than a firing squad. I didn't know what else I could say.

But once tied to the stake, both dogs turned immediately hysterical, trying to free themselves. They whimpered and plunged wildly, although they were tied too tightly to move more than a couple of feet in any direction.

I began to shake so much I nearly had to go to my knees. Mental illness had taken my capacity for making appropriate or rational decisions, but it had also taken too much of my weight and most of my physical strength.

The terror of these dogs was my own. Their unspeakable suffering was my own. I suddenly recognized the enormity of my mistake and longed to somehow change the whole outcome. But I found I couldn't speak; my mouth simply wouldn't work.

In any case, it was too late; Slive, standing some twenty feet away from the two lunging dogs, had leveled his rifle. I knew little about guns, but this deer rifle was a powerful weapon with large-caliber bullets.

The first shot was a quick kill. It went right through the nearer dog's shoulder and probably pierced its heart; the poor creature immediately slumped to the sandy area surrounding the post, twitched briefly and shuddered, then lay still.

The second shot was a different matter. The other dog lunged and twisted frantically as if it understood the reality of the event unfolding here. Slive had to wait some thirty seconds or so until this as-yet-unharmed dog came to a standstill.

Slive shot its lower jaw off.

The dog fell to its side, wailing pitifully. To make matters worse— much worse—Slive, with a sheepish look, told me he had only brought two bullets. I couldn't believe it and couldn't speak. He dropped his rifle and ran back along the cow path to the woods to his house. More bullets were there, he told me, calling back over his shoulder.

I sat down on the grass, listening to the wretched agony of the wounded creature shrieking its high-pitched cry of pain all the while, crushed not only by its pitiful suffering but also (or so I believed) grieving the loss of its companion.

Slive got back within two minutes or so, but it seemed like two hours. The dog's constant wailing didn't stop; it was as if all the suffering in all the world was burned into this point in time.

Slive shot the dog in the head from about six feet away, and that was that. Both dogs were dead, lying in the sand that had begun to darken with blood. "They're out of their misery now," Slive said flatly and headed back toward his house.

I don't know how long I sat in that spot, hearing that pitiful wailing over and over in my head each time I looked at the two gaunt corpses some fifty feet away, but I wouldn't be surprised if it was at least half an hour. I can still hear the pitiful wailing these forty-plus years later, which is why therapist Sandy felt I still needed to talk it through and perhaps, as she is wont to say, "work through it."

But I have never worked through it, largely due to my own feckless, incapacitated behavior at the time. I simply felt overmatched by the world itself and often have many times since. I sat in that grassy spot, wondering if Victor or his wife (or Judie for that matter) had witnessed the dreadful drama from a window; I concluded Victor and wife must have been away from home. There was no way they could not have heard the desperate crying out or the gunshots.

Eventually I turned my attention to the next step: What to do *now?*

Finally I got up, went inside the house, and unspooled two large garbage bags. I was still shaking as I secured each dog in a bag. They were warm and limp with drying blood clinging. I had to pick up the piece of jaw and slip it inside the bag of the second dog. Dead or alive, as I stared at their skin-and-bones frames and pitiful skin condition, I was reminded again how sick they had been. *At least their suffering is over,* I kept repeating to myself. *Eternal rest. Eternal rest.*

I dragged them into the woods; it seemed the deeper in, the better, but I had to stop and sit down to catch my breath more than once. I found a shallow hollow where I could cover them with dirt, leaves, and sticks, but I knew a couple of good strong windy days would blow most of the cover away.

I made my way back home, so late in the morning now I was sweating in the summer heat. I went inside and sat on the couch. I leaned forward with my head in my hands. Now the tears came, along with uncontrolled sobbing. The world was a terrible, merciless place, a place of constant sorrow and little hope for respite or sanctuary or even comprehension.

"Why is daddy crying?" our toddler Jason asked his mother. I couldn't remember how many times he'd asked her that same question during this terrible year and a half of the Curse. At least he had no idea what had just happened.

Still sobbing, I managed to blubber out the words, "We have to go home. I can't go on with this. We have to go home."

My comforting wife, she who had endured the broken lives my disorder had shaped, was rubbing my back. "I know," she said softly. "I know."

"I can't do this anymore. We have to go home."

"I know."

"I mean go home for good."

"I know."

IN 2016, in more than one counseling session, Sandy asked me to share my feelings about that deeply disturbing afternoon. She wanted quick answers, not the usual ones where I spent too much time "thinking."

"I was irresponsible," I said. "I felt at the time—and still do—more guilt and shame than at any other moment in my life."

"And that's why I think that awful day is worth exploring. Remember, you were sick."

"My fears overwhelmed my judgment."

"You were sick."

"I could have followed Earl's advice, put the dogs in the car and driven them to a vet. In fact, our vet lived about a mile or so down the road from us. We knew him pretty well."

"But that wasn't his office."

"No, but I knew where his office was in town. I could have made a *man's* decision and taken responsibility."

"Could you really?"

I got the point. "I don't know. Maybe. What if those pitiful dogs belonged to someone who was desperately searching for them? Just the way Judie and I had done in the March blizzard when we lost our special family dog?"

"Then those people, if they existed, wouldn't have had to see their dogs in that pitiful condition."

"You're trying to find my way out of this."

"No, I'm just saying you had a serious disorder, why would you expect to behave normally?"

"I don't know."

"Can you forgive yourself, knowing the condition you were in?"

"No."

"If you could do it over again, what would you do?"

"I would be a man. I would put those dogs in the car and drive them to the vet."

"You would be different. Even though you were sick, you would be different. Is that realistic?"

"It's what I want to think."

Repeat dialogue, time and again. There has never been a "breakthrough" or a "working through" the experience. I'm sure there never will be. I have nearly always felt hopeful and willing during talk therapy sessions, but they've never really had a lasting effect. Maybe it's my fault. Maybe I'm as poor a candidate for talk therapy as I've often been told. I know Sandy has always meant well.

The next day, I went to Jack's office to hand in my resignation letter. He said quietly, "I'm sorry it has come to this, Jim. I'm also sorry for all you've been going through. You've been a good teacher here, don't forget that."

I had not been a "good teacher" for three entire semesters, but I didn't say that. I simply thanked him for all his support. He got up from behind his desk, came out, and shook my hand. He patted me on the back. "I wish you the best of luck in whatever you do."

I stepped outside of Morrison Hall for the last time and gazed around the campus. A few people moved across the way but not many; summer school always had far fewer students and faculty. This place, with its competitive salary and robust package of benefits, had been at one time the most rewarding professional situation I'd ever known. I would never experience its equal again. This small college had brought me a level of financial and emotional security I would never know again the rest of my life. I felt myself tearing up.

We spent the next three days making the rounds of our closest friends to say goodbye. None of this was easy.

The day before we left was Sunday. We had an emotional leave-taking from our House Church family; we formed a circle and held hands. We sang "One in the Spirit" with tears stinging our eyes. Judie and I held Dick Dutton, his wife, Pat, and their children for a long time. "Never give up," Dick said to me. "I'll have you in my prayers."

I hated to leave him. No person outside our family had done more to help me or shown me more clearly the nature of Christian love.

The following day we loaded (with the help of good friend Phil Reiss) all our belongings into a sixteen-foot U-Haul truck. We hooked up our yellow Volkswagen Squareback to the back of the truck and headed west. As we drove along Interstate 84, I felt numb, almost out of body. I knew precisely what I was leaving behind, but what lay ahead? Would going home actually make any difference? Was this a for-real decision or merely a swap-out of problems? I tried unsuccessfully to dismiss these thoughts.

I cannot imagine living without dogs.
They are wonderful and, I think, man-
datory for decent human life.

—Gary Paulsen

Nanook

EIGHTEEN MONTHS EARLIER, I learned 1974 would turn out
to be the year that changed my life forever. I couldn't see it coming.
How could I? But the sudden and mystifying change had a lasting
effect; it not only defines the person I've been for most of my adult
life, but substantially accounts for what I've accomplished—or been
unable to accomplish—as a person, teacher, family man, and author.

On a cold and snowy morning in January, even before I got out
of bed, I was overcome with terror and panic. I sat up on the edge
of the bed and planted my bare feet on the cold wooden floor of our
Orange County, New York, home. I shook my head as if to clear
it—something was terribly wrong! I had simply awakened as on any
other day, but feelings of terror ripped at my stomach.

"What the hell?" I blurted out.

I got out of bed. My stomach was constricted, my pulse rapid. I
was short of breath, and my heart was palpitating.

With no warning, I was undergoing a major mental breakdown
characterized by runaway anxiety and depression, although it would
take some time and interaction with mental health professionals for
me to understand that depression was part of the equation.

I could not know on that bewildering morning my life would
never be the same again.

Downstairs, our eleven-month-old son Jason was smearing his
cereal around his high chair. When I told Judie what I was feeling,
the two of us took a brief inventory of what was currently transpiring

in our lives to see if we could identify a cause for these gripping fears. No. My job was secure and rewarding; in fact, I had just been promoted to associate professor. Our son was healthy and happy.

Then why was my stomach constricted with a nameless dread? What was making me sweat and shake? What was causing the beads of sweat on my forehead? "I don't know," Judie said. "I don't know what to say."

I took our lovable family dog Nanook outside into the backyard, where she eliminated, then romped a while in the snow. A Labrador-Malamute mix, she was born for this weather. I was getting cold, so I whistled at her and she came. We stared at each other briefly before I remembered to go inside. I'm sure she thought I looked just fine. Once inside, I gave her one of her Milk Bones.

I forced down a couple of bites of corn flakes but, that was all I could eat. I drank some coffee. The panic did not let up; it roiled my insides the rest of the day. That evening, I only ate half a slice of bread and downed half a bottle of Pepsi.

"Maybe it'll all go away just as fast as it came," Judie said in an effort to reassure me.

It did not go away. The terror continued for the next several days and nights. It was altogether mysterious and terribly frightening. Each night I went sleepless, trembling in bed. My pajamas were soaked with sweat. Judie would lie beside me, sleeping soundly, while I curled into the fetal position and shook with fear, hour after lonely hour until dawn finally came, when I would try to face another day. It did not seem possible my life had taken this turn.

In the middle of the night, I would begin to imagine all manner of fearful things. I was losing my mind. I was breaking down completely. I would no longer be able to hold my job. I would never recover. Very soon, I would be locked up in the local state mental hospital, confined to a padded room. My wife and son would come to visit me, their eyes full of shame and resignation. My body was pumping adrenaline so relentlessly I was going to die soon, probably of a heart attack.

One night in the now-normal panic, I went downstairs and lay on the couch. I was sobbing and didn't want to wake my wife or son.

Nanook came near the couch and sat beside me; she rested her head on my arm, while I scratched her between the ears. She looked at me with soulful eyes as if she understood my suffering and wanted to help. There are people—many of them engaged in canine research—who believe dogs can sense the suffering of their owners or special people. My experience over time has convinced me they are right.

We had adopted Nanook (it wasn't too long before we just called her Nanny) the previous spring, when our vet, Jacob, told us of a litter of mixed-breed pups a farmer friend of his was giving away. Jacob lived a mile or so down the road from us and before long became a friend we often consulted informally about our pets. He was a good man as well as a perceptive one.

He knew we had a new baby and would want a dog that would provide gentle companionship as well as safety for our son Jason. "These pups are Malamute/Lab mix. I can practically guarantee their gentle nature will never cause your little one any harm," Jacob assured us. He made this point specifically because he knew all about our unfortunate dog experience from the previous fall.

We had driven to a farm in another part of the county to have a look at these pups. We found them in a long run framed by posted chicken wire. One of them, a fluffy, chunky little black-and-tan scooter came bounding along the chicken wire to greet us, until she finally reached the gate. The other three pretty much lay in place and yawned. The farmer picked her up and put her in my arms.

I got a good face licking, and so did Jason, who was in his mother's arms. He didn't enjoy it much, flinching and closing his eyes, but Judie and I were convinced immediately that this was the dog for us.

We had decided to adopt a female dog due to the unfortunate experience we'd had with our Scottie, Fleance, some six months earlier. Fleance had undergone a major and mysterious personality change that caused him to become dangerously aggressive. Eventually, we had had no choice but to put him to sleep. It was a crushing chapter in our lives.

Therefore, we had agreed to go with a female the next time around even though this litter of pups would almost assuredly be docile and affectionate no matter the gender.

We had named her Nanook (of the North) even before we finished the drive home. As the days passed, we found all of Jacob's assurances to be true. If Jason was in his carrier seat on the couch, Nanny sniffed him out of curiosity and nuzzled him a little bit, but Jason invariably flinched at this show of affection. He was only two to three months old at the time.

A little later, when Jason was able to sit on the floor, she would crawl in his direction to get close. Sometimes when he was nibbling on toast, Nanny would get her fair share, but she took her bites gently. Then it became a game that actually found our little boy belly laughing. He'd give her a snippet of toast with his fingers; his hands were never damaged in the process. No mark, not even so much as a scrape on a finger.

When he was a few months older, they often sat on the floor together. Jason found great pleasure in pulling her ears, although the ears weren't long. We tried to break him of that habit, but Nanny always tolerated the game; she never seemed to mind. By October, she was getting large. She often rolled over on her side against him, spilling him to the floor and nearly squishing him. It almost seemed like she knew what she was doing, gently asserting her position in their interaction. For his part, Jason never seemed to mind, although getting back into a seated position was often more than he could handle.

No matter; she was the dog for Jason. The two of them would grow up together, and she would become "his" dog.

I discovered Nanny liked chasing sticks. Our stone house was in the country, with plenty of large trees on the property so there was never a shortage of branches—big and small—on the ground.

We took her to Jacob for her shots and dog license. We bought her a collar and had a tag made with her name and our phone number, because we had decided earlier we'd allow her to explore the nearby woods on her own. That was a decision that worked well until it didn't. But I'm ahead of myself.

Nanny, the rapidly growing pup, liked to join me on walks in the woods, and I was happy to have her company. She proved to be an intelligent dog well suited for exploring; she was exuberant and full of life but also cautious. She sniffed the ground carefully and sometimes came to a halt, especially when we came across forest rot or piles of decaying debris.

By the fall, she had grown to nearly three-fourths of full adulthood, at fifty pounds. She sat next to Jason's high chair and was gifted with morsels of toast, eggs, and cereal. Judie and I were very happy. Our boy and his special dog were going to grow up together. They would be inseparable pals who would form a lasting bond.

At this time, we began letting her loose on her own to explore the nearby woods and pastures. Since we were living in that country setting with meadows and woods all around, it seemed like an ideal opportunity to let a dog enjoy freedom of movement. Furthermore, she seemed highly intelligent. The county road that ran past the front of our house had little traffic. Combining all those factors, it seemed a shame to keep a quizzical, strong dog confined to the house. We felt like we owed her some of the joy of freedom dogs thrive on.

She seemed to handle it well, often content to come home within an hour or two. On other days, she hardly left the backyard at all. The farmer's dog, Sargent, soon became her partner in forest investigation. Sargent was an outgoing, friendly Pointer mix, a slim, shorthaired black dog with some white markings on his chest and face. If Nanny was going to live free, why not a good-natured partner?

It wasn't long before both dogs spent large chunks of each day stretched out in our backyard. In addition to his friendship with Nanny, Sargent had discovered our yard bestowed another benefit: The milk bones we tossed to Nanny usually left one or two extras for him. Over time, we became so fond of Sargent we missed him when he wasn't hanging around.

MEANWHILE, THE "CURSE" (as I had now begun to call this disorder) didn't relent. I was taking Valium at night in a relatively small dosage, but it offered very little help. Shaken and unable to sleep, I would go down to the couch.

It wasn't long before my sleepless trips down the stairs and onto the couch in the middle of the night became standard operating procedure. Nanny joined me, big as she was, and stretched out along-side. Some nights, I could hear Jason crying, then Judie's feet as they padded on the wooden floor; she was on the way to his crib to change and/or nurse him. Listening, I felt the sorrow of loss; I curled up more with feelings of inadequacy and guilt. *I need to be a part of this,* I told myself.

Nanny and I prone on that couch at the same time made for a tight fit. But she was so warm, and the winter was so deep. She was a docile dog who didn't do much tossing or turning. And even though lying on the couch with Nanny didn't bring serenity, it somehow felt *safe*. At that point in time, I got more comfort from her than from any human.

I still couldn't sleep or eat. I still felt the unidentified terror every minute of the day or night. After some two weeks of this alarm-ing disorientation, I sat beside Judie on the couch. "There has to be something," she said.

"I know there has to be something. This can't just happen for no reason. But I've gone over and over every part of my life and every part of our life together. If there's anything at all that could be caus-ing these feelings, I can't tell you what it is."

Then she said softly, "We're going over the same ground again and again." It was at that moment I saw clearly how much all this was disturbing her. "I know," I said.

"All we're doing is repeating ourselves." She took my hand and squeezed it.

"I know, I know."

"Maybe you'd better get some help. A counselor or something."

I knew she was right, but the world of professional counseling was so foreign to me it seemed scary. What if a mental health profes-sional confirmed that I had a mental illness so profound that I would need to be committed for good and all? How would I ever get out of that box?

But I knew I had to try. I started by sharing the condition with a priest named Father David, who was also a teaching colleague at Orange County Community College, where I was an English teacher. He listened with compassion but seemed as clueless as I was.

He advised me to seek help at a community mental health center by speaking to a counselor friend of his named Dick Dutton. He also told me to "keep a close counsel."

"What do you mean?" I asked.

"Don't spread this around to everybody you know. Keep your sharing where it belongs—with your wife, your very closest of friends, and mental health professionals who truly might be able to help."

I decided okay, at least it was a word of advice.

When I met Dick Dutton, he told me he was an ex-Baptist minister who had left parish work to become a mental health professional. I wasn't really enthused about counseling with a Baptist preacher, but he was a compassionate listener with the kindest of demeanors. I spilled it all to him. I just poured it out—the fear, the panic, the disorientation, the lack of any apparent cause. I remember how good it felt just to unload on somebody who might be able to help, although I had no idea what "help" might look like. Or feel like. Before I was finished talking, I started to cry.

Dick listened carefully then reached over and put his hand on my knee. "Something has to be causing these feelings," he said. "We just have to figure out what." Then he stood up. "I'll tell you what," he said. "We have a psychiatrist who is with us one day a week. It so happens he's here today. I'd like you to talk with him. Would you be willing to do that?"

"Sure," I said.

Dick went to get him. My spirits soared when I realized I would get to talk with a psychiatrist.

Here would be an answer, I thought.

The psychiatrist was a very fat Irishman named Dr. O'Malley who had oily hair and was unkempt. It didn't make a good impression, but I told my story again, just as I'd done with Dick. It comforted me when Dick chose to stay in the room.

When I was finished, O'Malley nodded and said, "You are having an acute anxiety attack. You need medicine to calm you down, then you need psychotherapy."

It seemed overwhelming. O'Malley got to his feet to leave. "I have other patients," he explained. This "diagnosis" didn't help at all.

In fact, it left me feeling utterly despondent. There was my answer: acute anxiety attack. It sounded so trivial, like the temporary apprehension of calling up a girl for a date. For feelings that were tearing my guts to pieces, it just wasn't adequate. I had an "answer" but certainly didn't like it.

I would learn later, over years and years of counseling and reading, that the condition is usually labeled acute generalized anxiety, or free-floating anxiety. A person who suffers from generalized anxiety has chronic, persistent symptoms of panic and apprehensiveness, but those symptoms do not stem from any cause that can be identified. At times, the feelings of apprehensiveness are more acute than others, but they are always present at some level.

Even later, I would learn that acute depression was hiding within the seemingly dominant anxiety condition. And even later than that, I would learn that attention deficit disorder and obsessive-compulsive disorder were also typically parts of a more complete diagnostic profile.

But after O'Malley left the room, I turned back to Dick. "Where would I get this medication and psychoanalysis?"

"Well, unless you're rich, your best bet would be the county mental health hospital in Goshen."

A patient in a mental health hospital? I was dumbfounded; my stomach churned all the harder, and I began to cry again. I had never been a crier, and this now-frequent phenomenon embarrassed me. *What are you, a big baby?*

"Does that scare you?" Dick asked.

"Yes, it does," I answered quickly while blowing my nose.

"Don't let it scare you. It's probably the best help you can get." He put his hand on mine again. "But think it over. Talk it over with your wife. Call me if you want to talk again. I'll help you in any way I can."

I drove home full of panic and confusion. Was I about to become an inmate in the puzzle house? When I got home, the first thing I did was head upstairs to look at Jason napping in his crib. He would be celebrating his first birthday in less than a month. For several minutes, I watched him sleeping. My heart ached. Would I even get to celebrate that birthday, or would I be locked away on the funny farm? The tears streamed down my face again.

I went downstairs and talked the whole thing over with Judie. She thought I should follow Dick Dutton's advice.

"But it's a mental hospital," I moaned.

"But maybe that's what it takes to help you get better."

I thought long and hard. I was teaching at the college, but we were between semesters; it would be ten days or so before classes resumed. It provided some room to maneuver.

Finally I said, "I'll go, but only if I can be a day patient. I'm not going to be a resident and spend my nights in a hospital bed." I knew I could call Dick again and ask him to work that out.

"Okay," said Judie. "That's a decision then. Do you want something to eat?"

"I'm not hungry," I said. I was never hungry, never had appetite. I was starting to cinch my belt a notch tighter.

I bundled up and went out to the backyard with Nanny. I threw the stick she liked to chase, plowing her way through the snow. She was a eighty-pound dog by now and plenty strong; her thick coat made her oblivious to the cold. We played this game for the better part of an hour. It made me feel a little better, and there was no doubt she relished it.

"Maybe you are part of the answer," I said to her before I let her inside. "Maybe the biggest part." And maybe I believed it.

When I got inside, I said to Judie, "I'll go, but only if I can be a day patient."

"You already said that."

"I mean it though."

Nanny was sitting by my legs, on her haunches, staring straight at my face as if to ask, *Okay, where's my milk bone?*

I have found that when you are deeply trou-
bled, there are things you get from the
silent, devoted companionship of a dog
that you can get from no other source.

—Doris Day

Nanook: Part Two

DICK DUTTON was, in fact, able to arrange for me to enter the county mental hospital as a day patient. It was about a half hour's drive from our country home. The daily schedule began at 8:00 a.m. and concluded at 5:00 p.m.

My school schedule allowed me to spend eight days in the hospital before second semester classes resumed. I stopped after five.

The entire ordeal was all the more devastating because the first years we spent in Middletown, New York, from the summer of 1968 through January 1974 were the most satisfying and fulfilling in our lives. We were Illinois transplants living in a brave new world. The Catskills were wondrous to behold for a pair of flatlanders from Illinois; we often took drives up and down the slopes simply to drink in the bold and beautiful hillsides. Orange County has a flavor of New England—stone fences surrounding meadows (sometimes for grazing cattle or sheep), horse farms in beautiful condition with gleaming regular white wooden fence lines. Occasional picturesque villages with white church spires nestled among the slopes.

We were lucky enough to rent a charming stone house built in 1780. It had its original hand-hewn walnut beams, original floor planks of various widths, and original metal latches instead of door-knobs. The walls were very thick; windowsills probably measured eighteen inches in depth. It had its original stone fireplace and a flat back porch made of fieldstone. It was actually more like a patio.

Judie and I bought a couple of Adirondack chairs for that porch because it was a peaceful place for reading and/or gazing across the acres and acres of meadow and woods. Although the house and rooms were small, it was a charming dwelling. The galley kitchen was thoroughly modern, as was the upstairs bathroom.

Good friend Bruce said on a visit, "There were probably some Revolutionary War skirmishes still going on in the area when this place was built." The house did feel like history.

It sat relatively close to the county road, maybe fifty feet back, where traffic was light. Landlord Victor often said he and his wife planned to move in there when they retired, but they had already retired; I guess they'd become accustomed to their much bigger home, some two hundred yards away, and were comfortable there.

The drive to Middletown's city limits was about eight miles. Along the way, there were occasional houses set back from the road and surrounded by deep woods. Any farms in the area were dairy farms, as the ground was essentially too beset by stones to allow for growing crops effectively. As a matter of fact, our stone house itself was actually situated on a dairy farm. A hundred yards or so beyond the landlord's house stood a large barn used by the tenant farmer, named Slive, for milking and feeding cattle. His house was in the woods nearby.

The Orange County Community College (now named SUNY Orange) campus was a warm and collegiate collection of some seven or eight buildings joined with many mature trees and landscaped shrubbery. There was an open, grassy green or quad.

The campus actually stood on the property of a former wealthy estate, with a huge stone mansion serving as the administration building that also housed a large number of faculty offices. For the first time, I had my own office. Not too far away was the stone carriage house that the college had converted to classroom space. A dozen or more large maple trees provided splendid fall colors, while in winter, snow hung along the boughs of the evergreens.

It was not my first community college teaching job, but it was the best one. I enjoyed my students, and they enjoyed me, even when I had to hand out low grades. The educational advantage of community colleges is the availability of one-on-one working sessions with classroom professors, whose sole responsibility is teaching, not grinding on esoteric research with student interns or publishing material in dry education journals.

I spent many hours working in my office (located in the mansion) individually with struggling students. Most of the courses I taught were freshman composition with occasional sophomore-level literature courses. In this respect, my teaching duties were similar to those of my colleagues.

I was very good at my job. Students, peers, and administrators agreed on that. But most importantly, I knew it. I was an effective professional and a confident man.

We soon became part of the college community. Colleagues became friends, and close ones. Some of them I even connect with to this day. We had more fun social life than we've ever had before or since. Scarcely a weekend went by without a party at someone's home, usually involving students as well as faculty members. I did a bit too much drinking in those days, although I limited it to the party events. At times, I had to stumble through Saturday or Sunday morning hangovers.

Occasionally, we hosted the Friday or Saturday night parties. A group of twenty was not unusual, including approximately ten faculty and an equal number of students who were often older, non-traditional students. There are always plenty of those in community college ranks.

The college, located as it was so near to New York City, also provided frequent intellectually stimulating personalities from speakers, musicians, and theatrical personalities. I recall a moving one-woman performance by noted Irish actress Siobhan McKenna, featuring passages from James Joyce's *Ulysses*. We were also blessed with major authors who spoke in the campus auditorium and even did some class visiting. Anthony Burgess and John Barth are two who come to mind.

The late sixties and early seventies were electric on most college campuses. Ours was no different. We often hosted controversial political speakers such as radical attorney William Kunstler, had student boycotts, as well as spontaneous rallies on the quad protesting the Vietnam War and/or pushing for civil rights.

Judie and I (as well as many of our friends) were active in the Vietnam War protest movement. Some of my students were young men who had served in Vietnam; most of them were members of Viet Vets Against the War. We participated in protest marches ending at the local armory, as well as several candlelight vigils.

When we first moved to Middletown, we liked the fact we were only about seventy miles northwest of The City, "the center of the universe," as Mayor LaGuardia had once claimed. The first year or two, we drove frequently to the City for theater, museums, and other attractions, but our visits there tapered off considerably due to cost and the fact our own campus provided so many opportunities—at no cost—for provocative programs and intellectual enrichment. We didn't really need to leave town to trade in rich life currency.

SUMMERS in the Catskills found me writing fiction, often four hours a day or more. I completed one novel that never got published and never should have. It was rejected quickly by the three or four publishers who actually agreed to read it. In those days, you could submit manuscripts directly to editors; nowadays most publishers won't agree to evaluate a book unless it comes by way of an agent.

Although I was always good with dialogue, I didn't have command yet of vision and purpose. I wasn't yet capable of writing a mature novel. That would come much later in my life, and with a level of success I found nearly intoxicating.

Nevertheless, I kept shopping my book to publishers and agents. I wanted to forge a relationship with a good literary agent because even though authors frequently submitted manuscripts to editors, doing so through an agent was always the best bet.

A colleague of mine had published a successful crime novel a couple of years earlier, and he convinced his agent to read my book. Within a couple of weeks, I got the manuscript back in the mail. A polite paragraph preceded the bad news: "But I'm returning your book because I honestly don't think I could place it for you. You have obvious talent, but you haven't really honed it yet. It seems to me you're still struggling to find your 'voice.'"

I was discouraged but not devastated. I knew well how competitive the book publishing industry was, as well as the particular difficulties involved for previously unpublished authors. Judie consoled me by saying, "Well, there's a lot of publishers out there. You'll just have to keep trying." I knew she was right; I had known how difficult the path to publication would be from the time I wrote the book's first page. I simply went to the college library and used *The Writer's Digest* to find more publishers to target.

But during that time, our lives were touched by six dogs, two of them family pets whose lives brought us some joy, but a great deal more loss, sorrow, and regret. Our stone house dogs did not tell tales with happy endings.

I WISH I COULD report that my time spent in the county mental facility was productive, that it gave me some significant relief. But such was not the case. About all I learned there was how to smoke.

Daily group sessions (at least mine) included a couple of licensed therapists and about a dozen patients. Some of them were psychotic and delusional. One man believed the television was reading his thoughts. Another believed he heard voices telling him what to do from the bathroom faucets. Most of the other patients were victims of depression; they were melancholy people who felt helpless and hopeless. Some of them were so thoroughly medicated they fell asleep through lengthy periods of the sessions.

The resident psychiatrist (who was rarely available for consultation) urged me to take more and stronger drugs. But like many patients experiencing mental health disorders for the first time, I was reluctant to go that route for fear of becoming an addict.

Besides, I would soon see too many patients drugged up and zombie-like in group sessions. Immediately I would come to fear that would be my fate and render me completely dysfunctional. I had a job to protect (somehow) and a family; I needed to function if possible.

Each time these delusional/paranoid people spoke, I became even more panicked; was this the fate that was in store for me? Was acute anxiety attack just a prelude to a more drastic, crippling disorder? Counselors told me no, but their attempts at encouragement didn't eliminate or even reduce my level of fear.

In the group sessions, each patient wanted individual attention, but with twelve or more of us, it wasn't easy to make that happen. Part of our duty was to help our fellow patients with questions and suggestions. I wasn't very good at that. Like the other patients, I was too knotted up, too compromised by the terror within.

It seemed nearly everyone in the circle was a smoker. These meeting rooms were thick with the blue haze of hovering cigarette smoke. Even most of the counselors were smokers. This was not surprising or unusual in 1974.

After three or four days of trying to make this program work, I accepted a cigarette from a fellow patient. It wasn't long, however, before I began buying my own and smoking nearly a pack a day. Smoking calmed my nerves a little bit. Soon, cigarettes were my constant companions during the long, lonely, and sleepless nights at home. Smoking went with pacing.

Even vocational therapy involved smoking, as a common arts and crafts project was making ashtrays out of small ceramic squares.

Each afternoon, when I drove home discouraged and terrified, I told Judie about my day. But it was always the same story: I wasn't getting better. I wasn't getting any relief or reason to feel optimistic.

If lack of sleep was discouraging, lack of appetite was no less so. I could usually get a couple spoonsful of Jell-O down and sometimes a soft-boiled egg. I couldn't eat cereal or soup, but I did manage to spoon down a small bowl of beef broth. I tried bananas but nearly choked on them. Cottage cheese was another food I could spoon down piecemeal but only if it was mixed with applesauce. It was a blend Judie thought up. It was essentially baby food.

I drank a lot of milkshakes. The last day I spent at the hospital, I weighed myself. I had lost fifteen pounds since the first day of the breakdown.

WHEN SECOND SEMESTER began at the college, I found myself struggling distractedly to get through each of my classes. It did seem as if engaging with students brought some temporary relief, but only till the end of class.

At home, I discovered that intense physical activity could bring temporary relief. I launched myself into chopping firewood and stacking it on the back porch. The wood chips flew, sometimes twenty feet or more, and Nanny went chasing after; here was a delightful variation of her stick-chasing game. I cut firewood furiously by the hour until my back and shoulders ached. Nanny, of course, never tired of this new fun. Sometimes Sargent, Silve's dog, showed up to join in the fun. Both dogs enjoyed chasing snowballs I made, then pawing them to smithereens. My dog and her friend were about my only sources of fun.

Whatever we lacked that winter, we wouldn't come up short for fireplace wood.

What seemed to alleviate distress even more was physical vigor that involved other people in a group activity. It had the capacity to absorb me. I approached a friend who taught P.E. and asked if I could join his jogging class. I became a jogger. I can remember pounding along snow-packed streets wearing borrowed sweat clothes.

Our course was about a mile and a half. I was weary and bleary-eyed from the endless sleepless nights, but I managed to finish the course just like all the students. While I was running, draining myself physically, I found I could shove my feelings of panic into the background. Until the class was over, that is.

I took up the game of racquetball, which I had never played before. I had no problem finding playing partners, usually faculty members who were close friends. We had a new athletics building with outstanding resources. Nobody used them more than I did. The faculty locker room became like my second home.

I even played on the faculty basketball team during noon hour. All these activities had to be dovetailed into my classroom and tutoring duties; the combination made for a tight daily schedule, which was what I craved. Down time or alone time (such as grading papers or class preparation) was the most fertile ground for escalating fear and anxiety.

The downside, of course, to all this physically exhausting activity, was weight loss. I was burning calories rapidly but taking few in. By St. Patrick's Day, I had lost thirty pounds.

When I sat at the college cafeteria for lunch with friends and colleagues, I usually just downed a milkshake. Others talked and laughed and swapped stories, while I was weeping inwardly with despair. It was terribly discouraging. Some of my closest friends asked me why I was getting so skinny. I remembered Father David's advice about keeping a close counsel, so I usually waved it off as exercise induced.

I longed to have fun too, just like my friends were doing. But there was no fun. There was no joy in life (I couldn't even muster much for my own cherished son) and no pleasure. There was fear, loss, and 24-7 discouragement.

If I could get even two hours of sleep at nights (it didn't often happen), I considered myself lucky. Most nights I still found myself downstairs on the couch again, sleeping with Nanny. I wrapped my arms around her like a small child with a teddy bear and told her of my suffering in plain (and often crude) language I couldn't use in other settings.

Sometimes she caused me to remember Fleance, our loving dog that simply didn't "work out." That loss now dated back over a couple of years, but I frequently relived the intense sorrow of the wrenching decision we'd had to make. I told Nanny about the dog she'd never known. "We still loved him," I told Nanny. "He was never really bad, just confused." She looked at me and often cocked her head, the way dogs do when they appear to be puzzled. Although I knew she couldn't understand what I said, I often pretended that she did.

Dick Dutton and his family became even more important in my life, not only because I maintained the counseling relationship with him, but also because he was the organizer/leader of a unique House Church experiment. I guess he still needed the pastor experience even though he had changed careers. The group was almost beyond ecumenical—we had Unitarians, Baptists, Methodists, even Jews and agnostics.

We met each Sunday morning at his home or the home of one of the other members of the group. We sang hymns while he strummed his guitar and had informal discussions about faith, the lack of it, prayer, and individual, personal struggles usually involving the loss of faith.

I was getting religion. Or desperately trying to. The mental hospital didn't help, maybe God would. Although I had been an agnostic since my freshman year in college, I soon began praying. Day and night. Maybe God could take this curse away. Maybe many Christians were right—God "wipes away all tears" if you just had the courage to lay your troubles at the Throne.

Those first prayers were ones of desperation. Even before dawn, I often bundled up and went outside, standing in the snow with the loyal Nanny by my side. We looked at the sky on frigid, starry nights while I gushed out to God all my fear and despair:

"Why? Why, God, why is this thing happening to me? Have I done something wrong or evil? Is this a punishment?"

I pleaded with Him to deliver me from my suffering. These were cries of despair as much as they were prayers, but I was determined to continue seeking God's grace.

I also began reading self-help books one after another, most of them Christian in nature. I could never read for long at a sitting and often tried to read while I was pacing. Each book seemed to promise relief from suffering if we only put our faith in the Lord and laid our troubles at his feet. Every day I was trying to do just that as sincerely as I could, but relief never came.

In addition to the Christian material, I read books by Zen masters and other Eastern religious materials and tried to learn the practice of meditation. It didn't work well because of my racing mind. This condition is common to many who suffer from mental illness, as the attempt to quiet the mind and focus is terribly difficult. The racing mind is also one of the biggest obstacles to sleeping.

I had a book of daily meditations by John Baillie that Dick had given me. Each morning after I got to my school parking space, I sat in the car and read that day's meditation. The meditations were profound and well written, so I hoped they might help me move into the Christian life and find a path to hope.

HOUSE CHURCH was a place of love and acceptance and capable people. It gave me more relief than the mental hospital ever did, but as always, the relief was very temporary; by the time we drove home, the Curse had claimed me once again.

There was a particular moment at House Church that moved both Judie and me to tears. On February 9, Jason had his first birthday. Dick decided we needed to have what he called a dedication service for him. "We can't really call it a baptism," he told us, with a sheepish smile, "but it can be just as important. We get commitments from all members to love and cherish him and pray for God's blessings on him. Not for just a day but throughout his entire life."

When the Sunday morning came, for the first time the group met at our house. Judie prepared coffee and juice, while I bought several large bottles of soft drinks. House Church was very informal; people sipped and munched on cookies or other snacks as we conducted our unconventional worship service.

That morning, everyone formed a circle with Jason standing in the middle. We sang his favorite church song, "He's Got the Whole World in His Hands." Jason clapped his hands as the song moved along, but when our little man figured out he was being singled out as the center of attention, he looked around in all directions, mystified. He began to cry and ran to Judie, who held him and soothed him until the tears stopped.

When he stopped crying, Dick took him in his lap and put his hand atop the little towhead. Nanny decided it was time to bark; I don't know what her reason was, but she didn't bother getting to her feet. She rarely barked at anything, so that in itself was surprising.

I can't remember all the words Dick spoke, but I remember he concluded by saying, "Lord God, we ask your blessings on this little boy now and throughout his life." Then I began to cry silently, with the tears streaming down my face. Jason asked his mother, "Mommy, why is Daddy crying?" He was precocious with language.

(Many years later Jason asked me if he'd ever been baptized and the best answer I could give him was a summary of that cold Sunday morning in Orange County, New York.)

After this dedication, it was time to get the sweets out. It was a birthday party after all, even in the midst of Sunday morning worship. Three women had brought cupcakes, and there were cookies as well. There were about a dozen children ranging in age from three to thirteen; some of them were very casual about eating and holding the cupcakes. Nanny took three or four tours around the circle, startling a few of them. It was her size, I suppose, that caused them to flinch.

She was enthusiastically eating the cupcake morsels as they fell. When chunks of cookies were dropped, she was more than happy to scoop those up as well. Her sweets intake that morning was substantial. At least she kept the floor clean.

I continued counseling a couple of times a week with Dick, but by this time, we were spinning our wheels by trying to identify a *cause.* Did I hate my father or my mother subconsciously? He knew I had had significant estrangement from my father dating back to my teen years and doggedly pursued that phenomenon. Had I ever been abused as a child?

More than once, he asked me about my dreams and nightmares, but I had to remind him a person has to go to sleep to have those. We were tinkering at the edges of the Freudian/Jungian tradition, but it didn't take. Talk therapy—even with a psychoanalytic bent—was simply not helping me.

Somehow I struggled through most of my classes. Sometimes I simply couldn't make a go of it and dismissed classes early. Knowing that my department chair and other administrators would not take kindly to this habit was simply one more thing to escalate my anxiety.

Weeks of despair were grinding on me in so many ways. Sometimes I choked food down in small amounts, not because it tasted good or because I had appetite, but Judie and I both knew it was imperative for me to try and eat. I had the shakes most of the time and often lost my balance. Flashbulbs popped behind my eyes. By this time, I was nearly a completely dysfunctional person, frightened and bewildered. I was thirty-two years old and out of hope. I had fallen deep into the blackest of black holes.

Close counsel or not, by this time I knew I had to share the crisis with my department head. Judie and I went one evening to Jack's house, a large Victorian home on one of Middletown's tonier streets. He and his wife, Eva, took great pride in their two giant Schnauzers, who sniffed us to death, no doubt getting a whiff of Nanny on our clothing.

It actually felt good sharing with Jack and Eva; he was a caring and compassionate man who told me I should just do my best, as surely this disorienting event in my life would soon run its course. "It can't last without any cause," he said. I found his words mildly heartening, although I had already begun to think otherwise.

But then Eva spoke up with a different agenda: "You must take medication," she said bluntly. "Medication is the only solution." She seemed so earnest, as if she spoke from experience. Maybe she did. I didn't ask.

For reasons I've already mentioned, this was not advice I wanted to hear. I cringed at the thought of becoming a drug addict. Many, many years later though, I learned how right she was as well as the reasons for.

I didn't answer her but told Jack how grateful I was for his understanding and support. It wasn't likely I'd be fired for neglect of duty. On our drive home, I told Judie how much I appreciated Jack's encouraging words and how little I appreciated Eva's two cents. She agreed with me on both counts.

Then, when I was least able to cope, along came a late March blizzard whose consequences would be devastating for all three of us.

Brothers and sisters I bid you beware
Of giving your heart to a dog to tear.
                        —Rudyard Kipling

Where's Nanook?

IT WAS about St. Patrick's Day when I had lost so much weight, was still so tightly in the grip of withering anxiety (it would be much later before I understood the depression component of this disorder) that Dick Dutton suggested I check myself into the hospital for some testing. He couldn't let go of his conviction there had to be a *cause* for what I was struggling with, and to tell the truth, neither could I. There simply *had to be* an answer. "Something doesn't come from nothing," he liked to say.

I always wanted to agree with him because if a cause could be identified, then the cure would surely come shortly after. "I already tried the hospital," I reminded him.

"I'm not talking about the mental hospital in Goshen, I mean Horton Hospital here in Middletown."

The only time I'd been in Horton Hospital had been at the time of Jason's birth. "What kind of testing?"

"Neurological testing. Maybe the problem is physical, not mental."

I was in the mood to try just about anything, so I agreed. I checked myself into the hospital and ended up staying there three days. I was poked and prodded. I had numerous x-rays and the kinds of brain scanning that were available in 1974. Doctors had me swinging the tips of my fingers together and hopping on one leg and even trying sit-ups and push-ups.

I couldn't eat much of anything at the hospital but drank a lot of juice. I was given bottles of nourishing products like Ensure.

I choked down some soft-boiled eggs and applesauce. Nurses kept urging me to eat more. I couldn't sleep either; I spent most nights pacing the halls and smoking. The nurses got tired of even having me around.

At the end of the third day, Dr. D'Antonio, the chief neurologist, told me all my tests had come back normal. Whatever was wrong with me had no neurological etiology as far as he could see.

It was not encouraging to know that my body was healthy. It was just more discouraging news; information but no answer. I just wanted to be home.

I kept struggling through classes, most of the time finishing them but not fooling myself. I was distracted and ineffective most of the time. In my office, I could grade only five essays at a sitting. I had to move. I had to pace. I had to smoke. And the essays that got graded lacked the useful constructive comments I had been so good at in the past.

At times I wondered if I would die soon. At other times I hoped I would. It would be devastating to leave a wife and child and lovable dog behind, but at least I wouldn't be a miserable shell hanging around.

Then the last week of March, the blizzard came.

Judie and Jason had driven me to school that morning, as she had followed weather reports and wanted to do some shopping to stock up on basic grocery necessities.

The snow began about ten in the morning and by noon was blowing. Maintenance people on campus scrambled to keep walkways clear, but they couldn't keep up with the storm. As soon as they cleared an area, it was covered again.

My final class ended at 3:00 p.m. Judie and Jason drove into town to pick me up. "The driving is awful," she said. "You can hardly see the road." I drove on the way back and could see how right she was. "I let Nanook out before I came because I didn't want her stranded inside in case we got stuck or the roads became impassable."

I felt a little punch in the gut hearing this as I didn't like to think of her outdoors in this storm. But I knew her decision was the right one. A dog stranded inside a house for hours and hours was not in a position to function.

With the snow deep on our county road and blowing snow creating near white-out conditions, I gripped the steering wheel tightly and snailed along at about twenty miles an hour. The Curse had another wicked dimension: it magnified all problems far out of proportion and intensified my levels of anxiety. The knot in my stomach grew ever tighter, and my palms sweated.

As time passed, I would become more and more aware of this terrifying side effect. Nothing roils the guts of a mentally ill person more than conditions that feel out of control or not amenable to a quick and decisive conclusion. The need to feel in control, even in very small ways, fuels the phenomenon of obsessive-compulsive behavior. There has to be a solution, no matter good, bad, or indifferent, and it has to happen quickly if not immediately.

It was nearly 4:00 p.m. when we eventually made our way home. When I got out of the car, it seemed as if ten or twelve inches were already on the ground, while drifting snow covered most of the yew bushes in front of the house. It was a freakish storm for the last week of March, but it was real.

We looked outside for Nanny but couldn't see her, and any footprints she might have left behind were long since covered up. We called and called for her, but there was no response.

About seven o'clock it started to get dark, but the snow had stopped, and the wind was diminished. I bundled up and went into the small meadow beyond the fence. I called and I called and I whistled. Nothing. No movement of any kind I could see. I went up and checked the barn; the cows were there but no sign of Nanny.

When I went back inside our house, I asked, "What do you suppose has happened to her? She knows the area, she's used to being outside, and she's absolutely built for cold weather."

"I don't know," Judie answered. "It could be anything. Oh! I feel so bad. She's out there in this blizzard somewhere. She could be hurt on a road somewhere or even shot. And what about the traps? There are traps in the woods. I hope she's not suffering." And then my wife began to cry, upsetting Jason seated in his high chair at the table. He began crying too.

And at that moment, I understood clearly how the Curse had impacted Judie dramatically and even Jason to a lesser extent. Maybe even Nanook as well. All the mysterious suffering had taken a toll on my wife, try as she might to maintain strength and support. Like any person, she had limits. It wasn't just that *I* had a problem; our whole family had one. Other than bringing home paychecks, what good was I for my own family? I was dragging everyone into a very dark place, and there was nothing I could do to turn around and find the light switch.

Thinking about Nanny, I was gripped by panic. It felt like my heart was pounding so hard it would burst right through my chest. It was as if my nameless fears had grasped this event eagerly in order to have a fresh target.

About the time we went to bed, Judie said, "I'm real worried about our doggie."

"I know."

"I'm just afraid something terrible has happened to her. There are people who steal dogs and sell them to labs for experiments." I put my arms around her, feeling more fear than she but not wanting to show it. "She runs through the woods a lot," I reminded her. "She'll probably come home during the night." But I didn't believe a word of it.

I turned out the light and curled into the near-fetal position, ready for another sleepless night only tormented this time by the crisis in our home. *We may never see our dog again.* My heart pounded away, and my palms began to sweat. Eventually, when I heard Judie's light snoring, I got up for more rounds of pacing and smoking. I went downstairs and was greeted by an empty living room, an empty couch. No Nanook. I looked out every window to see if there was any sign of her. There wasn't.

I had the shakes, and in that woeful condition, I made a very bad decision. Even though the kitchen clock said 2:00 a.m., I went looking for her.

47

Many types of mental illness, particularly severe mood or affective disorders, drive people to make drastic decisions. The powerful, sometimes even hysterical urgency to find or even create results overwhelms the person's sense of judgment or perspective. And so it was with me at that moment.

I bundled up and headed outside. I felt literally powerless to do otherwise. The thermometer at our front door read twenty-two degrees, but it was no longer snowing, and the wind had stopped. A clear sky with a bright moon gave pretty good light. I started down the road, walking south. The snow was so deep and drifted because the road hadn't been plowed; there were occasional tire tracks, and I tried to keep my footing in them when I could.

I walked two miles, calling at each of the six farmhouses I passed. There was no answer or movement of any kind. It was a silent night of deep and silent snow. I decided to head back to the north through the woods, even though it was another bad decision. I called and called for the dog desperately, knowing inside it was futile.

Much deeper into the woods, I suddenly realized I might freeze to death here. My hands and face ached with the cold. Snow had worked its way down inside my boots; my feet were wet and freezing. I decided I had to get back to the road. I headed back to the east. I was seized by a terrible panic: I might not make it. My body was sluggish as I sank deeply into the snow with every step. I was stumbling, and small tree branches frequently whipped me in the face.

The fact that I was now in a predicament that threatened my life was squarely before me. I knew all about frostbite and hypothermia and knew that I could freeze to death. All the fears and terrors of the many weeks swept over me, and I trembled. I wondered if I had come out here to die—maybe this was just a form of suicide. But I didn't want to die. I knew I wasn't going to find Nanook; I just wanted to get back home somehow and get warm again.

Then I saw the road. I crossed the ditch and headed north. Frozen and exhausted, I still had at least a mile and a half to go. It seemed to take the rest of the night, but somehow I managed to get home. The parts of my body that didn't ache were numb.

I stumbled inside, but the banging of the storm door awoke Judie; she came down the stairs white with panic. She asked me what was happening, so I told her. The clock said five. I had been gone three hours. My fingers were not functional. She had to unzip my coat and pull off my boots. "Why did you do this? Why would you even think of doing it?"

I had no answer. She pulled off my boots and partially frozen socks then ran a dishpan of warm water. I sat in front of the fireplace and put my feet into the water. I held my hands close to the fire. I felt not only a physical misery but I was devastated by my terror and irrational behavior. My fingers and toes were frostbitten. For several years they would cause me discomfort, even in summer months.

Then I began to cry. "We're not going to find her. We're not going to see her again."

"Why? Just because you went on one stupid search? This is only the first night. She hasn't been gone for even twenty-four hours yet."

Even though she made some sense, I could only shake my head while using a towel to wipe away the tears. After I had warmed up a bit, even though I was exhausted, I went upstairs into Jason's bedroom. He was fast asleep in his crib. I pulled up his covers even though they didn't need pulling up. He was sleeping blissfully, and I watched him for several minutes while the tears rolled down my cheeks and into my mouth. *What good am I to you?* I thought. Two months had passed, and I was still the same wretched man. Nothing had changed.

I was looking straight into the terrifying fact of a nearly eviscerating reality: I could not continue my own life on my own resources. A person's life *can suddenly simply spiral out of control.*

THE NEXT MORNING the college was closed, as were all Middletown public schools. A warming sun was out, sending temperatures into the forties. Our road was finally plowed, and I knew the sun would help clear it more. It would be possible to drive, and I was determined to travel any road I could to search for Nanny.

I drank some chocolate milk and ate some applesauce. When I weighed myself on the bathroom scale, I was down to 140 pounds. In two months, I'd lost forty pounds.

We called Jacob to tell him of our missing dog, and he said he'd pass the word to the other vets in town. "Don't be completely pessimistic," he said. "She may have just gotten lost in the storm and will find her way back today in the sunshine." I vowed to try and see it his way.

Judie called the local radio station and the newspaper to take out a classified ad. She also called the pound, the police, and the sheriff's office. I notified the Humane Society where I'd been working as a volunteer Sunday mornings, cleaning cages and walking dogs.

We did not see Nanook that day. I went back along the meadow to the edge of the woods. With the trees bare, I could see the tenant farmer's A-frame, some fifty yards back in. I called and called and whistled. Sargent, often Nanny's running partner, came running out to greet me, but he was alone. I scratched his head. "If only you could talk," I said to him. "If only you could talk."

I made my way to the small house and found Slive's wife at home. She was a sweet young woman who was sympathetic when I told her of our plight. She promised to keep an eye out. I often wondered why she'd ever married Slive, who seemed like a slug to me, but then again, I didn't really know him well enough to judge him. In fact, I'd never even learned his first name.

The next day was the same, and the day after that as well. I called Judie three or four times a day from the college to see if there was any news. There wasn't. It was so discouraging having no news; it was the pins-and-needles stress of *not knowing*. No answers, no information, and no conclusions.

I struggled through my classes by letting students talk (and argue) about current events, telling them I was letting them lead the way to good writing topics. The truth was that I was essentially avoiding teaching just so I could get through the hour.

I still ran with the jogging class, played racquetball, ate little, slept little, hoped little, and lost weight. My eyes were usually blurry, and I continued having the flashbulbs-behind-the-eyes phenomenon. I was constantly distracted and dysfunctional.

A week passed and then another with no sign of Nanny, no piece of information.

Still, even though we had little hope, we renewed our notices in the radio stations, newspaper, and dog pound, and every Sunday morning I checked apprehensively at the Humane Society shelter.

Even in House Church, the congregation prayed for her safe return. We always had time to lift up individual prayer concerns. Jason often asked where she was. We always told him the truth: she had gotten lost in the storm, and we were searching for her.

Warm April weather came late in the month. I began digging in my garden with the spading fork. It was physical work that to a modest extent absorbed me. But when it came time to plant the beans, I was firmly in the grip of apprehension and stomach-churning anxiety. Planting beans suggested I had a future, a right to expectations, and a reason to hope. But I had no hope. I had no reason to believe in future expectations. That mentality was for other people.

I remember making several more half-hearted, desultory trips through the woods thinking but not believing I might find Nanny. But I had given up even if I resisted admitting it. So had Judie. One day she said, "I only hope she didn't suffer. That's the thing I hate thinking about the most."

"Me too," I replied. "If only we could know. If only we could know what happened, even if she died somehow."

"I'm not going to think about that. I have to believe someone found her, took her in, then decided to keep her and love her. She's in someone's home right now being loved and cared for, that's what I believe."

I didn't remind her Nanook had a tag with her name on it and our phone number; I preferred to look at it her way. It was the best possible outcome and something to cling to, hard as it might be.

The loss of Nanook intensified my disorder. Now, when I found myself pacing and sweating in the middle of the night, she wasn't there to hold and stroke. She had always seemed to understand how I was suffering and snug up in support. Now I was truly alone in the night and in the dark. The situation seemed so sad and helpless. I longed for her unlikely return and prayed for her safekeeping.

By the time my birthday rolled around (April 25), it was warm enough to sit on the back porch and grade papers. Since my ability to concentrate was so poor I could never grade more than five at a time, sometimes less. Then it was time for more pacing and smoking. And staring. I frequently just stood in place, staring across the meadow and into the woods, hoping against hope that I might see Nanny come bounding out, heading home. I knew it was wishful thinking, but it didn't stop me from indulging the fantasy.

Often, Sargent, our neighbor's dog, would wander into our yard and stretch out on the grass. It was as if he were looking for Nanook to accompany him on a romp in the woods or join in for a game of catching wood chips. Or maybe he just liked me better than Slive the farmer. I'm sure I gave the dog more attention and affection than he ever did.

I found myself scratching him between the ears and talking to him: "You miss her too, don't you, buddy? You wish you had her back, just like we do." He usually cocked his head as if trying to understand me. Dogs are smart creatures, but they don't speak English.

There were leftover milk bones in our kitchen; we refused to throw them away. We also refused to throw away Nanny's favorite blue blanket. We even kept it folded neatly on the couch. I usually gave Sargent one of the treats, which was no doubt one reason he liked coming to visit, although I chose to believe his loneliness was the bigger part of his motivation. He dropped by to commiserate, I thought. His visits were always welcome but always bittersweet.

But then there came a time when we didn't see Sargent for quite a while, at least a week or two. His visits stopped. One evening when I was working in the garden, I spotted Slive walking along with the cows, headed toward the barn for milking. The cows always walked so slowly, but they knew the way. I approached Slive and asked about Sargent. "He hasn't been over to visit for quite a while," I said.

"That's because he's dead" was Slive's answer. He spoke in a monotone with little facial expression. He could just as well have been talking about the weather.

"Dead? How?"

"He got hit by a pickup on the road. The driver told me, so I went to look. He was layin' next to the road."

"Was he dead?"

"No, just all busted up. I had to shoot him."

"Shoot him? You didn't try and take him to the vet?"

"Didn't have the time, didn't want to spend the money. I put him out of his misery."

I was about to ask him if he missed his dog, but I pretty much knew what the answer would be. I wanted to tell him he should have made the time and spent the money. In the hospital, the professionals told me I needed to learn to be more assertive; they thought it would be a way to release some of the roiling conflict in my subconscious. They were big on the role of the subconscious, but I never was. I don't think I ever believed it or understood the *why* of it.

In any case, I just turned and walked away. I had had enough of Slive for one day. And I grieved for the loss of his friendly, affectionate dog even though it was clear he didn't. Or at least didn't seem to.

I told Judie the news about Sargent. "Oh, that's so sad," she said. "He was such a nice dog, and he was Nanny's buddy."

"I know."

"Was Slive sad?"

"I don't think he gives a damn. I doubt if he even tried to bury him."

"Maybe he does care but just doesn't show it. I don't think Beth would have married him if he didn't."

"Maybe," I said. Judie had had plenty of interaction with Slive's wife. She was a stay-at-home mom, and Beth was the typical farmer's wife, so they had the time.

Both of us had the same thought: *I hope and pray Nanny didn't die like that,* but neither one of us said so out loud. But moving forward, I knew the backyard would seem to me as empty as the downstairs of our house in the middle of the night. We would miss Sargent and grieve the way he had to die.

But it was more than that. I couldn't ignore my sense of the world as a place of suffering, grief, and sorrow. A place without hope or at least without *credible reason* for hoping. My newfound commitment to Christianity notwithstanding, I was heading toward a full-blown melancholy agnosticism that would eventually become my permanent spiritual location. It would, however, take me many years to get there.

And dogs would play a part in nudging me in that direction. In addition to the sorrowful endgames with Fleance, Nanook, and Sargent, my volunteer work at the Humane Society exposed me constantly to a grim narrative of loving canines victimized by neglect and abuse.

THE CURSE was so unrelenting I made another appointment to talk with Jack, my department head, in early May. I told him I was afraid I'd have to resign. Of course I'd already shared with him (as well as his wife, Eva) what I was going through, so he had some history.

"I think you might be a little premature," he said. "Give the whole thing a little time." I couldn't have had a more caring and supportive boss.

"I can't tell you how hard it is for me to get through a class. And let's be honest—I'm not doing a good job."

"You're probably doing better than you think. I haven't had a single complaint."

"But it's what I know inside," I said.

"I still think you need to put off a decision that drastic right now. Have you found any medication that helps?"

"You've been talking to Eva about this."

"Yes, but she knows something about all of this. She's been on medication for depression for a long time."

"But I don't have depression. I have acute anxiety disorder. I'm taking some Valium every night."

"Is that all?"

"That's all."

"Even so, I have to say it's worth looking into a little further. I am worried about all your weight loss though. That can't be healthy. Pretty soon you'll have to buy yourself a whole new wardrobe."

I was now down to 130 pounds, a fifty-pound weight loss. "I just keep tightening my belt and live with shirts and sweaters that hang on me like coat hangers."

"Don't give up," Jack said. "Don't give up."

Don't give up was already my only strategy, and one I'd honor for years to come. *Don't give up.* What else did I have to cling to? All the prayers in the world, all the studying of meditation techniques, all the Dick Dutton sessions, all the House Church support had not alleviated this disabling condition in any manner.

I reported the conversation with Jack to Judie, and she agreed with him.

"You can't make such a drastic decision right now. You have to get better first."

"What makes you think I'm going to get any better?"

"Well, you have to. You just have to. If you resigned your job, what would we do? Where would we go?"

"We could go back home." We had been on a visit to Illinois in January, a few days before the breakdown. Now when I thought of "going home," it just seemed so safe. Counselors often ask, "What is your safe place?" Right now, especially without Nanook in the middle of the night, I didn't have one.

"Back to Illinois? What would we do, and where would we live?"

The fight-or-flight mechanism intensified. "I don't know."

"But you can't just give up."

"I won't ever give up," I said evenly. "But I've given up hope."

She didn't answer, but she was tearing up.

I saw a psychiatrist a few days later. I don't even remember his name. He increased my Valium dosage but said he didn't want to go beyond that until enough time had passed to see if the increased dosage would kick in. There was very little satisfaction in that. And nothing ever kicked in.

Not a single distressing night passed when I didn't think about Nanny and pray for that happy ending that Judie had scripted. Sometimes I included Sargent in a prayer. My love and compassion for dogs had always been an important part of me and, as it turned out, always would be.

Dogs' lives are too short. Their only fault, really.
—Agnes Sligh Turnbull

Where's Nanook,
Where's Sargent?

SOMEHOW I made it through the rest of that spring semester of 1974 and even (as it would turn out) beyond, through another complete academic year. To this day I don't know how, but classes were better than no classes; they were interaction with other people and therefore absorbing to a limited extent. I guess it was the *never give up* mentality. For temporary (usually momentarily) relief, I leaned on the usual activities. I was attending group therapy sessions led by Dick Dutton. Cutting firewood. Working in the garden. The jogging class. Racquetball. House Church. Volunteering at the shelter.

When I drove back home, I took an alternate route along county roads somewhat distant from ours. Each time I passed a house or a clearing, I slowed to a crawl to look for Nanook. It was about six weeks since she had disappeared in the storm, but I hadn't given up hope altogether. By this time I probably should have, but I still missed her, every day. My heart ached each time I recalled that frozen night when I searched frantically (and foolishly) for her.

Taking these kinds of alternate and unfamiliar routes had become a routine. I looked and hoped. Maybe I'd spot her running somewhere near the road or across an open meadow. She had meant so much to me during the early months of my breakdown, had provided so much warmth and comfort, had been such an important part of our family, my heart just wouldn't let me quit. My brain told me otherwise.

My only solace, such as it was, was to hope Judie's hypothetical narrative—that Nanny had been taken in by responsible, loving people—could become my conviction as well. But it was a hard sell; a part of me always doubted it and wouldn't let go.

Frequently, I talked on the phone with my mother, who, along with my father, had moved back to my childhood home of Monticello, Illinois. She was very anxious to see Jason, now nearly a year and a half old. I told her we would drive back for a visit as soon as summer came. She and I both looked forward to it with warm anticipation. In these conversations, I never told her about the Curse; I didn't want to worry her. She had always been the best mom a growing boy could ever have. My dad was a kind and good man but somewhat distant; it was hard to know him. So if we talked on the phone, it was always briefly, and only about the most superficial of things, such as the weather or the Cubs and Cardinals.

When I stood on our back patio, looking toward the distant timber, I always felt Nanny's loss sharply and would for weeks and months to come. It was intensified when I allowed my mind to wander to Sargent, her daily companion and the other dog that almost seemed like ours as well. I could never dismiss from my memory how that friendly and vital dog's life had come to such a pitiable end—crippled by a moving car, then shot to death on the spot. How long had he lain on the pavement suffering before Slive "put him out of his misery"?

DURING THIS PERIOD, the few moments of joy or hope to come my way occurred in the time I spent with Jason. He was smart and precociously verbal, and he loved being read to. Judie and I had made a habit of reading to him well before his first birthday. He was now nearly a year and a half.

We had put together a small library of books just for him. Like most toddlers, he wanted his favorites read repeatedly. We had copies of *The Listening Walk*, *The Very Hungry Caterpillar*, *Brown Bear, Brown Bear, What do You see?*, *Green Eggs and Ham*, *Goodnight Moon*, *The Runaway Bunny*, and half a dozen others.

Sometimes in the evenings, I took him to the Middletown Public Library, where we read together. One night we read the Steven Kellogg classic *Can I Keep Him?* He giggled each time we finished the book and demanded "Again!" I held him in my arms and squeezed him. At that moment (and for several minutes after), I felt a soaring kind of euphoria blending with the hard-core anxiety. I had no name for the feeling, which was simultaneously joyful and painful. But later would have such episodes again from time to time and recognize them as manic. Eventually, years later, one of my diagnoses (I would have several different ones) would be bipolar disorder.

We checked out the Kellogg book and another classic, *Where the Wild Things Are* by Maurice Sendak, to take them home.

When I had free time, I could always find an excuse for driving to town on errands. Shopping, even if for only one or two items. Trips to the bank. The drug store for mouthwash or a bottle of Tums (I ate a lot of those.) Each time, I took Jason with me, locking him down in his car seat. I carried him in my arms through each establishment, watching the joy and fascination spreading across his face each time he eyed a toy on a shelf or a colorfully wrapped sale item, even if it was only a household cleaning product or a case of drill bits.

I just wanted to hold him close. Holding him seemed a little safe somehow, a sliver of encouragement, even the remote possibility of a future. He had one for sure, maybe I could ride with him. And I always prayed he'd inherited the core of his genetic code from his mother, not from me.

In fact, I was already becoming dependent on him, and that dependency, in a small and often hidden pattern, would last the rest of my life. By the time he was twenty-five and with a family of his own, he was the competent adult I could only dream of being.

I found myself getting a little sleep at night—at times up to two hours. Eating was still the same problem. Try as I might, I couldn't get food down. My weight had slipped just below 130 pounds. My ideal weight, prior to the breakdown, was 180 pounds. At that weight, I was fit and strong, even athletic. Not surprisingly, I was usually very fatigued. I was also continuing to lose strength while having frequent dizzy spells.

But I was finding it harder to accept the idea that my faith would deliver me—even if only partly—from the disorientation and suffering of the Curse. So much of the material I read claimed a belief in God and Christ, if sincere enough, would lift any burden. I read this often enough to hold fast to it, despite my doubts. The reading I did came in fits and starts; my concentration was becoming ever poorer. Sometimes I could only read a page or two before I paced and mumbled with agitation.

I developed the habit of going to the chapel on the St. Albert's Seminary grounds (practically adjacent to the college campus) and praying on my knees in front of the altar. As I had done many times before, and would many times again, I implored God to take this suffering away. Or at least reduce the intensity.

I had never been exposed to Catholic houses of worship before, so the crucifix above my head was unfamiliar. But it seemed important in that it underscored suffering and the promise of recovery. At times there were others at prayer too. When I was alone, though, I often made the sign of the cross as I had seen Catholics do so often. Anything that might help take away the suffering. *Anything*.

One afternoon, after genuflecting, Father Dennis joined me. "How do you do this?" he asked. "How do you keep this up?"

I told him I didn't know; it was a question I asked myself every day. He was talking about my scarecrow physique of course, and I'm sure he noticed the bleary eyes.

"Are you getting any counseling?"

"I talk to Dick Dutton fairly regularly. That's about it."

Father Dennis nodded his head in approval. The two men knew each other. "He's a good man. Do the talks help you?"

"They help a little when I'm talking to him, but nothing lasts. Afterwards, I'm right back where I was."

"How about medication?"

"I was taking some Valium but gave it up."

"Why?"

"It wasn't doing any good. I still can't sleep at nights. Why should I keep taking it?"

He waited a few moments while he stared at the large crucifix. "I'll keep praying for you."

He was praying for me. It never occurred to me that someone might be doing that, other than Dick and my parents. "You pray for me?"

"Oh yes. I keep you in my prayers. I've seen you stop in at the seminary for prayer of your own. At least that's what I assume you're doing."

"Do you think the prayers do any good?"

He put his hand on my shoulder. "Most definitely. I believe God can lift this burden you're carrying."

"You do?"

"I absolutely do. I've seen it happen."

I had a few moments of hope, but the hope didn't last long.

I also read some books and guide books by Buddhist and other Eastern religion gurus that seemed more practical; they offered specific meditation exercises designed to lead to inner peace.

I remember two of them rather vividly. Both recommended sitting still in the lotus position, up against a wall if necessary, to guard against intrusive back pain. One of these exercises involved staring at a lit candle in order to rid the mind of negative thoughts or images. Another advised closing the eyes and imagining a blank screen. These techniques didn't work well for me; I was simply unable to quiet the racing mind or keep my focus more than a minute or two.

It was also true that such meditation techniques were admittedly part of a long journey to inner peace that could take months or years. I was far too agitated to keep faith with long, mind-altering patterns of meditation. And besides, I had no person to guide me in any of this or any person to share in the "making good practice." My own resources were far too impaired to immerse myself in or maintain a long-term spiritual journey.

One afternoon in May, while counseling with Dick, I told him that Judie and I planned to head back to Illinois in June and visit our families. "I'm glad to hear it," he said immediately. "That might be the best thing for you right now. Jason needs to see his grandparents, and they need to see him."

"I know."

"It might bring you some relief." Then he smiled and said, "You might come back with your batteries recharged."

I wanted to believe that, but hope seemed to be moving further and further away.

In early June, some two weeks before we were scheduled to drive back to Illinois, I tried writing fiction again. Like countless English teachers, I was dedicated to writing the Great American Novel.

Summers had always been for writing, but now, disabled by the Curse, I found it to be a hopeless proposition. Agitated and with the ever-present anxiety gnawing away at my insides, I couldn't sit still or focus. I couldn't wrap my mind around a plot, develop a character, identify a setting or a theme. I paced and I smoked and I threw notebooks around the room (I had always used the smallest bedroom as a study). Finding my voice was impossible.

I did make a set of notes that turned out to be important much later in life. When I had been a patient in the mental hospital, I had several conversations with a nineteen-year-old girl named Sue. She said I was a good listener. Sue had a difficult panic disorder. Unlike me, who was terrified of *nothing*, Sue seemed terrified of everything life had to offer. To her, the world was a very scary place.

She was a sweet girl who had seemed especially fragile and vulnerable. In short, she seemed overmatched by life itself. I made a page and a half worth of notes about her that I used many years later to write a critically acclaimed young adult novel titled *I Can Hear the Mourning Dove*.

But writing—or even trying to make notes for a manuscript— required me to assume I had some sort of a *future*. It was always hard to imagine I did.

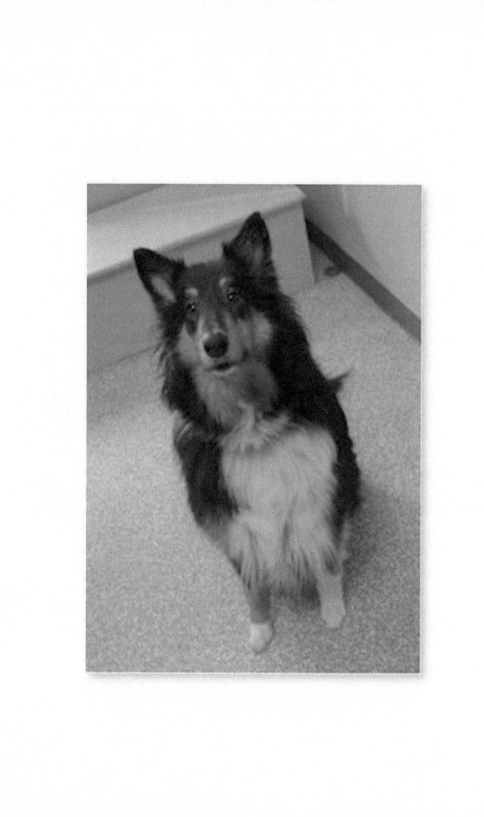

Sometimes you find a dog, some-
times a dog finds you.

—Anonymous

Shep

GOING BACK HOME seemed like I was doubling up. I was not just in Illinois; I was in Monticello, the small town in Central Illinois where I grew up. I had gone from first through eighth grades in the old brick Washington School building.

The scenario was an unusual one. Dad had been appointed to serve the Methodist church there, the one he'd loved so much. He and Mom were right back home in the same parsonage they'd occupied from 1948 until summer of 1956. This was a very unusual appointment for him, but the terms were that he would serve there for the three years leading up to his retirement.

The Methodist parsonage was a big house, located on a large corner lot on Main Street, a block off the town square. The church was just across the street. It was a large church, with approximately one thousand members in a town of some three thousand people.

For the week we were there, it did feel comforting. My generalized anxiety was simmering in the pot rather than boiling over. I even ate and slept a little better. There were nights when I slept for three hours, sometimes even four. I found I could eat a couple of soft-boiled eggs and a few bites of toast for breakfast. I could usually eat some pudding.

My parents asked me why I was so skinny. I had written them a fairly long letter before we left Middletown, describing the breakdown as well as I could, but my appearance still shocked them both. Mother was always a good and sympathetic listener, so I summarized the breakdown in some detail. "But there had to be something to cause this," she said.

"Not necessarily," I told her. "It can just happen on its own. It could be a chemical imbalance that opened its floodgates for no reason we will ever know."

"But what does that mean?"

"It probably means my brain is just wired wrong. And it may never get better."

She asked me about counselors and psychiatrists. I summarized. It seemed like there were so many, many details I couldn't possibly know how to cover them. Talking it through with my mother made me feel better. I knew she would share the story, as well as she could, with my father. It had always been difficult for me to share feelings and emotions with him, which was ironic because he spent a good deal of his time counseling troubled parishioners.

Mom spent every moment she could fawning over Jason and taking him for walks. She had seen him for the first time the previous Thanksgiving when they came to visit in New York, but in the six months since, he had grown into a highly intelligent, highly verbal toddler. He wasn't a baby anymore. Mom and Judie spent a great deal of time pushing him around town in his stroller, taking him to a local park, and making visits to the Dairy Queen.

Monticello was a wonderful place to grow up—even for a preacher's kid. The town was, and is, a prosperous community with a Norman Rockwell courthouse square, church suppers, and school-centered activities. In truth, churches and schools were the town's nerve centers. The locals were enthusiastic supporters of the high school athletic teams, as well as those of the University of Illinois, located some twenty miles to the east.

I talked over old times with several friends. I had a standard answer for each time I was asked why I was so thin: "Just some poor appetite and lots of intense physical activity." I visited my old elementary school, so unchanged it seemed like time had stood still for the past twenty years. I checked out the Little League ball fields where I had played so long ago. With regret and loss gouging at my stomach, I stared at the high school I'd never had the chance to attend. Sometimes I took solitary walks around town, identifying the homes of former friends and recalling memories of pick-up baseball games, games of kick the can, or even hide-and-seek. I could almost feel Shep at my side along every street or driveway.

In short, this homecoming was a witches' brew of happy memories, grief, disorientation, and apprehension all stirred into one. I tried talking to Judie about the back-and-forth of all these memories, but I couldn't really find the words. Maybe it was just too much to absorb for a man undermined by a mental disorder that was now clearly chronic and locked into place.

I remember sitting on a park bench on the town square in the warm sun for long periods of time. Sometimes Jason and/or Judie sat with me with ice cream from the Dairy Queen. Jason usually ran out of patience with all this sitting; after all, he was still so young.

When I found myself sitting alone on the square, I felt like Grover "caught upon this point of time" in Thomas Wolfe's *The Lost Boy*. Caught upon this point in time, but living in the past, cradling memories big and small, important and trivial, joyful and sorrowful.

So many of the memories locked on to dogs. Mom and I shared fond memories of Shep, and she didn't waste any time reminding me that she had been the one to identify the scenario that had probably led him from his working duties to our front porch. And I still remembered Nanook with sinking sorrow, even after three months.

SHEP CAME TO US In the spring of 1954, when I had just turned twelve. I went down to the front porch to get the morning paper. (I was already an early riser, spasmodic sleeper, and avid reader.)

There was a dog lying on our porch. It was a long-haired, good-sized dog with the white-and-yellow markings of a Collie. He had plenty of German Shepherd in him too. The dog wasn't wearing a collar and was a little dirty. This stray dog thumped its tail up and down as I approached slowly but leaned to one side, turning its head away. It seemed like the body language of a dog used to being cuffed around or smacked.

When I began scratching the dog's chin, it turned to lie on its side, so I could see this dog was a male. The chin scratching seemed to reassure him; the tail thumping increased. "Who are you, boy?" I asked. "Where are you from?" The dog didn't answer but rolled back up onto his stomach. This was a gesture of confidence. I stroked his head for a little while before I said, "Are you hungry, boy? Are you thirsty?" He cocked his head in puzzlement at my words.

I went inside and got a couple slices of bread and brought them out to the porch, along with a water dish. Standing up, he ate the bread quickly and drank some of the water.

Immediately at breakfast, I asked my mother if we could keep him. "No, of course not" was the answer. "We don't know anything about him, not where he comes from or who he belongs to. Just leave him alone and he'll probably find his way home. And don't you dare feed him!"

I said okay, I wouldn't feed him.

The following day I didn't see him around, so maybe my mother was right; he had to come from somewhere, and the somewhere probably included an owner. Even so, my youngest sister, Martha Jean, age six, had already named him Shep. And the name stuck. And although we couldn't have known it at that moment, he would turn out to be a vital member of the family circle for the next eight years.

The day after that, he was prone on the porch again. That was when my sister and I began beseeching our parents: "Please, can we keep him?" I had given him more bread, of course.

They wavered a bit. My dad said he'd contact the police and sheriff to check on any missing dog reports they might have. Eventually, enough time passed that my parents were able to satisfy themselves through the available channels there wasn't an owner searching for him. The vet told us he probably wasn't older than three or four years, based on an examination of his teeth.

It was clear by this time that we never adopted him. He adopted us, somehow, some way. Meanwhile, our entire family was drawn to him. I caught my mother brushing his coat out on the porch once. When I said "I told you so!" she just waved me off.

It wasn't long before Shep was my constant companion. When I rode my bicycle to school, he trotted alongside. When school was out, I found him waiting for me beneath a huge maple tree on the grounds of my school. I went to Little League baseball practice, and Shep was there. On Saturday mornings when I pedaled around town, baseball glove looped around my handlebars, looking for the location of that day's pick-up baseball action, he jogged along next to my bicycle.

Sometimes he overdid it. He followed me to an actual game that spring and lay down in the outfield close to me. The umpires said he'd have to move off the field. I knew they were right, but I also made an important discovery that day: Shep responded to hand and voice signals. I told him to get up, which he did, and waved my hand for him to move, and he did. He walked about thirty feet and lay down beyond the foul line.

We discovered that he responded to other commands as well. Sometimes, when it seemed like it would be best if he didn't follow me to a particular destination, all I had to do was raise my hand and say "Stay!" and he would simply gather himself, lie down in the grass, and stay put. Obviously, he'd had some training; this kind of disciplined behavior didn't happen by accident.

After a while, when other pieces of evidence showed up, my mother came to the conclusion that he'd once been a working dog. She later suggested he might have been a sheep dog or herder of some kind.

There was plenty of evidence to support her conjecture. For instance, when Martha Jean was playing outside in the yard, Shep would get up and move to a better position to watch her if she moved out of sight. He did this on a regular basis. Once, when I was watching, a long-eared dog that looked like a coonhound came walking up the driveway near to where Little Sister was digging in the dirt. Shep bolted and ran down the side yard, low to the ground, to take up a position near the driveway. He didn't attack the intruder but stood rigid and braced; he bared his teeth and growled a threatening growl in a low voice. The coonhound turned and jogged away. Shep maintained his position and body language until the dog disappeared from view.

It was the first time we'd seen him run fast, and it was fascinating. Either he had a strong protective instinct or training. Or both. On another occasion, when Mother cooked lamb chops for supper, we watched, puzzled, as Shep moved restlessly from kitchen to dining room to living room, then repeated his path until he was in effect walking laps. All the while, he was panting. I asked my parents what this behavior meant, but they didn't know. He was accustomed to getting beef bones or pork chop bones to gnaw on, but when Mom offered him the lamb chop bones, he backed away slowly, one measured step at a time, while crouching near to the floor. He was ultra-focused and alert.

What could this mean? We all wondered. It was such peculiar behavior. The next morning when I got up, I let Shep out the back door. Mom had left the chop bones in the backyard, assuming he would return to normal behavior and feast on them. But he didn't touch them. Instead, he sank low to the ground and actually *guarded* them, glancing furtively in all directions. As I set out for school, he didn't follow. That, of course, was unusual. When I beckoned for him to come, he took a few steps in my direction then a few steps back, as if he didn't want to abandon his post. He went back and forth like this until I felt sad. Somehow he was faced with a difficult choice.

When I told Mom about it, she said, "This just confirms what I think about his past. He might have been a sheep dog that had an unfortunate incident or incidents."

"What kind of incident?" I asked.

"I don't know. Maybe he lost part of the herd and got punished by his owner. Maybe that's how he became a dog without a home, but I just don't know."

All we could really do was speculate; we still knew nothing about where he might have come from and nothing about how he might have been treated. Neither did anybody else around town, it seemed. This knowledge was something we could never have. "If only you could talk," I said to him. But maybe it was best that he couldn't speak; if he'd been abused, I didn't want to know about it.

There were other events suggesting that Shep had been trained to take care of business and protect. Once in a while, Mom would give Martha Jean a nickel so she could buy a small cone at the Dairy

Queen, located on the corner of the town square. It was only a block from our house, but she had to cross two streets. They weren't busy streets, but there was occasional traffic.

When Shep accompanied her, he came to a full stop at each corner. I don't think Martha Jean understood that he was leading, but the stop usually got her attention; she was safer even if she didn't fully understand the behavior he was modeling. The trip back was the funny part. Shep's head was higher than her waist, and she was careless about holding the cone. We never knew who got more ice cream, the little girl or the large dog.

But there was a scary event as well. One day, Martha Jean came up missing, and my parents were visibly shaken. Mom had been watching her from the kitchen window but looked up one time to find her gone. She moved quickly around the entire house, checking the shrubs and bushes to see if Little Sister was hiding (something she liked to do). But no. Mom made a flurry of phone calls to all the usual people and places, while Dad cruised the streets in the car. I cruised the neighborhoods on my bike. No luck. She was missing.

Then I noticed Shep was gone as well. Mom and Dad couldn't help thinking the lost little girl might have been taken. As in kidnapped. It was scary. For about an hour, none of us was home; we were all searching, in various ways and in various places. Finally, Dad went to the sheriff's office to report her missing. When he got to his destination, he found Shep sitting upright on the sheriff's porch, as if standing guard.

Sure enough, Martha Jean was inside, talking to a deputy. "We've been trying to call you for a while," the deputy told my dad, "but the line was always busy." The three of them walked home together, a trip of about four blocks. Martha Jean got a good switching that day from a piece of the bridal wreath bush, but before that happened, I heard Dad say to Mom, "I can't tell you how relieved I was when I saw that damn dog sitting there. I knew right away everything was okay. It was almost like he was standing guard."

It was the first time I'd ever heard my father curse and the first time I'd heard him praise Shep, the dog who brought more than affection and loyalty; he brought purpose and aptitude as well.

SHEP WAS also my loyal (and comforting) buddy in a difficult period of my young life. In the sixth grade, we had the teacher from hell, an aging woman named Miss Shell, who doled out corporal punishment with a wooden paddle nearly every day. She was a stern taskmaster straight out of the "spare the rod, spoil the child" school, and I was a poor math student. Not a good combination. We were trying to learn advanced fractions, and I was falling ever further behind.

Miss Shell and my mother (traitor that she was, I remember thinking) decided I needed to do extra math work on my own. Miss Shell mimeographed several pages of fraction problems and sent them home with me. I didn't want to work on them after school, when I always played baseball, either organized or pick-up. After supper, I wanted to watch the new television my parents had recently bought, and/or work on non-math homework assignments.

That left early mornings. My mother was skeptical about this arrangement, but she agreed to it on a trial basis. She got me up at five each morning but then went back to bed. I sat at the dining room table at (or before) the crack of dawn, staring apprehensively at the mimeographed sheets. I felt sorry for myself, and I also felt disoriented and distracted. My mind wandered as soon as one of the problems began to lose me. I often got stuck on the same problem for half an hour, mostly staring into space as the frustration mounted.

Had I been a young boy in the twenty-first century, I'd have been diagnosed with attention deficit disorder (ADD). But in the mid-fifties, I was simply an undisciplined child who let his mind wander.

My one consolation on those lonely, discouraging mornings was the dog stretched out by my feet. Shep was always there. Sometimes he would sit up on his haunches so I could scratch him between the ears, feeling tugs of anxiety in the pit of my stomach as the clock moved forward, but solving fractions didn't. Little by little, my apprehensions increased until they began to disrupt my sleep at night or at least make it difficult for me to *get* to sleep. I was experiencing my first spell of disproportionate anxiety, not knowing of course how this state of mind would later become a tortured way of life.

Miss Shell decided to start keeping me in from recess so I could work on my math workbook. It was extremely disheartening to sit at my desk to work on obstinate math problems, when through the window I could see my friends playing kickball or dodge ball. I felt anxious with Miss Shell staring at me; it wasn't surprising, therefore, that I made little progress on workbook pages.

One day, when I was staring through the window, longing to be outside with my classmates, I suddenly felt myself flopping like a rag doll; Miss Shell had me by my arms and was shaking me violently. "When will you learn to pay attention to your work?" she demanded loudly. "Does your mind ever stop wandering?"

I felt my face turning crimson. Naturally, I had no answers for her questions, which were essentially rhetorical, after all. Before the shaking, I had felt alienated and despondent; now I felt humiliated as well. I told her I had to go to the bathroom. "All right," she said flatly while slumping in her desk chair, "but make it quick."

On shaky legs, I made my way down the two flights of stairs (the restrooms were in the basement) but had begun to cry by the time I entered the boys' room. That was what I didn't want her to see. It was what I didn't want any of my friends to see. But most important, it was what I didn't think could even happen. I was twelve years old now and should have been able to withstand any punishment a teacher could mete out.

But by the time I got back to the classroom and parked myself in the lonely situation, I had remembered that after school, Shep would be waiting beneath that tree so we could go home together. It was a comforting thought.

Somehow, I survived sixth grade math, although with a low grade.

The next year, I started a paper route. Shep would jog alongside as I cycled my way to the forty-some porches. He was by now a very important part of my life—loyal friend, consistent companion, source of love and reassurance. It seemed like I rolled around with him on the floor nearly every evening.

Although he was usually waiting for me after school, even in cold weather, I discovered he made his rounds about town during the day, often accompanying my father when he went to the coffee shop on the town square. He waited patiently outside the building for Dad to emerge then walked with him back to the church. Sometimes he stood guard on the church steps as well. He also frequently followed my mother to the grocery store, waiting patiently on the sidewalk until she came out with her groceries. Then he joined her on the walk home. Still, on most days, he anticipated the time school dismissed and was usually waiting.

Somehow, for some reason, this loving and patient stray dog had targeted our house and our family—all four members. It was enough to make you believe in destiny. We never knew his how or why, or how far or how long, but the extent to which he enriched our lives would have been difficult to quantify.

THEN, in 1956, just after I finished the eighth grade, we moved. We moved from Monticello to Bloomington, Illinois. Dad had been appointed to the position of district superintendent, which meant he wouldn't be serving a particular church. Instead, he would be overseeing and aiding some eighty Methodist churches spread out over a large geographical area. Troubleshooting for these churches was a big part of the job, perhaps the biggest. He was gone a lot, driving to different communities several times a week.

I hated leaving Monticello. It was traumatic for a boy who was just about to enter high school. Friendships I had forged over an eight-year period were left behind. Since we moved in June, I would be missing out on my intermediate summer baseball league and arriving in Bloomington too late to join a team or league there. I was shy by nature and inclined to withdraw once the move was completed.

Bloomington was a much larger city than any of us was accustomed to. It had a population of forty thousand and, coupled with twin city Normal, approached some fifty-five thousand residents. This "big city" intimidated me, and it was not a setting for letting dogs wander free. Most people walked their dogs on leashes, something we'd never had cause to do with Shep in Monticello. But since he obeyed commands so well, we could leave him untied in the yard.

I did make a couple of friends about the middle of the summer, who introduced me to the daily wiffle ball games in a park about a block away. This was a destination close enough to home that Shep could go along with me. He just stretched out in the sun while the games took place.

Since there were swing sets and a merry-go-round in the park, it was also a favored destination for mothers and their young children. As soon as they found how approachable Shep was, they soon delighted in petting him and scratching him along the chest and belly.

Martha Jean, now in fourth grade, often went to the small neighborhood grocery store at the end of the block to get a candy bar and/or a cold soda. Since there were no streets to cross, it was safe for Shep to walk beside her. As a rule, though, when we left home, we had to signal him to stay put. Which he did. He never approached people who walked along the sidewalk in front of the house.

I entered high school as a timid and anxious young man who felt miserably out of place. We (Mother, Martha Jean, and I) joined a large Methodist Church that had a youth program. I did make a few friends there, but none of them lived close, and my shyness prevented me from cycling around in this strange city to build on the friendships.

I did poorly in schoolwork from the get-go. My concentration was spasmodic. As usual, I was easily distracted most of the time, found it hard to finish homework, and if I did finish a homework lesson, it was usually flawed or misguided. I often lay on the screened front porch with an open workbook with the faithful Shep beside me. He didn't exactly give me confidence, but his presence tended to reduce my homework anxiety, if only a little.

Most of the time, I got Cs, with an occasional B or D. My parents were thoroughly concerned about my substandard academic performance and made sure I heard about it.

Over time, Shep gradually became Martha Jean's dog. She spent more time with him than any other member of our family, petting him and holding him. He developed the habit of sleeping in her bedroom.

I didn't mind too much. By the time I got my driver's license, I had full-blown adolescent hormones calling me. I had discovered why girls were important but lacked the confidence to ask them out. I was gone from home more. I had the typical teenage issues and independence agendas. Little by little, I didn't look for dog comfort except when I was struggling with classwork. And of course, due to urban traffic volume, Shep could no longer be my walking or bicycling companion.

WHEN IT became time for me to go to college, I enrolled at Illinois Wesleyan University, whose campus was located only about four blocks from our house. I really wanted to go away to college rather than live at home, but the financial package at IWU was too good to pass up. The school knocked off half of my tuition because Dad was a member of the university's board of trustees. Because I had done a good job with the Bloomington High newspaper, the other half was paid for by the local newspaper, *The Daily Pantagraph*, after the newspaper contracted with me as a future journalist.

I started working at the newspaper as a part-time sportswriter. I even got paid. But my living at home as a college student yearning for freedom and independence wasn't easy for any of us.

I stayed on campus as much as possible, spending time in the library or campus grill when I wasn't in class. Most of the time, I could even eat my lunches and suppers there with my *Pantagraph* income. I didn't have many dates, and the few I did have were usually limited to the campus grill or some on-campus movie. I had plenty of interest in girls, but I was still very shy and uncertain

As usual, my grades were below average. I was usually frustrated by a repetitive grind of trying to connect the dots—Who was Metternich, and exactly why was there a Russia and a Prussia?—over and over without grasping the material.

An ongoing consequence of that pattern was frequent low-grade anxiety bouts leading to restless nights. But by junior year I declared an English major because I had always liked to read, and my writing skills improved dramatically from my work at the newspaper. Before long, I was suddenly dean's list material.

The time came when I had to spend more time at home, like it or not. But I didn't resent it even a little bit: Shep, who by this time had essentially become a house dog, needed me.

He had begun to hobble around. The vet said he was developing arthritis and possibly hip dysplasia as well. As the months went by, he occasionally lost control of his back legs and stumbled while climbing or descending stairs. Martha Jean was distraught because she'd become so bonded with him and was accustomed to having him in her room at night.

It wasn't too long before he sometimes needed help to climb stairs. At first, it was a simple matter of holding him under the chest; with this arrangement, he could walk up and down stairs if we went slowly. Everyone in our family could manage this simple maneuver.

But by my sophomore year at IWU, when Martha Jean was a high school freshman, Shep needed even more help. He developed a limp as he moved slowly from room to room. It was getting painful to watch him moving laboriously from place to place. There were times when his back legs failed him so completely that Dad or I had to carry him outside and/or back in.

I talked it over with my mother and agreed to come back home frequently on days when Dad was on the road. Heavy though Shep (probably about seventy pounds) was, we had to carry him; neither she nor Martha Jean was strong enough to manage this. The easiest way was to pick him up on the front porch and then carry him down the five or six steps to the sidewalk. It could be a tricky maneuver because he cried out in pain if you happened to grip his hips by mistake. The best bet was to pick him up under the chest and simply let his back half hang free.

That was the arrangement we followed for the next few months. Each time, it seemed, when I came home to help him, I spent a little more time with him. Either on the porch or living room floor (depending on the weather) I sat down while he lay his head and front paws in my lap. I scratched his head and chin, sometimes for as long as half an hour while talking to him quietly. *I wanted to remember. This time, this place, and this touch. I wanted to remember.*

Because our whole family knew what was coming, and that time not far off, I told him how sorry I was for neglecting him over the past couple of years. I reminded him of all those wonderful times in Monticello we'd shared together. He lifted his head while I talked, looking straight at my face as if he understood every word I said.

One last time, I asked him where he'd come from in the beginning, what his life before us was like, and why he'd picked us out to be his family. He sighed, turned on his side, and licked my hand. *Oh, if you could only talk*, I thought for the umpteenth time.

We continued this arrangement for the better part of six months, until one day I came home and the house was completely empty—no mother, no sister, no dog, and Dad on the road. Right away I knew. I sat on the front steps and got my tears out of the way. I was a twenty-year-old young man and didn't want anyone in my family to catch me crying.

That wasn't the case with Martha Jean when she and Mom came driving home. My little sister had tears flowing freely. My mother told me what the vet said, that his condition had worsened to the point where the only act of love was to put him to sleep.

"How did you get him in the car?" I asked.

"John helped us," she said. John was a big, strapping construction worker who lived next door.

I was not a hugger, especially when it came to members of my own family, but just this once I couldn't resist holding Martha Jean to let her sob it out on my chest. Shep had been *my* dog, then *her* dog. But through all the eight years, this gentle, loyal, and highly intelligent creature had truly been *our* dog. As a matter of fact, in subtle ways and over time, he had brought my sister and me into a closer relationship than that usually shared by siblings with such an age gap.

While I was still holding Martha Jean, I said, "He came to our home when he didn't have one. He found that home and a loving family. For eight years, he had a terrific life. That's what we have to try and remember." At that moment, my words might have been adult and accurate, but they didn't really resonate with me; they just sounded like clichés. There was too much heartache. I looked at my mother; even she was misty-eyed.

There was plenty of lasting sorrow in our home. We all looked for him, in various places at various times, but he wasn't there. Martha Jean looked next to her bed, but he wasn't there. In the early morning when I set out for the campus, I couldn't stop from turning around at the corner to signal him to stay put. Even Dad confessed to missing him in the study room where he conducted church business, mostly on the phone. Shep was a vital part of our family, and once he was gone, we seemed to understand that better.

I will always remember this warm and wonderful dog who happened into our family circle unexpectedly and wanted nothing more than to be part of it.

*I heard somebody define heaven once as
a place where, once you get there, all the
dogs you ever loved run to greet you.*
—Robert Parker

Buster

BEFORE WE LEFT Monticello to head back to Orange County, I sat one last time on the front porch steps and gazed at the spot I'd first seen the big yellow-and-black dog. The day we'd found each other. I found tears streaming down my face. Jason asked Judie (as he'd done many times before and would do again), "Mommy, why is Daddy crying?"

My parents gave us goodbye hugs. I didn't want to leave. I didn't want to go back to Middletown and the college, as they now seemed to represent only fear and failure. I wanted to stay here, in this quiet little Midwestern town, and live through ball games, the companionship of so many friends, and screen door summers.

But of course the idea was absurd. There are no cocoons in life. No places to hide. No time travel. What could I possibly do here to earn a living or provide for a family? That opportunity was still at the college, no matter how much it might scare me.

"I hope you get better," my mother said. "You should keep working with that counselor friend you've talked so much about." She meant Dick Dutton, of course. Dad told me he'd pray for me, and I knew he would; in his steadfast Christian heart, it was the most profound of all promises.

Back in the lovely stone house in the Catskills, I found the Curse still plaguing me day and night. Going without sleep or food, I saw my weight bottom out at 120 pounds. I could no longer avoid buying some new clothes. Or at least different ones. I spent my money at thrift and consignment shops to save. But for whatever reason, it seemed like I bottomed out at that weight. Although I rarely ate more in a day than a soft-boiled egg or two, some bowls of broth, and applesauce or pudding, I was holding steady at the 120. The bad news seemed like good news.

We had picnics with our friends from the college that summer and even some makeshift softball games, but I felt little motivation to participate. I mostly kept to myself, often lying on a picnic table off to the side while trying to *breathe* my way through especially intense anxiety attacks. When friends asked me what the matter was, I retreated to my standard answer, that I just wasn't feeling well. Good times and camaraderie all around me but unable to participate, I felt terribly discouraged. *Every day of this is one day of your life checked off,* I told myself, with a deep sense of sorrow and disorientation.

I spent more time working at the humane society shelter, cleaning cages, walking and feeding dogs, picking up poop. It was busy work that helped alleviate the anxiety for a short period, but it also put me in an environment full of dogs that needed a home. I thought often of Nanook with tears flowing in my belly. But it was busy work, and it was physical—the kind of activity I prized and relied on.

I made many errand runs with Jason and took him frequently to the library so we could read picture books together. I loved holding him while we read.

Then a day came at the shelter when a new dog showed up in one of the cages. He was a brown-and-tan shepherd mix, about eight months old. His name was Buster. Unlike many of the other dogs that became animated when humans came near, Buster just lay still in his cage and stared up with those sorrowful dog eyes, almost like a prisoner longing for a get-out-of-jail card.

A couple of nights later, I told Judie about Buster. She and I both wanted that perfect dog to be Jason's growing-up companion. Besides that, we were both certified dog lovers. "Do you think it's too soon?" she asked.

I knew what she meant. This was late August, some two weeks before the first semester would begin at the college. I put my face in my hands. "It's been five months," I said.

"Could Nanny forgive us?" It was the kind of question that only make sense in a conversation between dog people. Dog people bestow human qualities on their favorite canines without a moment's hesitation. Judie was asking me if Nanook would feel betrayed should we adopt a new dog.

It took me awhile to put together an answer. "I think she would," I finally said. "I think anything that would make us happy would make her happy." Judie was nodding, but there was still doubt in her eyes. "Take me out to the shelter so I can see Buster."

We brought Buster home just before Labor Day. After we introduced him to Jason and watched his face light up, we felt better. Buster was soft and cuddly and seemed to enjoy being held. We still felt a sense of guilt associated with our wonderful Nanny but decided we needed to find a way to move past it.

The second day we had him, we took Buster to our friend Jacob, the vet, who examined him and declared him healthy. He weighed twenty-five pounds. "He's basically still a pup," said Jacob. "He'll get bigger."

"His sheet says he's eight months old," I said.

"Yeah, he may eventually grow to forty. He's got some German Shepherd in him but probably some Border Collie too. In terms of disposition, it should be a good blend."

But over the next couple of days, the dog's "disposition" was discouraging. Although he was never aggressive or touchy, he also seemed disinterested. Bored, even. He never objected to being picked up and held, but he didn't seem to enjoy it either. And once we put him back down, he simply walked to a spot along the wall he'd picked out and lay still. He didn't even look in our direction; he simply took a deep breath and put his chin on the floor between his paws.

As the days and nights passed, Buster didn't respond to us. He didn't respond to affection by returning it. He pooped and peed on the floor, but we expected that; he was young and had to be trained. But when I took him out in the yard and offered him a dog treat if he "took care of business," he tended to just ignore the treat and turn his nose away. He never wagged his tail. In fact, when I took him outside to try and get him to play, his tail was never up.

"It's like he's never had any socializing," Judie said.

"I know," I said. There were a couple of nights when, unable to sleep, I came down to the living room for the usual pacing and smoking. I brought Buster onto the couch with me, to see if he might return my affection that way. But it didn't happen. As soon as I took my arm away, he simply got down from the couch and made his way back to his spot along the baseboard. It was so disheartening.

We tried to tempt him by tossing sticks or a tennis ball in the backyard, but he didn't react. He just lay still. And his behavior didn't change when we tried to coax him to come from just a few feet away or tried to tempt him in our direction with a dog treat.

It was as if Buster had no interest in human contact at all. He was a cute little dog and probably a "good blend," as Jacob had said, but seemingly bored with us. Naturally, his behavior caused my anxiety level to spike. The Curse, which had begun from nothing, now seemed to inflame everything.

After two weeks, we took Buster back to Jacob for a consultation. Holding him on the examination table, the vet looked in his eyes and ears. "He seems healthy," said Jacob. "So that's not the problem."

Once more, we described his behavior. "I think maybe," said the vet, "he's what we call a kennel dog."

"A kennel dog?"

"Yes. He may be unresponsive because he spent his life alone before he came to the shelter. It may be he never had human interaction or socialization. Sometimes, a dog left alone all his life simply loses the will to live. He's never been a part of anything, so he goes into a psychological shell. I've seen it a few times. Every shelter gets a kennel dog from time to time."

I looked at the little dog lying listless on the exam table. "No one ever loved him," I said, "or held him."

"About right. We can't know his background in any detail, but it's my opinion he never knew life, and he may not have the will to know it."

It seemed so sad. Judie and I were not ready to give up on Buster quite yet, though. We took him back home and, for two more weeks, tried to find some stimulus that would get him to respond. But it didn't work. Nothing changed. A month's worth of urging, coaxing, and cajoling didn't impact the little guy in any way.

With heavy hearts, we left Jason with a neighbor and took Buster back to the Humane Society. "It just didn't work out," we told the shelter manager. "Our vet thinks he's a kennel dog."

The manager furrowed her brow while nodding her head. "It happens," she said. "Not often, but it does happen. I'm so sorry the little guy didn't work out. He's a cute little thing, though." That was true. He was.

When we got back home, the two of us sat on the couch and wept. Not just for our loss and disappointment, but for the fact the little dog, although only eight or nine months old, had simply lost the will to live. "He'll be euthanized," Judie said through her tears. "Maybe not right away, but sooner or later they'll decide he's not an adoptable pet."

I knew she was right. We were sitting in the same spot, with the same tears, where we had mourned the loss of Fleance some years earlier. "One dog that turned vicious," I blubbered, "and one that simply had his spirit broken by neglect and loneliness."

She was nodding. "And one that got lost in a blizzard and never came home. "Maybe you and I are just not supposed to have a dog." It was so much sorrow. We wept some more before I went to pick up Jason.

When we got him home, we told him about Buster.

"Is Buster coming back?"

It twisted my heart. "No, he's going to live at the shelter again."

"But why?"

"He wasn't happy," Judie said. "Maybe he'll be happier if he's living with other dogs." I couldn't bear this conversation. I turned on the TV. *Sesame Street* was on.

I thought again about writing a letter of resignation but resisted the urge. I went into the backyard, stared at the woods on the other side of the meadow, and let the tears flow.

SOMEHOW, I survived two more semesters. The Curse never relented. The gnawing knot of fear in my stomach, the sleepless nights, the pacing and smoking, the tiny amounts of food, never a pause, never a respite. And never anything close to an answer. It had all come at once for no reason and never gave an inch. I couldn't imagine what vital toll this was taking on my body. How long could I live like this? How long could I survive? I didn't want to die young, but each dreadful day made such an outcome seem all the more likely.

At the college, I threw myself into the usual draining activities when my schedule allowed. Jogging class. Racquetball with my usual partner, a friend named Ron Richardson, a geography teacher. I played on the faculty basketball team. I played with an intensity far beyond that of everyone else. It was just recreational basketball, after all. I was the leading scorer, and it didn't mean a thing. As soon as each game was over, the Curse devoured me again.

Near the end of January 1975, I realized I had now been battling the disorder for a full year. And making no progress. The sleepless nights found me downstairs in the living room again, curled up in the couch. The cold temperatures and deep snow seemed to make the fear and loneliness all the more intense. *Where was the big dog to hold?* I lay on my side often, shivering and shaking. I dozed off a few minutes from time to time but mostly watching the clock moving ever so slowly, longing for the first light of early dawn.

For the first time, I began having suicidal thoughts. With death would come peace. No more suffering. But the standard methods, those involving guns, ropes, knives, were much too scary. If we had a garage, I sometimes thought, I could just drive the car in, close the door, and turn on the engine. Death would come slowly but surely. The suicidal thoughts never went very far. Although my life was dominated by suffering, it included too much family love. Too much Judie and too much Jason. I could never inflict that kind of pain on them, and besides, suicide would mean giving up. Giving up was not something I planned to do. Ever.

I began withdrawing from campus social activities—the Lyceum lecture series featuring significant authors, the college theatrical concerts, speeches by politicians, and more. We went to fewer parties and social get-togethers. I couldn't find the motivation; it was easier to simply stay at home and curl up into a ball.

I still had the shakes a lot of the time, along with the occasional dizzy, lightheaded spells. The flashbulb effect behind my eyes came and went from time to time.

In classes, I wasn't really teaching. Many times I had the students write in their journals; the idea was to examine their lives and make notes for future essays. It let me off the hook. In literature classes, I had them read ahead while I sat at a desk and made notes under the heading "stone house dogs." One day, I began to tear up when I made an entry about the neighbor dog Sargent and the brutal end that had claimed him. I had to leave the room. In the hallway, I wiped my tears and blew my nose before returning.

I graded the journals, maybe two or three at a time, before my agitation had me up and pacing.

I knew that I couldn't possibly go on beyond the spring semester of '75 since I was too disabled to actually do my job. I discussed it with Judie from time to time. She understood, but the conversation usually ended with "If you quit your job, what would we do? Where would we go?"

"Back home," I usually replied.

"Back home to where? To what?"

And I knew she was right. Was there any reason to think a change of scenery would reduce the intensity of the Curse? In these conversations and others, I was reminded again and again how my condition was taking a heavy toll on my wife. My feelings of guilt were significant and ever present. Jason seemed happy-go-lucky, as if he were safely removed from it all, but I knew that couldn't be so. It was all affecting him in ways that didn't show.

I have a vivid memory of the St. Patrick's Day party we attended at the home of Phil Reiss, history teacher and good friend. We joined about twenty colleagues, friends, and students. The idea was to wear green and have an Irish story to tell. Phil and I had a semiprivate conversation off to the side. For some reason, he asked me about the outcome of our dog Nanook. The question surprised me.

He was in the sympathy business at the moment, but his question prompted me to look at the calendar on the wall. It had been a year, almost to the day. Twelve months without her hadn't taken away the keen sense of loss. I excused myself and went to the bathroom, locking the door behind me. Immediately the tears began to flow. For a good five minutes, I sobbed and blew my nose. *Somebody found her and took her in*, I told myself. *Despite all odds, she's in a good home with people who love her and care for her.*

Some people, including mental health professionals, say crying is good for us when we're hurting. I could never see how it was good for me, but at least at that moment, I didn't have to hear Jason asking Judie, "Why is Daddy crying?"

ABOUT A WEEK before spring break came an invitation from my colleague and close friend Ron, a physically adventurous guy and my most frequent racquetball partner. He wanted me to go with him on a canoe trip to Maine to navigate the Allagash. I lied. "I'll think about it," I said. I didn't intend to put myself through a trip like that, far from home.

A couple of days later, he changed it to the West Branch of the Penobscot River. "I found out the Allagash is too challenging, too many difficult whitewater passages," he said. "I don't think you're experienced enough."

"So you're looking out for my best interests."

"Something like that."

When I told Judie about his proposal, she encouraged me to go. "It sounds like fun," she said. "Why don't you go?"

"I wouldn't feel right, going to someplace like that and leaving you and Jason at home."

"That's not the real reason. You're afraid to go." She was developing a sense of when to be firm with me, when to support and when to push.

"Okay," I said. "I'm afraid."

"Of what?"

The mounting pressure inside turned to anger. "I'm afraid of being somewhere else! I'm afraid to be without control, in a situation I can't control! I'm afraid of something different."

"But why?"

"Because I'm terrified of the unknown. I don't trust myself to accept what is spontaneous or different. I cling to activities I'm sure of, that I'm used to. Whatever makes me feel in control, if only a little bit."

"But you can't spend the rest of your life living like this. Where will you ever have any fun? What will you enjoy?"

"Fun? I don't even think about fun," I told her without a moment's hesitation. "That's for other people. I care about surviving. I do whatever I have to to survive."

"Don't you see, Jim? That's why you *should* go on the canoe trip. You might prove something to yourself. You could show yourself that you can deal with a situation that's out of the ordinary. Maybe you could even enjoy life a little bit instead of fighting with it."

There was no question her advice made sense. I knew it and had often urged the same advice on myself. I promised her I would think about it.

For two days, I did think about it. I argued with myself one way, then the other. The longer this dilemma played out in my head, the more pitiful I felt. I was being ripped apart by a decision most people were capable of making with very little apprehension. I talked it over with Dick Dutton, who also thought I should go. But he added a very important piece: "I think you should do it for Judie."

Immediately I knew what he meant. "She needs to be away from me for a while."

"Well?"

I had to say it: "She needs a break from me. All this suffering and disorientation is dragging her down too. I can't tell you how many times I've thought of it."

"Well?"

"It doubles my guilt. Or maybe I should say triples it."

"Have you ever talked it over with her?"

"Some, but not enough," I answered quickly. "I'm also scared I'm doing damage to Jason."

"How so?"

"Well, even though he's only fifteen months, he's perceptive. He's reading people. Whenever I'm in tears, he asks his mother why."

"That's natural," said Dick. "Any toddler would ask that question."

"Yes, but what if I'm setting him up for emotional problems of his own later on?"

"This is too much. You're overthinking again. Let's deal with the original topic. I think you should go on the canoe trip and give Judie a break."

I had to agree with him, although my apprehensions were nearly hysterical.

That night I slept restlessly for an hour or so, then got up around midnight and stumbled downstairs. I lay down against Nanny's blanket on the couch; if I couldn't have her, at least I could have her blanket. We also had a framed eight-by-ten photo of her on the mantel over the fireplace. I turned on a light so I could look at it. Looking at the picture gave me a profound sense of loss, but I pounded a fist into a palm. "I'm going!" I declared to the night. "I'm going, I'm going, I'm going on that canoe trip."

The next day Ron and I went to the store to buy supplies; we would be sharing the cost. We bought everything canned or in tins so we could conserve space by avoiding a cooler. Enough food for four people over a ten-day period would have to fit in two canoes. Ron was bringing his teenage son, who was bringing a friend.

I stood by the Dinty Moore beef stew with terror clutching me. I got so dizzy I nearly blacked out. But I braced myself against the shelving. "What's the matter?" asked Ron.

I had not told him of the nature of my ordeal over the past fifteen months. It was that "close counsel" policy. "I'm a little worried," I said.

"About what?"

By this time I was used to lying. "I'm a little worried about leaving Judie and Jason back at home alone."

His answer came quick: "They're the ones with all the doctors and hospitals. They're the ones with neighbors and firefighters. The four of us will be the ones in the wilderness without resources."

His answer terrified me. I pictured myself in the wilds of Maine, alone and afraid. I nearly backed out of the whole thing, but Ron got me interested in other supplies. From time to time he asked for my opinion about purchases. I always said, "You decide. You're the one with more canoe trip experience." It got me off the hook. I was incapable of making a decision. But I did insist on two six-packs of the chocolate-flavored Ensure nutritional drink I leaned on nearly every day.

"We won't have room for that in the cooler," Ron said.

"I don't care. It can be warm." And that ended the discussion.

We started out early the next morning in Ron's car. His son, Andy, and Andy's friend Gary, both about fifteen years old, were already in the back seat. We had supplies and two tents; we would get the canoes from an outfitter in Maine.

We drove north throughout the day. Fear clutched my stomach as we went deeper and deeper into the wilderness. The only roads were dirt logging trails maintained, more or less, by the paper companies. Late that night, when it became obvious we couldn't reach the outfitter until the next day, we pulled off and decided to sleep by the edge of the road. I ate a few spoonsful of cold ham and beans from a can we all shared and drank the first bottle of Ensure.

We didn't know it, but we were lying next to a stream. The mosquitoes were deadly. We spent the whole night swatting bugs and not sleeping. It was an unexpected nuisance, and I reacted with palpitations and sweat. But it was too late to decide not to make the trip. There was no turning back now.

The next day about noon, weary and haggard, we reached our destination. Ron arranged with the outfitter to rent the canoes and transport us upriver. With my eyes burning and heart pounding, I looked at Ron's car and longed to drive home. I did not want to embark on even a single day of canoeing, let alone the five or six days the trip on this lonely river would likely take. I was about as lost and miserable as I had ever been during these past fifteen months. I gave myself a stern pep talk that had no beneficial effect.

The outfitter, a greasy fat guy with bad breath, loaded the two aluminum canoes atop his big Jeep and took us deep into the timber upriver. We started our trip along the West Branch of the Penobscot.

For five days, the four of us floated our way through the wilderness, using basic maps Ron had thought to bring. Most of it was smooth sailing, although there were modest rapids from time to time. We did not see another human being during that period of time.

We paddled our way (I was not completely inexperienced) through that pristine environment looking at elk, deer, waterfowl, and many square miles of pine forest. I did not enjoy the experience; I did not prove anything to myself. I was in terror throughout the trip. I suffered through night after night without sleep, curled into a ball in the small tent with my heart pounding. It was the worst five days of my life, and it filled me with regret because it confirmed the Curse was more eviscerating than ever if I lacked my support system. And of course, I didn't have a dog in my life. There was no Nanook, and there never would be. A loving dog just seemed so essential for living.

One morning Ron said, "You look lousy."

"I feel lousy."

"Why? Not getting enough sleep?"

"That's pretty much it," I said, without exploring the subject further.

On the next to last day of the trip, a couple hours after noon, we found the river widening into a small lake. The wind was strong and the water rough with whitecaps. Suddenly, the boys' canoe tipped over. Ron and I jumped in after them. The four of us were soaked to the bone as we pulled both canoes to a nearby island and rescued most of the remaining supplies.

The island was sandy with a few scrubby pine trees. We stretched out the tents to dry, then we stripped off all our clothes to let the sun and wind dry us. It was chilly, though. It felt strange to be standing naked outdoors, but there were no people nearby, nor were there likely to be. "You're really getting skinny," said Ron.

"You're skinny yourself."

"Yeah, but I've always been that way."

"Well, now we're both that way." End of discussion. This was now the manner in which I dialogued with most people, including my best friends.

Later, we put on our dry clothes, built a fire (there was plenty of dry driftwood lying around), and cooked some canned stew. I was able to eat a few bites of it. I drank the last bottle of Ensure.

Ron went into the woods to answer nature's call, and when he returned, he said, "Look what I found in the crook of an old tree." He was holding an old cigar, half-smoked. "Look what the natives left behind."

We sat on the warm beach, watching the sunset. We smoked the stale cigar, passing it back and forth. We heated up some coffee. For a few minutes, I felt some calm for the first time on the trip. It was an odd set of ingredients that generated this short period of relative peace, but that was what happened. Plus, I knew the next day we'd be back in Ron's car and headed home.

When the trip was over, I was exhausted, shaken, and grateful to be back home. I hugged Judie and Jason until the tears began running down my face. I did not enjoy the trip, nor did I have any fun. When Judie told me she was worried about me when I was gone, it didn't even seem as if her vacation from me had worked out.

It was now abundantly clear to me that I had grabbed on to a lifestyle that could only be called *rigid defense*. The weapons I had developed to fight back were now my whole life. I was consciously structuring every day, right to the hour if possible, with predictably absorbing activities. Every day had to be programmed. I made certain that no day allowed for free time because it was a threat. Anything that caused me to rearrange my schedule or required spontaneity was equally threatening. It was very disheartening to see the kind of prison I had built for myself, yet I felt that I had to survive, and I knew no other way of doing so. I was doing what I had to do.

More than forty years later, it's still the strategy I cling to. I don't believe I could survive without it.

Two days after I got back from the canoe adventure, I typed out my letter of resignation and put it in an envelope with Jack's name on it. But for some reason, I didn't give it to him that day or the next. I put it away in a desk drawer for the time being.

When the semester was over, Judie and I planned another trip back to Illinois. Then came the terrible June day when I was sitting out behind the house, trying to read the movie review.

And the mailman came around the house to tell me he had a package that needed a signature. I signed it.

As he turned to leave, he asked, "What's the story on those two dogs?"

"What two dogs?" I asked.

Those two dogs layin' in your stairwell there."

"What two dogs?" I asked again then stood up to take a look.

*Once you have had a wonderful dog, a
life without one is a life diminished.*
                                    —Dean Koontz

Dogless in Urbana

WHEN WE MOVED back to Illinois, we moved in with my parents
in Monticello while storing all our belongings in their garage. We
knew this was only temporary. I had an urgent need to find employment as we only had about $4,200 saved.

There were no job options in a small town, so each morning
found me driving the twenty miles east to Champaign-Urbana, home
to the University of Illinois. Since I was still a devoted Christian, or
at least wanted to be, I began visiting the religious foundations on
campus; maybe I could find something that emphasized Christian
life and/or programming.

In each case, I talked with the director of the foundation to
determine what staffing needs it might have and what I might be
qualified for. Most people tried to be helpful. If they had nothing
available, they promised to keep an ear to the grapevine for me. But
it soon became clear that the nation's sluggish economy was being felt
by campus religious foundations, just like everybody else. In most
cases, they were being forced to cut back, not expand, their programming operations.

One day, as I was leaving the McKinley Foundation, I looked
back at the large banner hanging above the entrance with these words
of scripture: "If God be for us, who can be against us?" Inside, I
felt a surge of encouragement. I knew that in the days and weeks to
come, I would need to remember that banner. Whatever developed,
I longed to believe I was not alone, and with God's help, sooner or

later I would find what I needed to get better. I think by this time I had given up on the idea of getting well.

After a month, Judie and I agreed it was time to move to Champaign-Urbana. After a few days of hunting, we located a small house for rent in Urbana. It was exactly what we wanted, and the rent was modest. But we had to convince the landlord that he should rent to an unemployed family. I explained to him that I had bachelor's and master's degrees. I told him I was a good worker. He was a local businessman and reluctant to give in, but he finally did.

I realized all along that my job hunt would be made even more difficult because of my emotional disorder. My anxiety attacks were often so severe I literally could not sit still. The thought of being trapped in an office terrified me. In addition, I had been a community college teacher for ten years. I had always had at least a modicum of freedom to set my own hours.

There were several interesting leads I followed. I applied for a job as an editor for the medical school at the university, but I was in competition against a number of highly qualified people. I investigated the academic possibilities for part-time work at the University Athletic Association. The AA had positions for academic tutors who worked with athletes. I had lots of experience teaching remedial English and lots of knowledge about athletics. But nothing opened up. Urbana was a university community bursting with educated, capable people. Many of them were forced to take jobs that did not challenge them or match their capabilities.

My search continued in this fashion for two to three weeks. I prayed every morning and every night for God's help. The first of September came, and we still had no income. We were about to find out what the stress of real poverty was like. Because I was still not having any luck, I signed up with Manpower. I was about to become a day laborer.

It was necessary for me to go to the Manpower office early in the morning and wait there for employers to call. I carried a sack lunch, never knowing if I'd actually need it or if I'd be able to eat much of it. It was a depressing office without energy or any sense of purpose. Three secretaries who answered phones and handed out job assignments sat behind a cracked vinyl counter. Crushed cigarette butts littered a dirty vinyl floor.

The applicants were young and old, black and white, thick and thin. Some of them had no teeth and had not shaved. They looked like they had stepped out of a Depression-era breadline. Some of the men played cards, others read newspapers, and still others smoked cigarettes and gazed out the window. The room was hot, without air conditioning or even a fan. As was our house. We had to buy a couple of box fans.

I learned from conversations that sometimes you could wait all morning and not get a job, whereas on other days, you might get a job the minute you walked into the office. I was out of luck my first day and, about noon, drove home miserable and lonely. Some three months earlier, I had taken home a robust paycheck every two weeks.

The next day I forced myself to go back and try again. It was wretched, but I couldn't think of anything better to try. That morning I got a job assignment immediately. Along with three other men, I rode to a large grain elevator west of town. We spent the day shoveling corn from bins and onto waiting trucks. It was hard work and hot, but I was glad to be doing something. The job lasted a few days. After a couple more days of idle waiting, I was assigned to the Champaign Park District, mowing grass in the city parks. This too was hard work, but it was out of doors and very physical. It was pleasant to be working in fresh air, no matter the heat. That job lasted a couple of weeks.

But the pay was very low, and of course, we had no benefits such as health insurance. The savings were going fast and we knew that very soon we would have trouble paying basic bills.

Judie started looking for work also. Somehow we would need to find a way to make ends meet. But her efforts created a logistical problem: We only had the one car. She started using it while I began riding the city bus to the Manpower office. That meant we had to find a place to care for Jason. We had no friends to turn to, so we located a group babysitter. It turned out to be a negative experience for our son. All the children did was watch television. It was not at all stimulating; he was nearing three years old and was very advanced in verbal, social, and learning skills.

Once or twice he asked, "Where's Nanny?"

And Judie usually told him, "She went to live with someone else."

"Why?"

And she usually answered, "We thought it would be better if we didn't bring her to Illinois."

He had other disorienting issues. Each morning as we left the house, Jason turned to me and asked, "I don't have to go to the babysitter's today, do I?"

"I think we better," Judie and I said.

And then he began to cry.

Judie tried to console him by suggesting, "Maybe it'll be fun with the other children today." He just cried harder. I felt ripped by guilt. I felt dispiriting guilt every single day, but this was more intense. It was because of me that we were here in this unfamiliar community, without prospects. Why should our little guy suffer this disorientation and confusion? It was because of me that Jason had to be placed in a negative environment. It was because of me that my wife was suffering apprehension, discouragement, and lack of direction. It was because of me that she ached for our little boy.

The next morning, after another day of no work and another night of no sleep, I drove to the Wesley Foundation on the university campus. I knew there was a progressive nursery school housed there. It turned out they had room for another little one. Jason adapted immediately. The children sang songs together, played games, worked on art projects, and had outdoor recess. It was essentially a preschool environment for children too young to enroll in an actual preschool. Jason always came home with fun stories to tell, finger-painting projects to show and encouraging notes from the teacher.

My relief was immense, as was Judie's. But we had to pay for this opportunity, and our savings were nearly gone.

OUR BIG BREAK came the next week. The director of the McKinley Foundation called to tell me a large Methodist Church in

Urbana was looking for a youth director, and the church was willing to consider a layperson.

I went quickly for an interview. The church was an old one, a large stone building in the Gothic style, located downtown. The senior pastor, Bob Mulligan, knew my father well, so I had a connection. Mulligan interviewed me and said I was what they were looking for. Although I had no experience in youth ministry, I did have extensive background working with young people as a teacher. The only hitch was that the position was half-time, at half-time pay. My annual salary would be slightly less than six thousand dollars, or about a third of what I had earned as a teacher in New York.

But this was a job in Christian education—youth work—in a church. It was essentially what I had hoped to find when I first began my job hunting a couple of months earlier. Furthermore, the church also needed a part-time secretary, and they wanted to know if my wife might be interested.

For the first time, I felt as though God had answered my prayers. I was flooded with hope—more hope than I had felt for many months. When I told Judie about this development, she was as excited as I was. We threw our arms around each other. We would be working in a Christian environment, and although our working hours were not likely to match, we'd be sharing the same building and colleagues.

But we also knew that I would have to find some other part-time income, and we would still be living on the edge because we still would be without benefits. We could only hope and pray that none of us would ever need to go to a hospital or a clinic.

She told me how proud she was of me for all my efforts in grunt work enterprises, but I didn't feel the pride. Mostly I still felt the sting of failure. And so there it was again: I saw only the things I might have done better. It was the same message I had received from Dick often enough. I couldn't succeed because I was never good enough. I was simply not convinced of my own worth. These feelings were understandable but not helpful.

In mid-September we both began work at the church. I was extremely apprehensive because I had never taken on youth ministry responsibilities before. I was restless at nights, sleeping for two hours at the most while pacing the floor most of the time.

Change is difficult for anybody. For people with mood disorders, however, a major change is exponentially more challenging. Their fears and apprehensions are multiplied many times over. The inability to focus leads to an unproductive, racing mind that yearns for answers to anticipated problems large and small. It becomes nearly impossible to find a center or prioritize. And so it was for me; although a meaningful opportunity seemed at hand, I was consumed most of the time with fears and doubts.

Reverend Mulligan mitigated some of the fears by orienting me carefully and patiently. He took the time to answer all my questions and was always reassuring. I have never forgotten his sensitive role in preparing me for my new duties and responsibilities. Other church people were equally helpful. And despite the fact I had much to learn, I kept reminding myself I had my chance to serve God. I wished I could tell Dick Dutton about it.

I think, given all my mental/emotional difficulties, my frequent confusion, and my inability to concentrate over time, I did a pretty good job as a youth minister. I helped the church's teenagers design and carry out their activities. We had educational experiences, recreational experiences, and service projects. We had canoe trips, pizza parties, guest speakers, worship services, and even theatrical productions. We did work projects for elderly members of the congregation. Frequently, we helped and entertained in nursing homes, where we led patients in activities that ranged from bingo to worship services.

In the church school program, I also had a role. I taught some classes and worked on teacher recruitment and training. I designed and led workshops for church school teachers. I was a good teacher with strong experience. I felt my contribution to the church school program was substantial. Judie's job as part-time secretary went well. She answered the phone, took messages, typed newsletters, and helped with program scheduling.

But despite the emotional rewards of these activities and relationships, I was still in the grip of the Curse, day and night. Even though I found myself able—little by little—to eat a little more and sleep a little more, I was still experiencing full-blown apprehension and anxiety. The Gordian knot in my stomach, still wound tight, would lodge in place for years to come, no matter what success or apparent success I might achieve.

Since my small office was in a church, I often went to the sanctuary to pray. I begged God to lift my burden, to cure my suffering. So many active Christians had told me that would happen, but it never did. At times I wished desperately that He would, and at those times I was impatient with Him. Eventually, I think I resigned myself to the fact that lifting would not happen. But it didn't stop me from maintaining a commitment to the Christian life. I believed—or tried hard to—that God truly respected my courage, my willingness to work on solutions to my problems, and my commitment to a life of faith *no matter what*. Some pastors (including my father) had told me that was what true faith amounted to. Such reassurances were not helpful.

In all situations, though, whether in a corn bin or a church sanctuary, my concentration scattered. Sometimes when I was praying in the sanctuary, my mind drifted back to Nanook. In those moments, I missed her terribly. I could picture her out back of the stone house, chasing sticks or snowballs, charging out of the woods with Sargent, or wrapping up with me in the middle of the night, relieving some of my terror if only for a little while. *I wish she was with us here*, I often thought. *Oh, how I wish it.*

But then, inevitably, my mind spun off course and tormented me with images of the two dogs executed at the stake. And I would make a feverish, usually unsuccessful attempt to dismiss that grisly episode from my mind.

I still needed to make more money. I tried the Manpower office again from time to time but usually not before the afternoon, when jobs were scarce. It was a dead end. Somehow I scraped enough money together to buy a push lawnmower and found several takers, mostly elderly folks who were members of the church. I worked at the church throughout the mornings then spent afternoons mowing lawns. I charged five dollars per lawn, the typical working price at that time.

The part-time afternoon work enabled me to program nearly every day, right to the hour. Again, it seemed like control—anxiety attacks were certainly a lack of control. Free, unstructured time was still the enemy. I was not capable of spontaneity; my defense system had no provision for it. I was an authentic, generalized anxiety neurotic. I was still in jail and, in fact, afraid to leave the cell.

One summer afternoon as I finished one of my lawns, I sat down on the curb and unwisely allowed myself to reflect on my situation. Here I was in my mid-thirties with a master's degree and years of teaching experience, mowing lawns for five dollars. A couple of years earlier I had been earning eighteen thousand dollars a year teaching in community college. I had friends, colleagues, and students in a reliably warm and stimulating atmosphere. I had a pension and other benefits. We'd had a special home with charm and character. It had only been four months, but it all seemed so long ago and so far away.

Now I was mowing lawns as I had done twenty years earlier—my first job as a teenager! What I needed at that moment was a dog. A big, snuggly dog that would rub against me. One that I could put my arm around. One that would press its muzzle against my neck. As the tears ran freely down my face, I counted on my fingers; for eighteen months now, Nanook had been gone out of our lives. I remembered the cold, lonely winter nights and her warm presence. Her clean smell. I remembered . . . I don't know how long I sat on that curb in my T-shirt and blue jeans, in the hot sun until the tears finally stopped.

During our two years in Champaign, I did have opportunities to share time with Jason. Someone had put a little red wagon at the curb as bulk waste, but I snatched it up and brought it home. It was a bit rusty, but a little oil and it was good to go. He loved it when I pulled him around the block. We went to University of Illinois hockey practice and some of the games (they were free of charge.) We often went to watch the university's marching band practice (free as well). It was exciting, especially to Jason, but also very special to me. Ever since my breakdown when my very real fear was separation from him and Judie, I had cherished every moment I got to share with him.

None of this, however, alleviated the poverty we were trying desperately to struggle through. Our income was so low we were barely surviving from paycheck to paycheck. We were often in need of clothes and shoes. We were robbing from the utility money to pay the rent and vice-versa. The closest thing we experienced to a luxury was an occasional trip to the Dairy Queen. We always bought the smallest cones. I'm sure we could have qualified for food stamps and/or other forms of public assistance, but those kinds of opportunities never occurred to me. We did manage to keep Jason enrolled in his nursery school; somehow we always managed to pay for that.

The economic predicament brought constant stress. I came home one afternoon and found Judie in tears. "I don't have enough money to buy the groceries we need." She sobbed.

My heart sank. I put my arm around her. "I know," I said. "I can't get the car fixed either."

"I hate being this poor," she went on, through more sobs.

"I know it's bad," I said. The guilt I felt was nearly overwhelming.

She began to cry harder. "I need a coat and shoes. Jason needs a coat. He's only got that little baby thing, which doesn't fit, and anyway, I'm tired of shopping at the Goodwill and the other thrift stores. Just for once I'd like to buy him something new and special."

I felt a deep sadness inside on top of the guilt. My mental disorder had caused us to rearrange our lives in ways that forced us to live in poverty and try to endure the fear that goes along with it. Or rather, I had *let* my disorder cause these changes; I could never truly let myself off the hook, mental illness notwithstanding. I didn't know what to say. I had no words.

After a while, her sobbing died down. "I know it's not your fault," she said. "You didn't *make* yourself have a breakdown."

"But you can't help resenting me, can you?" I asked.

She started crying again. "I don't want to have any resentment," she said, "but I'm afraid I do."

"I don't blame you."

"I'm so ashamed to have any resentment," she said again. "I know this is not your fault."

I put my arm around her again. I felt hollow inside, like my soul had been drained. I was a failure. A failure as a man, a husband, a person, and a father. My life had spun out of control, and the consequence was this poverty and dislocation for our whole family. Three lives—not one—sacked.

"I know this must make you feel terrible," she said. "Deep down inside, I know it's the illness that's to blame."

"Yes, but maybe you need to say it," I said. "Maybe it's important for you to acknowledge the feelings you have."

"Maybe, but I know it makes you feel terrible, and I don't want you to. I want you to be proud of yourself for your courage and determination."

I was incapable of feeling pride, but I didn't say so. The timing seemed wrong. With a lump in my throat, I simply kept my mouth shut.

"I want you to feel proud of yourself, not guilty," she said again.

I brushed her hair back. She had stuck by me throughout the whole ordeal of these months and now years. "You have to resent this," I finally said. "You're a human being, and you have to resent living like this. I resent my emotional disorder every day. You can't help having the resentment, and there's nothing wrong with saying that you do."

"I don't want to make things harder for you."

"You're not making it harder for me. I know it's there, and I need to hear it. It's probably good for me to recognize it. And for you."

This was a problem Judie and I would have to work on and for the long-term, not the short. Getting it out in the open seemed helpful, although I've never been exactly sure why. Maybe it just helped me understand her suffering better.

When a big dog licks your tears away, then
tries to sit in your lap, it's hard to feel sad.
—Kristan Higgins

Toes

QUITE UNEXPECTEDLY, in the summer of 1977, a new opportunity presented itself. Reverend Mulligan called me into his office to tell me that East Bay Camp would be needing a new resident manager as the current one planned to move on in the fall. He urged me to apply for the job.

"I thought I was doing a good job here," I said.

"You are. You're doing a very good job. But this job at the camp would be full-time work with a full-time salary and a benefits package. It would bring you much more security for you and your family." This preacher was a good man. He had trained me carefully and supported me in all ways possible.

As I was about to leave his office, I turned and said, "You're being awfully positive about this. But all I'm about to do is apply."

He smiled and said quietly, "I might have put in a good word."

My heart leaped up when I thought of East Bay Camp. It was then (and still is) a large youth camp and conference center on the eastern edge of Lake Bloomington, located near the twin cities of Bloomington-Normal. It was (and still is) the water supply reservoir for the city of Bloomington. Best of all, I had connections there from my past. As a child, I had attended church camp there several times; as a high school boy I had held summer jobs at the camp, washing dishes and mopping floors in the main dining hall. I knew the camp well and had fond memories of it. In my spare time, I had gone swimming at the beach on a regular basis with the current love of my life, a girl named Sharol, who also worked in the dining hall.

Besides that, I had graduated from Bloomington High School, earned a BA degree at Illinois Wesleyan University in Bloomington and an MA degree at Illinois State University in Normal.

If I landed this job somehow, it would truly be going home.

Immediately, I told Judie about this possibility. After I described the camp and summarized its mission, she was enthused and urged me to apply as soon as possible. I called Reverend Steve Clapp, who was coordinator of camping for the Central Illinois Conference of the Methodist Church. The conference, which spread across Illinois from border to border, was the actual owner of the camp.

The next day, Steve called me back to offer me the job. I accepted immediately. The salary would be very modest, but it was a good deal more money than I was currently making. In addition, the camp provided an on-site home free of charge and also paid all the utilities. And many free meals would be available in the dining hall; grocery shopping would be a very minor expense.

I have always thought my dad had some influence in all this; he was a highly respected pastor in the conference and had served for many years on the camp's board of trustees. When I asked him several years later if he had used his leverage to help me land the job, he usually said, "Why would you ask me that?" I didn't pursue the matter again; what he left unsaid seemed to tell a tale all its own.

Once again, we had to move. We packed up another U-Haul truck (the church generously paid for this) and headed for the newest adventure. We moved into a small ranch house at the camp that would serve as our home until the fall, when we would move to the big house provided for the camp manager.

Naturally, confronted by this major change and huge responsibility, I was extremely anxious and apprehensive. The camp had more than one hundred buildings, many of which were basic unheated cabins, while others were heated and able to accommodate camping and retreat groups year-round. I slept badly, wondering restlessly through our first nights there about all the responsibilities I would have and projecting countless scenarios that would be beyond my capabilities.

Judie was thrilled by the camp's scope and natural beauty. It was (and is) more than five hundred acres, consisting of individual camping areas full of mature trees of all kinds separated by wooded areas. An aging wooden footbridge spanning a narrow part of the bay connected the northern sections from those on the south side. The bridge was the access route to the south side dining hall. Beyond the outer limits of the camp property itself were hundreds of acres of undeveloped woods, some with occasional footpaths worn.

It was a unique situation for raising a child, with woods and trails for Jason to explore with the friends he would soon make. (There were hundreds of private homes around the large lake beyond the borders of the camp.) There was a beach on the north side, so our little guy and any friends could enjoy that as well.

Since Jason was four years old now, the time was right to get him a bicycle to ride on the camp's numerous blacktop pathways.

It was also the perfect place to bring a new dog into the family. In mid-July, we discovered that a nearby farmer had a litter of pups that were half Labrador and half German Shorthaired Pointers. When we went to check the litter out, we found a group of four black pups with occasional white markings.

The only female was a bit smaller than the three males and a bit more timid as well. But we still wanted a female, largely because of our earlier disheartening experience with Fleance's unexpected pivot to aggressiveness. The preference might have been illogical since we had no facts to measure canine male versus female aggression.

We brought our little girl home and held our breath; our most recent experiences with a family dog had concluded with sorrow and loss. Still, we said it again: now our little boy would have a special buddy to grow up with, to share the trails and woods, maybe even the beach. The new arrival was nearly all black, except for a small white marking on her chest and white markings on all four feet. Her toes were white. Almost immediately, Jason was calling her Tiptoes.

From the beginning, Tiptoes was frightened at night. She began crying as soon as the lights were turned off. We had prepared a bed for her by spreading a blanket in a large cardboard box, but the crying was nonstop. She was a lonely little creature far from home, why wouldn't she feel afraid or abandoned? We tried using the ticking clock strategy, but it had no effect. Judie and Jason seemed to sleep through it (the new dog's bed was in the kitchen, as far from our bedrooms as we could locate it), but I couldn't. Of course, I wouldn't have slept well even if conditions had been utterly quiet.

And so, plagued by my own insomnia and Tiptoes's lonely cries, I got out of bed, picked her up out of the box, and settled on the living room couch, holding her against my chest. Our bonding started that quickly. Immediately, my thoughts sped back to my original breakdown, our special stone house, my nightly pacing, and holding Nanook tightly on the couch. On those occasions, I was the one suffering terror and loneliness, and she was the comforter.

Now, holding Tiptoes on another couch in another house, in another state, in another time, she was the one terrified by perceived abandonment, and I was the comforter. But not really; my own rampant apprehensions about our new lives in this unique place and my fears that this new job, with its broad range of unfamiliar responsibilities, would be beyond my capabilities meant that Tiptoes and I were comforting each other.

Whereas Nanook was so large (but warm) she nearly crowded me off the couch, Tiptoes was small and warm; I could encircle her against my chest with her head tucked against my chin. She usually fell asleep quickly on the couch while my racing mind prevented me from sleeping at all. Still, one thing was clear: Jason's dog was already my dog as well.

And for the next thirty-eight years, our family, three of us then two, would have a loving family dog. And no tragic endings, even though there would be rough spots as well as the inevitable grieving and loss. That's the guaranteed pain you sign up for when you bring a dog (or any pet) into your life. You just think it's so far down the road there's no need worrying about it.

SINCE WE'D ARRIVED in midsummer, the camp was in its busy season, swarming with youngsters of all ages. Most camper groups stayed a week, then others replaced them. The weekly camper population in summer months ranged from three to five hundred. Some twenty summer staff employees, most of them college students, were on payroll as dining hall workers, maintenance people, and lifeguards. The current resident manager, a very kind man named John Braun, oriented me carefully as his busy schedule permitted.

Much of the orientation occurred in the camp office, located adjacent to the camp's main lodge, Pilchard Hall. John walked me through the procedures of camp contracts, scheduling practices (often the camp hosted three or four separate groups at the same time), outreach procedures to new groups or potential ones, billing, budgeting, and the like.

All campers, as well as their counselors and directors, had to be fed, housed, provided access to shared areas like the beach and the large athletic field, and cared for medically (in summer months the camp had a full-time nurse with her own office and living quarters). Reports had to be filed, work orders approved, and cash receipts (mostly from vending machines) had to be accounted for. Regular reports had to be filed with the conference.

Many of the groups that contracted with East Bay were church youth groups, while others were secular. Every summer the camp hosted special-needs groups like United Cerebral Palsy and the Muscular Dystrophy Association. These groups stayed in Pilchard Hall, which was handicapped accessible. Other secular groups included school associations, planning retreats, and even large family reunions. East Bay was a very busy place, even in off-season, although that was when most groups contracted for weekends only.

Meanwhile, Tiptoes was coming out of her shell. She romped around with Jason near our house, running at his side and jumping up. We had gotten him that new bike, and he rode it with Tiptoes jumping and running alongside. She was growing rapidly; no surprise there, as we knew that eventually she would be a pretty large dog. By this time, she was sleeping peacefully in our bed or Jason's.

The lone exception came during thunderstorms. She was always terrified of them and would scramble to get to a safe place, usually under the bed. Later, when she was too large to do that, she would try to scramble inside a closet, digging her way through shoes and scattering them. If I lifted her up onto the bed or other furniture and held her, she was never pacified; she always trembled and panted as long as the thunder and lightning persisted.

After a while, we let her tag along with us when we went to the dining hall to eat with staff members. She pretty much stayed put out by the dining hall loading dock until we came out. We were confident with this arrangement because she never wandered far or even out of sight. We weren't ready yet by a long shot to let her roam free, although that time would come eventually.

The college kids on summer staff adored her and gave her plenty of affection. Even better, they gave her cookies and biscuits. She was a smart dog and learned plenty fast how rewarding it could be to hang out near the dining hall, especially when the dinner bell rang. Summer staffers showed us how much she liked chasing Frisbees, trying to catch them in midair. She was still too small to master that maneuver, but the time would come when she could, and on a somewhat spectacular scale.

As an adult dog, her speed and jumping ability were nearly amazing. But she was still a pup and a small one at that. Some of the summer staff young people began calling her Toes. We all seemed to like the shorthand, so from that point forward, we merely called her Toes.

Although I was always fatigued due to lack of sleep, I spent the rest of the summer helping out with grunt work of all kinds whenever John was too busy to engage in periods of orientation. It was physical labor like mowing or scraping paint or cleaning, so it satisfied that now-familiar need to absorb myself in activities that engaged my body completely and thus my mind if only partially.

In September, shortly after we moved to the centrally located big house and I was now the boss, a weekend planning group of a physicians' association was a guest in the main lodge. At lunch in the dining hall, I spied a familiar face, a Dr. Fred Cunningham, who had been our family physician when I was living with my family in Bloomington and I was in high school. He had actually been a close family friend.

The Curse still held me hostage in a very dark place, so I shared my story with him at lunch one day. He immediately prescribed some Triavil, one of the traditional drugs for depression, although I explained to him in firmest language that anxiety, not depression, was my problem. I tried taking the medication anyway; it must have been a significant dosage because the side effects were immediately debilitating. I was so profoundly drowsy most of the time I could scarcely function. I nearly fell asleep during conversations. At nights I fell asleep fitfully for limited periods of time but always felt like I was walking through a haze throughout the day.

It was simply not a workable situation since I was operating equipment like mowers and driving pickup trucks around the camp. So I quit taking the medication, confirming once again to myself that medication would not work for me. But what would work, then? Prayer? Talk therapy? Anything?

THE DAY Jason started Kindergarten in the nearby village of Hudson, Judie, Toes, and I waited with him at the end of our drive-way for the school bus, by the edge of the narrow county blacktop that made a sharp loop around the east end of the lake. Part of the road actually went through a section of the camp on the north side. All three of us watched him board then disappear from view when the bus turned sharply. It was an apprehensive rite of passage famil-iar to nearly all parents. We hoped he wouldn't be scared, at least for long, hoped nobody would tease or bully him, hoped he would begin the important process of making new friends. We hoped and then hoped some more. The three of us must have made some classic tableau standing there until long after the bus was gone.

Toes was more than a year and a half old by this time. Her breed mix was pretty apparent. She was fairly large, about fifty to sixty pounds, with a black Lab's coloring, but she had a narrower muzzle and leaner body type. That was the Pointer half. She was an energetic, intelligent dog used to spending her time with the three of us one place or another. I asked Judie, "Is it time to let her loose on her own?"

"Probably," came the answer, "but remember what happened to Nanook."

"I can't ever forget that. It's the main reason I have my doubts."

"But we can't let those doubts determine what we do now. There's always risk in life no matter who you are or what you are."

"No we can't," I agreed. "If there was ever a place for a dog to roam free, this is it." And so we gave her that freedom.

For several weeks—if not months—she didn't seem to know what to do with the freedom. She still spent most of her time in the house when we were there or accompanied us when we weren't. Our regular staff of about six people (during non-summer months) still broke away from our chores to have lunch in the dining hall each day. Toes didn't break her habit of waiting this out, knowing that goodies were probably on the way from the secretary or one of the maintenance men or me. Judie always thought it was a better idea to phase out the sugar-laden treats.

Slowly but surely, over a long period of time, I began to eat more. The dining hall seemed to help; there was always plenty of pudding and mashed potatoes and gravy, foods I could spoon down in significant quantities. I was sleeping three to four hours a night and beginning to gain weight again. I was up to 150 pounds after a couple of years on the job. It was as if my central nervous system was trying to fight back.

But this "improvement," if I can even call it that, was so gradual, so inch by inch, it was hard for me to grasp it was actually occurring. I was still enduring acute anxieties throughout most days and nights. If the bewildering Curse was actually abating, I couldn't recognize its decline. I was like a batter who occasionally hits a foul ball after a lengthy streak of striking out without even making contact. Or, as I told Judie and a counselor I was seeing, I often felt like a simmering pot, just waiting for it to boil over. In short, if I was making progress, it wasn't significant enough to bring me any real relief. Every day was still a fight.

Managing the camp was a unique type of work. Unable to focus properly for any length of time, I turned over the office work to our secretary. This enabled me to tackle the never-ending list of physical chores the camp demanded. There was no such thing as quitting time, especially during summer months. There was always mowing to do, firewood to be cut and split, painting and trimming, cabins and shower houses/bathrooms to be cleaned and repaired, toilets to be unplugged, roofs to be fixed, blown fuses to be replaced, landscaping like shrub trimming to be done, and so on. *Something* was never done.

I was always capable of interpersonal relationships with the numerous camp directors who came to East Bay. If they had scheduling needs, I was good at meeting those needs. If they had problems, I was a good listener and (for the most part) able to help get the problems resolved. It was an ability I always had, even when my disorder was extremely acute. I couldn't begin to count all the folks who told me over the years they had no idea I was suffering; I sure did a good job of hiding it, they usually said.

But there was no hiding it, at least no attempt to do so on my part. I was simply grinding it out, fighting through the haze, using people as a temporary outlet. As I've said before, working with other people was usually an opportunity to get outside myself, if only for a little while.

It kept me quasi functional to stay busy, sometimes for fourteen to sixteen hours a day, but it also exhausted me. The East Bay job was the perfect job for me and the worst possible one. A day of painful reckoning would eventually come.

Non-summer months brought a slower pace, with opportunities for free time, but to satisfy the needs of my obsessive-compulsive disorder, I found myself scheduling rigidly as always, targeting jobs like scraping and painting, both interior and exterior. There was always work to be done on facilities that had been occupied in summer, although much of this work would likely have been postponed or even ignored by a person not so driven or lacking consuming urgency.

A lot of this time I worked alone, like it or not. When the weather was warm enough, I often took one of the pickups to one of the camp's areas with basic cabins to replace worn-out mattresses or fit them with fresh covers. Toes was often my working companion; she loved riding with me in the truck till we got to our destination.

I would often play Frisbee with her as I worked, tossing the disc high and far, then watching her race to run it down, often leaping high to make the catch. It was a game we both relished, and since I was working by myself, her company was always especially welcome. I might have been working alone, but I wasn't lonely. I was a troubled man with sporadic functioning, but I had a buddy for sharing; we were constantly engaged in a one-sided conversation, although no one is ever sure what information a focused dog can understand. Smart ones do develop a fairly extensive vocabulary, but at what level and to what purpose? It didn't matter. I talked, and she understood.

I always made sure we got back to the house in time to meet Jason's school bus so I could enjoy watching the two of them jumping up and down and running around the area near our house. Usually, out came the Frisbee. By the time Jason was six years old, he could toss the disc as well as adults.

Eventually (by careful scheduling of course) I would come to make use of these free-time opportunities to spend time with Jason. It was a chance to spend time together, and I didn't want to miss the chance. We explored the woods together, usually with Toes at our side. We tossed the football around and kicked the soccer ball past each other to an imaginary goal, usually the steps leading to the dining hall's loading dock. He played on a children's soccer team coached by a very patient and understanding man. Eventually, I would make the time to coach the team myself.

In cold, snowy weather, we joined other staffers and campers sledding down a steep hill and then gliding some fifty or sixty feet over the frozen surface of the lake. Toes tried to join in, but getting traction on a frozen lake is a little more than even an agile, athletic dog can handle. Sometimes in warm weather, Jason and I went fishing, especially in May, when the spawning carp thrashed the water's surface in great numbers. Most people know that carp are not a sought-after game fish as they are too bony and their taste too fishy. It was so easy to catch them it almost seemed unfair, as if a pole and line were unnecessary; you could practically just scoop them up with a net.

Actually, he tended to do more fishing with a couple of our camp maintenance workers who were much more experienced with a rod and reel than I. They also had more free time, as I continued to drive myself as a way of life.

I remember watching Monday Night Football together with him when he was a little older. We always allowed him to watch the first quarter before heading to bed, provided he had done his homework for school. Some of his school chums lived in private homes on the other side of the lake, so we found ways to get him together with those youngsters. Otherwise, he would have been a pretty lonely kid. These boys always relished their visits to East Bay; they could explore the woods together, ride their bikes all over the place, and spend plenty of time at the beach.

In all these activities, I found ways to bond with my little boy even if I was struggling to wipe away the cobwebs of mental illness. I wish I could say I had fun with him. This connection with him helped me because it showed me that even with the ever-simmering anxiety, I could still be a father if my determination was strong enough.

But as much as I loved and cherished him, I had to recognize that duty and obligation were my primary motivators. I was still very much locked into survival mode. Fun was for other people. The closest thing to fun was the playful activity of tossing the Frisbee to our dog, usually with the participation and encouragement of camp employees, watching her leap ever so high on the dead run to snare a disc that seemed too high up and/or too far away.

Or tossing snowballs in winter for her to chase and paw to pieces, just as Nanook had done at the stone house in Upstate New York, so long ago.

As time passed, Toes was also spending much of her time exploring all the nearby wooded acres and even working her way around the lake, checking out the private residences. One summer, she began bringing friends home at dinner bell time. They wore collars and were no doubt lake residents' pets. We learned their names from their collar tags. One was a purebred male Labrador named Rocky. Another was a three-legged dog we called Tripod, a brindle gray-and-white shorthair built like a greyhound. These dogs quickly learned what Toes had known for a long time: hanging around the dining hall reaped the finest of rewards. Campers began bringing uneaten chocolate chip cookies out and feeding them to the dogs as well as many other delicious treats.

Tripod was especially friendly. He liked to roll onto his back and have his chest scratched. All staff—particularly the summer college students—enjoyed the dog. This endearing creature's amputation of its right foreleg was especially clean—right at the shoulder and no stump. It was almost as if the amputation was the work of a plastic surgeon.

I can recall many evenings when he and Toes entertained us at the large rec field by running and chasing. Toes was a fast runner, but Tripod, even on three legs, could keep up with her for a length of time until our dog would make a sharp turn left or right, and poor Tripod would take a tumble trying to match the turn. It was funny but a little sad too, as if Toes had decided to torment him. But it never took him long to recover; he was back up on those three legs again and ready to charge.

All three of these dogs could often be found swimming with the campers along the beach, as could Jason. The lifeguards developed a great affection for Jason and allowed him to swim with whatever group might be beach scheduled at the time. And he had "his own dog," a loving, spirited companion who would be his buddy for years to come.

Our dog also began bringing "trophies" home from the woods and (almost catlike) laying these treasures by our front porch steps. Most of them were rotting or partially decayed carcasses of squirrels, raccoons, or possums. One day she dragged home an entire deer leg, mostly bone. Camp staffers found it all amusing. It seemed harmless enough, if somewhat noxious, but the time would come when we would discover to our considerable dismay that the habit wasn't so inconsequential after all.

If you don't own a dog, at least one, there is
not necessarily anything wrong with you, but
there may be something wrong with your life.
                                        —Roger Caras

Toes: Part Two

ONE SEPTEMBER afternoon, our Toes came slowly limping home on three legs, with her head hanging. She was barely able to struggle to the front porch of the house, where she collapsed at the foot of the stairs. I saw this from the maintenance shop, while Judie observed from the kitchen window. Highly alarmed, we both rushed to greet her. I can remember thinking, *Whatever this is, I'm glad Jason isn't here to see it*; he was still at school.

There was a bloody hole about the size of a dime on her left front leg, just above the ankle area. The part of her leg near the wound was swollen and mangled; it was actually misshapen. My first thought was she'd gotten caught in a beaver trap but had somehow managed to pull loose from it. Trapping was illegal throughout the area, but everybody knew there were some lowlifes who ignored the law and set traps anyway.

But whatever the cause, the injury was obviously very serious. Judie was near to tears, and I could feel my stomach recoil into the tightest of knots while my palms began to sweat and my pulse raced. It was my usual physiological reaction to life's curveballs.

"We have to get her to the vet," I said. Judie just nodded. "Who could do this?" she demanded angrily. "Who could be so cruel?"

"I don't know. Later we'll have to call the lake ranger." I was able to lift her into the back seat of the car by turning her gently on her side, but she cried out and whimpered a couple of times. We set out on the fifteen-mile drive to Bloomington after Jenny McIntosh, our food service manager, agreed to meet Jason at the bus.

I was hitting eighty to eighty-five miles an hour on the drive to town. We'd had more than our share of crises with family dogs; we didn't need another.

"What if her leg has to come off?" I asked through shortness of breath.

"Oh, don't say that. Just don't say that."

When we got to Dr. Brunton's office, I carried the whimpering dog inside. The fact that her mangled leg was flexing no doubt caused her pain. I felt so bad for her and began to share Judie's anger.

Brunton took her into the exam room immediately, where he was joined by an assistant. "Mmmm," he murmured. "I don't like the looks of this."

Judie and I sat shakily in the waiting room for more than half an hour, wringing our hands. Pet owners know all about this. Anyone who owns and cares for a loving family pet will become well acquainted with veterinarians and their offices. Dogs (or other pets) get sick. They get injured. Or even, as we learned so sadly in the case of our Scottish Terrier Fleance, they can undergo a radical personality change. In that case, Jacob was the medical man whose kindness and understanding was a great comfort to us. Sometimes I think that vets are special people, and I'm not the first person to think it.

Because it was a fearful one, the wait seemed long. "What if he has to amputate?" I asked again.

"I told you, don't say that."

When Dr. Brunton, a sensitive and gentle man who would be our vet for many years to come, emerged, he had an unlabeled prescription bottle with him. He opened it and showed us a good-sized flattened metal disc. "Your dog wasn't caught in a trap," he said. "She was shot."

"Shot?"

"Yes, and what you're looking at is a mangled pellet of double-ought buckshot. Your dog is lucky that whole leg wasn't pretty much blown off. In fact, if whoever shot her had a little better aim, she'd be dead."

This information shook us up even more. *Did someone in the timber take dead aim at our dog to kill her?* The thought was nearly beyond comprehension. Hunting in the lake area was even more strictly forbidden—and the law more strictly enforced—than the prohibition on trapping.

My pounding pulse could hardly keep pace with my racing mind, which spun in many directions at once. *Who did this? Why? Why did our dog have to suffer like this? Would her leg have to be amputated? Would there be any chance to apprehend the perpetrator?*

Judie dared to ask the question about amputation.

Dr. Brunton said, "Maybe not. I'm hoping that won't be necessary."

That was equivocal enough to frighten both of us.

"Both the radius and ulna bones are splintered," he went on. "I'm going to try and pin them to see if I can get enough stabilization that way. I hope I can."

"Are the bones shattered?" Judie asked.

"No, I'll just stick with 'splintered.' If they were shattered, we probably would have to do an amputation. You'll have to leave her here for two or three days."

"What about when we bring her home?" I asked.

"She'll have a cast on that leg. You'll have to curtail her activities by keeping her inside or staying with her when she needs to go outside to eliminate. You'll need to keep her quiet and off her feet for at least a couple of weeks. That shouldn't be too hard because she'll obviously be clumsy. She won't be in the mood to go running and jumping with only three legs for support. I'll also send some antibiotics home with her. Then bring her back, and we'll take another look."

When we got back home, Jason was in the dining hall, helping Jenny mix some cookie batter. We told him about Toes' injury. "It's pretty serious," Judie told him. "Dr. Brunton has to fix her leg."

Jason was fidgeting. "Why would someone shoot our dog?"

"We don't know. There are people in the world who aren't very nice."

Jenny advised us to inform the lake ranger right away. But that was action for which we didn't need any prodding.

Given the seriousness of the wound, Toes recovered well and quicker than we might have hoped for. Judie was working as a teacher's aide in a school for mentally handicapped students in Bloomington, and Jason was attending school, so I was home alone, so to speak. Since it was off-season, I was able to free myself up to sit with her in the living room. We comforted each other; I needed help to soldier on during days when the Curse was rampant, and she was a help if just briefly.

Working at the school in Bloomington was good for Judie; it gave her something stimulating to do, and it brought home a little money. Raymond School was for developmentally disabled students exclusively, ages ranging from four or five clear up to twenty-one. Although she had no background or experience working with this particular student population, Judie found she enjoyed them,

But mostly it was good for her to get away from me, because most of our conversations were opportunities for me to spill my guts and treat her as a de facto therapist. What had worn me down over so many years of chronic frustration and fear had also worn her down. She needed a rewarding outside activity that didn't involve listening to the problems of her husband mental patient. The school job was that opportunity.

I never knew when bad days would come or why or how long they would last. The disorder had a life all its own, which was what made it so terribly discouraging. It brought intense feelings of helplessness and powerlessness. It is what causes people with chronic mood disorders to lash out at the gratuitous, uninformed directives of well-meaning friends or relatives to straighten up or snap out of it.

Toes needed caregiving through the healing process. For one thing, she had to be fed differently; we needed to put her food bowl up on a chair, as the clumsy cast prevented her from getting her head down to the floor. For another, I had to carry her down the steps that led to our front yard. Once she was on the ground, she could hobble well enough to eliminate.

For a very active dog, she seemed quite satisfied to lie down and remain still. Of course, she had undergone a major trauma that impacted her entire body. I often stroked her for an hour or more, fingering the plaster cast from time to time that already sported at least half a dozen signatures.

She looked at me with sad eyes as I talked with her softly about her leg and why Dr. Brunton was such a good practitioner that she would be able to make a full recovery. You never know how much a dog understands, but I'm sure the stroking and my tone of voice created a climate of comfort.

I know it helped me; one of the common misconceptions about a therapeutic relationship is that there is a giver and a receiver. In fact, any quality counselor/therapist will tell you that he/she receives as well as provides. Effective talk therapy is a partnership that nurtures both professional and patient. Thus, it was during those afternoons with Toes—in giving comfort, I received comfort, at least for the short term.

After a couple weeks of quiet time, the cast came off. Dr. Brunton was pleased with the healing process. But even without the cast, she still needed carefully supervised recovery time. Jason implored us to let him use his sleeping bag on the living room floor so he could sleep beside her. We relented, as young kids are always pretty much able to sleep in nearly any position on nearly any kind of surface.

Toes healed well. As the weeks went by, she was able to resume normal activities, which for her meant running, jumping, chasing Frisbees, swimming, exploring, and chasing Tripod or Rocky. She would, however, always walk with a slight limp, and her athleticism would be somewhat compromised.

We never knew who shot our dog or why. She might have wandered too close to a farmhouse with a chicken coop. She might have scrounged in the garbage can of a lake resident. In a dense part of the woods, she might have been mistaken for a deer. We would never know. She recovered; that was what mattered.

IN THE WINTER of 1982 to 1983, I decided to have another go at writing. At least on my "good" days. I worked in the camp office because in off-season, the camp secretary was only a part-time employee. To do this, I had to set aside about two hours in the morning. It was the only system that would work because of my inability to focus for any length of time. In addition, I soon felt guilt about neglecting all the many camp duties I had staked out for myself, only a few of which were ever compelling enough to truly warrant attention. It was the same old story of needing to get as busy as possible in a physically demanding job. Interior painting, snow shoveling, and chopping ice off the footbridge were the most common choices. Sometimes I helped mending frozen pipes.

My vision for this book was rather muddled. I wanted to write a book about the breakdown, and I wanted it to be a Christian book. I had been told by more than one counselor that writing about my difficult experience might be therapeutic.

The ironic part was that I was undertaking this project at a time when I was slowly but surely losing my faith. I had spent parts of every day for some eight years in earnest prayer, beseeching God to lift this chronic burden or at least reduce it. But that wasn't happening, and truth be told, I didn't think it would. This cup was not going to pass from me.

The closest thing to optimism or hope I could generate was the notion that over the long haul—the long, long haul—time would simply run out on this Curse. Somehow, someday in the distant future, my central nervous system would toughen so much that I might reach a point where my symptoms would become manageable. It's a word often used by counselors and other mental health professionals. I still dared to hope—though rarely—that one day I might actually find peace. That never happened. And still hasn't, these forty-odd years after the fact.

While trying to write a book with a Christian message, I was finding it harder and harder to believe in a god who would allow me to suffer at this level over this much time and leaving me too bewildered to understand the suffering.

It wasn't too terribly long before I became a confirmed agnostic. There was simply too much suffering in the world, and the Bible had no explanation for it that satisfied me. We don't live in a world in which the righteous prosper and the wicked suffer. A god of love and mercy, were he all-powerful, simply wouldn't stand by and watch a world of misery and devastation play out. Or at the very least, he would have created us with the capacity to understand the reasons for so much pain and sorrow.

All three of us were still attending church regularly, although I began to realize, for me at least, the regular activity was meant to benefit Jason. Whether or not I was still a true believer, I didn't want him to spend a childhood with no exposure to the Christian message or community. I was reading *The Interpreter's Bible* in little chunks and pieces as my concentration allowed, but I was also reading books on Eastern religions. I found myself fascinated with Buddhism, especially Zen meditation practice. I read several Alan Watts books as well as daily meditation/devotional books by Zen masters. I even tried practicing some of the sitting myself, but not effectively. I had no guidance because I was on my own and my racing mind teamed up with my knotted stomach to sabotage my efforts.

Not surprisingly, my book project was very slow going. I was pretty much a house divided as I started writing, in longhand on legal pads even though I had a manual typewriter at home and the office had an electric one. Then whenever I finished a chapter, I would type it out. (This was the same strategy I would follow much later when writing my first successful novels.)

It was sometime during that spring that we faced another crisis with our dog, only this time even more threatening. Toes had heartworms.

I let her out one morning to take care of business and happened to notice that she seemed a bit clumsy walking down the porch steps. I didn't think much of it at that moment, but as I was making a pot of coffee, I happened to look out the kitchen window, and what I saw broke my heart: Toes was walking—make that trying to walk—back toward the house. She was stiffening with each step, all four legs rigid and vibrating. She could hardly walk at all.

I was so shaken I woke Judie up to come and have a look, then went outside to pick her up. I knew that whatever was wrong would prevent her from walking back up the stairs to the porch. Inside the house, it was more of the same, as if all her legs had vibrating steel rods at their core. Then she fell down in a heap, panting madly. We had no idea what was wrong, of course, only that whatever it was was very serious.

Immediately, we knew she needed to visit the vet as soon as possible, but we didn't want Jason to have to see this. "I'll get Jason off to school," she said.

"What'll you tell him?" I asked.

"I'll just tell him Toes is sick and needs to see the dog doctor. I won't tell him what we just saw."

"Okay, okay. Tell the guys I've got their work schedules made out."

On very shaky legs and with sweaty palms, I carried our dear dog to the car, stiff as she was, ready for another emergency trip to Dr. Brunton. I remember driving very fast. The office wasn't open yet; I was too early. I could see Toes twitching in the back seat as I paced around and around the car, smoking a couple of cigarettes along the way. My legs were still shaking, and my heart hammered away at a rapid pace.

When Dr. Brunton pulled in, he was surprised to find us there. "What's wrong?" he asked. When I summarized for him, he frowned. "Bring her inside."

I carried her to an examination room and laid her on the table. Her limbs were still rigid and twitching, and she was still panting. Dr. Brunton looked at her then at me. "What do you think?" I asked quietly.

"What I think is heartworms" was the answer.

I could feel my stomach contract sharply even as my heart sank. My experience with dogs, especially from my days of working in rescue shelters like the Humane Society, told me this could be fatal. I also knew that heartworms could develop from a single mosquito bite. Since Toes ran free throughout many wooded areas, it wouldn't be surprising if she'd been bitten by mosquitoes many times. "Dogs die from heartworms," I mumbled.

"Yes, they do," said Brunton. "But they also get well. Let's not get ahead of ourselves here. We can run a blood test that will tell us pretty quickly. You want to wait, or should I call you?"

"No," I said immediately. "I'll wait."

I waited and fidgeted and paced in the waiting room for what seemed like an eternity but really lasted less than an hour. When Dr. Brunton came out, he was straightforward: "She came back positive. She's got heartworms."

I didn't know what to say, so I just sat down. He sat down beside me. "Do you give her the heartworm medicine every month?" he asked.

"Absolutely," I said. But having said so, I began to wonder: *Did we miss a dose? Did we forget last month or in February when we assumed the weather was too cold for mosquitoes to live and breed?* I couldn't remember for sure, but it was one more cause for concern.

"I'm sure she gets plenty of mosquito bites," I said. "That's what causes heartworms, right?"

"Most of the time. But I know she runs around the woods out there on her own. Does she ever chew on dead carcasses?"

"A lot. At least I think so. Sometimes she drags them home. Could she get heartworms from that?"

"It's possible, especially if the dead critter was already infested."

Once again, I wondered if we'd forgotten a dose of her heartworm medicine. "So where do we go from here?" I asked, my hands folded together between my knees and my head lowered.

"We start with pre-adult heartworm treatment."

"Pretreatment?"

"Yes. I'll be giving her antibiotics, some heartworm preventives, and a round of steroids immediately. I'll need to keep her here a few days to monitor her reactions. Then a little later, we'll begin the actual heartworm treatment."

"What does that involve?"

"It's a series of drug injections that kill the worms. It takes an organic arsenical compound that is injected into her lumbar, lower back muscles."

"Arsenic?"

"Essentially. Heartworm treatment kills the worms with poison. That's why the treatment protocol can be fatal to the dog. But it's usually not. I'm not trying to scare you here, but you deserve honest answers."

"Yes," I said, my mind racing frantically. "Honest answers."

"You're going to be running a hospital at home for quite a while, by the way. The treatment for heartworm disease takes at least sixty days to complete."

Sixty days, I thought. Far longer than the gunshot wound that fractured her leg. "Can you call me?" I asked.

"In a few days I'll call you and let you know to bring her home. If there's any complication or negative reaction to this first round of injections, I'll call you right away."

"Okay," I said, standing up. I wanted to call Judie, but I knew she'd be at her school. I decided to wait till I got back home.

When I got back to the camp, I shared the bad news with the five full-time staffers at lunch. They were all sympathetic and registered real concern. Toes was a popular member of the camp family as well as a vital part of ours.

The protocol for treating a dog with heartworms is lengthy and uncertain; through it all, the dog is living on the edge. Once the dog has completed the course of steroids, heartworm preventive, and antibiotics, like Dr. Brunton said, he/she is ready to start the actual heartworm treatment. Again, like our vet said, an organic arsenical compound is injected into the dog's lumbar, or lower back muscles, to actually kill the adult heartworms that are already growing to maturity and getting ready to breed and reproduce in the dog's heart and blood vessels.

After the first injection, the dog is given a follow-up shot thirty days later and another one on the next day. During this period the dog needs to stay in the hospital or veterinarian clinic for observation to make sure he/she doesn't have any serious reactions to the drug. Sometimes the vet prescribes a tapering dose of steroids such as prednisone for each month following the injections.

When the dog is home during the protocol (and afterward), its exercise has to be severely restricted. No running or jumping. The dog should go outside only for eliminations and shouldn't be allowed to do any roaming. If this means taking him/her on a leash, so be it. Even if the dog seems to want activity, it must be curtailed for at least four weeks following each injection. That's a total of eight weeks.

Coughing can occur as well as listlessness and loss of appetite, so the dog needs to be closely watched at all times. Spasms can also occur as well as rapid, labored breathing and rapid heart rate. The dog is likely to be pretty sore along the lower back where the injections were given, so the owner or caregiver needs to be mindful of that when picking him/her up or moving him/her.

This is what we were up against with Toes. There would be no shortcuts and certainly no guarantees. When she was home, one of us would be sleeping with her through the night. Since I was fighting persistent insomnia (beyond my typical level), I found myself moving downstairs most nights and curling up with her on the large sectional we had in the living room.

We both lay on our sides while I held her. She slept while I rested fitfully, alarmed each time she spasmed or coughed. I was a caregiver, but we were both suffering, just not in the same way.

Sometimes she needed to go outside during the long and lonely nights to eliminate. Other times she had accidents because her compromised range of motion and strength prevented her from reaching the front door in time. Luckily, our floors were either wood or tile. Cleanup wasn't difficult.

The fears and concerns I had were mixed with some guilt; neither Judie nor I could remember if we had given her the heart medicine in March. My anxieties were elevated to an extremely uncomfortable and disturbing level as I held her. My mind couldn't avoid drifting back to the awful winter of '74 when sharing the couch with our loving Nanook in the middle of the night gave me a feeling of safety that was temporarily reassuring.

During daytime hours, I took frequent breaks from whatever work I was involved with to sit with Toes and stroke her. For the first four to six weeks of the treatment protocol, she seemed content to simply lie still and rest—a good sign according to Dr. Brunton, since we wouldn't have to be working against her inclinations. When I carried her outside, I had to fold her legs up underneath her, much like a baby farm animal, to avoid touching her very sore back. It wasn't too long before she was able to walk outside and back on her own;

it was encouraging to see her do this without any more symptoms of rigidity or twitching.

We were moved almost to tears when camp staff dropped by to check on our patient. Her well-being was important to them too.

Sometimes her appetite was poor, so we sweetened the pot by adding cooked, loose hamburger or sweet cereal to her food. Jason liked sitting with her in the recliner while sharing French fries or pretzels with her.

But the entire recovery process launched me into a prolonged period of instability and heightened anxiety. This threatening condition was for me a crisis because, in addition to my troubling concern about our dog's recovery process, it disrupted my routines and forced me to make adjustments. That kind of flexibility was simply beyond my capabilities and (as I've said before) beyond the capabilities of most who suffer from mood disorders. Rigid scheduling, especially if you are able to stick with it, doesn't necessarily equate to control but often *feels like* control.

Eventually Toes got well, but not before spring had moved into early May. We could take her with us on work sites around the camp, but she was less inclined to roam and explore. As a rule, she stayed close at hand, seemingly content to be in our company. When I tossed her Frisbee, she chased it half-heartedly but actually came to a halt and turned her back on it if it sailed too far. In the afternoons, we found her lying peacefully on the grass between the dining hall, mechanic shop, and our house. She was well, with a clean bill of health from the vet, but she seemed to have settled into middle age.

A dog is the only thing on earth that
loves you more than it loves itself.
—Josh Billings

Toes: Part Three

EVENTUALLY, I found a publisher for my book, whose title was *A Quiet Desperation.* I had traveled the tedious (and time-consuming) process of submitting query letters to publishers and then, if I got a green light, sending the entire manuscript. Authors could still do that in the eighties, whereas nowadays, most major publishers won't even look at a book unless it's submitted by a literary agent. It can boil down to the chicken-and-the egg thing.

Thomas Nelson was the publisher that accepted the manuscript for publication but only if I agreed to remove portions of it that mentioned religious traditions other than Christianity. In its original form, the manuscript included my attempts to cope with my disorder by using meditational practices found in Eastern religions, particularly Zen. I made the requested changes because I desperately wanted to publish that first book.

It was an exciting time for our family since I had hoped for so many years to become a published author. I can never forget the day the box came in the mail from Thomas Nelson. Inside were twelve shiny copies of my book. *My* book. I was enthused about the cover art. On the back was my photograph and two positive statements from reviewers. Jason was in school at that time, but Judie gave me a huge hug. Toes barked at the two of us; hugging that didn't include her never pleased her. So we gave her a hug too.

I lined the books up on the living room bookshelf right next to Aldous Huxley, James Joyce, and Ernest Hemingway. "If this doesn't make you proud of yourself, I don't know what would," Judie told me. And I have to admit I had a soaring feeling that felt very close to happiness. This "soaring" feeling had implications for the future, but I wasn't about to worry about that now. For several days after, I made trips to the house just to stare at that lineup of books.

The book certainly didn't make me (us) rich. I received an advance of $500 but never got a royalty check. The book wasn't promoted or marketed aggressively, so sales were minimal. The book did get some nice review notices.

At approximately the same time, Judie had begun taking science courses on a part-time basis at Illinois State University in Normal (Bloomington's twin city). She wanted to pursue a long-held dream of becoming a nurse. Finishing some of these science prerequisites would make her eligible for nursing school. I encouraged her because I wanted something good to happen to her, something all her own that brought her satisfaction and pride. She had spent the past ten years or so serving as caregiver to a chronically dysfunctional spouse. Loving and devoted as she was, this role was a crushing load to bear and too taxing to manage. She too was suffering on a daily basis.

My reasons for encouraging her also included an ulterior motive: Achieving this goal would not only bring her satisfaction but also give her a marketable job skill. In case I came apart again, our family would have another (and better paid) breadwinner. Even after several years, I was still making only about $15,000 yearly, although free housing and utilities combined to make a package of greater financial value.

In any case, the prospect of having a nurse's salary in the family seemed to be important at this time because the job of managing this camp began taking a greater toll on me, mentally as well as physically. Frequently, I got calls in the middle of the night from guests who needed to see the camp nurse or to report blown fuses or toilets that were backing up. Even though I was still sleeping poorly, these calls for help usually made things worse.

When we (the camp staff) got calls about backed-up toilets, we usually groaned. It nearly always meant a sewer line was blocked. Since the camp had its own waste treatment facility, it had sewer lines running from various locations, often through wooded areas. Hair roots from trees were usually the culprits, but we never knew where along the line the blockage might be located. Manholes were in place but not nearly enough of them.

The job usually fell to me because maintenance staff people were involved in the work I had assigned them early in the morning. I was the one with the flexible schedule, although ironically, I was the one least equipped to be flexible. A wiser manager would have delegated the job anyway, but I was still a driven man. Later on, the consequences would be crushing.

The sewer-clearing equipment we had included the electric machine itself, which was about the size of a window air conditioning unit, and several spools of flexible steel cable. The loaded spools weighed at least eighty pounds apiece. Back in those days, I could carry two spools at once, one in each hand, and lift them into the bed of one of our pickups. But this got harder and harder; I wasn't getting any younger, and my on-again, off-again appetite prevented me from gaining weight and strength.

The manholes themselves tended to be about ten to fifteen feet deep, so getting the augur head on one of the cables into the right opening was tricky business right from the start. Then started the painstaking, frustrating job of spiraling the cable back and forth, advancing and retreating sometimes a foot or so at a time. There were so many trees we never knew if the blockage was thirty feet down the line or a hundred. The final breakthrough could take three to four hours or even longer. It was grueling work, and most of it (at least it seemed) in summer heat. We always had to stop from time to time to drink plenty of water.

One summer I worked one hundred days in a row, each day lasting ten to twelve hours or even longer (other staff were promised an eight-hour day). All those days I worked in extreme heat, mowing, cleaning cabins and gate houses, cleaning bathrooms and shower houses, or splitting wood for camp fires.

Judie warned me to slow down and learn to delegate, or I would burn myself out. So did a counselor I was seeing at the time on a weekly basis. This counselor was a former Baptist pastor, just like my dear friend Dick Dutton back in Upstate New York. His name was

Robert, and he was a good soul, a caring individual who was a careful listener. He frequently urged me to seek psychiatric help to find medication that would help me. I told him of my brief encounter with Valium in New York (which brought no relief whatsoever) and, more recently, Triavil (which brought disabling side effects).

One day he said to me, "You know, we've never talked about suicide."

That was true. "What about it?" I asked.

"Do you ever have suicidal thoughts?"

I didn't try to hide from the question: "Many times. Many, many times over the past several years."

"So tell me about that."

"I've thought about the various methods of ending my life. They all scare me more than waking up each morning tied up in knots, afraid to face the day ahead."

"What else?"

"I can never imagine leaving my family behind. Or my dog."

"Your dog?"

"I should say *our* dog. She's very precious to me. She's a loving family member, and we've worked through some very difficult crisis situations with her."

"You sound like a real dog lover."

"Sometimes I think it goes beyond that. Sometimes I feel like I *need* a dog in my life, and I've got one I love who loves me back."

"Have you ever been diagnosed by a psychiatrist?"

"Just that one time when I had the major breakdown. Acute anxiety disorder. Why do you ask?"

"I ask because I've never seen a case quite like yours."

"Quite like mine how?"

"I guess I mean the intensity of it and the duration. I've never known a patient to suffer from an acute anxiety disorder this intense or long-lasting. Usually it's a condition that dissipates relatively quickly. I don't mean to imply that the person finds peace and serenity, but their symptoms become manageable."

There was that word again. Maybe it meant the ability to eat. "Yesterday at lunch I actually ate a full plate of meatloaf and mashed potatoes," I told him.

"And? What do you mean by that?"

"You said manageable symptoms. Eating a full meal seemed relevant."

"Why?"

"Because it's the first time I was able to do that."

"The first time all day? All week?"

"No, the first time in ten years or more."

Robert actually squirmed in his chair. "You're not exaggerating?"

"No, I'm not exaggerating."

"How much do you weigh?"

"About 150."

"And what would be your ideal weight?"

"About 180. That's what I weighed back in New York right before I had the major breakdown. I played basketball and racquetball all the time, and that's the weight I maintained."

He shifted gears: "I'd still like to see you working with a psychiatrist. Medication may turn out to be the best weapon you have. What if you could actually experience some actual peace and serenity?"

As often as I had heard this, it didn't really feel convincing. My diagnosis had come from a psychiatrist, yes, but only based on a ten-minute interview and by a shrink not in private practice but one based in a clinic and therefore overworked. "Peace and serenity," I said bluntly, "are things I never expect to experience again. Not in this lifetime."

"I don't think it will help your cause to be that pessimistic." Then Robert urged me again to get an appointment with a good psychiatrist, revisit the diagnosis, and make an honest effort to find medication that helped.

"Okay," I said. It wasn't exactly a lie, but I knew at the time it was something I'd most likely put off long enough to put it off for good.

A DESPERATE turning point finally came during a particularly brutal cold day one January when the wind chill index reached nearly thirty below. It was so cold Toes refused to go outside the house. An exposed sewer pipe that stretched some twenty feet across a ravine froze. This went against assurances by our licensed waste treatment man, Elmo Page, that "Sewage can't freeze. Bacteria action makes it impossible."

In this instance, Elmo, who was nearly always right about nearly everything, was wrong. The sewage in that twelve-inch cast iron pipe was frozen. There was a retreat in the main lodge of some twenty adults, so the blockage had to be broken somehow. Jeff McIntosh, the brother of food service manager, Jenny, was our main maintenance man. It was his job to figure out how to free up the pipe.

I might add here that Jeff too, although a young man in his mid-twenties, had wide-ranging skills in carpentry, electrical systems, and mechanical systems. Much of the grunt work I did over all the years at East Bay I never could have done without pointers and advice from Jeff and Elmo. Once, Jeff and I built a wheelchair ramp along the front of the main lodge; another time we put a new roof on a large outdoor shelter. These jobs were both well over my head, so in both cases, Jeff managed the project, and I simply did what I was told.

But this blocked sewage pipe had to be freed up, and right away. We had to start by cutting a hole in the pipe to gain entrance with our very basic roto-rooter. Try cutting a hole in a cast iron pipe sometime. It took nearly the entire morning to cut such a hole, as we slipped and slid along the snowy, uneven ravine, hoisting and positioning the heavy, clumsy tanks that fueled the camp's acetylene torch. The ravine was located near the dining hall, so we ran inside every fifteen to twenty minutes to sit on the heat registers until we thawed out. Jenny always had hot chocolate waiting.

Eventually we cut a hole about six inches square, just enough to get the augur in, and sure enough, what we exposed was solid ice. At lunch, we told Elmo, who was nearing seventy and too old to join us in the battle, that the sewage was frozen. He shook his head and said, "It goes against everything I ever knew." That's how cold it was.

Judie had no science classes that day, so she was there to eat with us. "I have to force Toes to go outside," she said, "or she'd be doing her business right on the floor."

It took us the rest of the afternoon to force cable in both directions until finally the ice broke loose. Then Jeff had to find a way to rig a patch so the sewage wouldn't spill down into the ravine. It was one of the most miserable days of my life; I got frostbite on my toes and face. Sometimes it still acts up with a burning sensation.

It was past dark when I finally got back to the house, turned the thermostat up to eighty degrees, ran hot water in the bathtub, and started soaking my hands and feet. I left my coat on all the while; I thought I'd never be warm again.

I had the shakes. I also began to cry. I felt myself on the verge of another breakdown and couldn't think how to avoid it. "I don't think I can do this anymore," I blubbered to Judie. "There's only so much a man can take."

She took a stern approach with me, sympathetic though she might have been. "That's no way to think, not right now, not after you've had such a terrible day."

"There are too many terrible days, and I'm just not strong enough to keep it up."

"I've tried to warn you about delegating. You just refuse and drive yourself."

"I do what I have to do. It's called survival."

"Survival? Look what you've done to yourself. Does this feel like survival?" And then she left the bathroom. I figured she'd go downstairs and have a good cry of her own. And why not? How much patience could she have with me? And for how long? She was a strong woman, but how long could she subordinate her own feelings to pay homage to my disorder? *What kind of husband was I?* She deserved so much better.

I tried to re-psych, because she was right. *Don't think about decisions right now, especially major ones. Don't allow a bad day to cripple you even more. If you've learned one lesson from all these years of hurting and bewilderment, it should be, don't even think of major decisions when you're this vulnerable.*

But this pep talk didn't last. At least not for long. For the next few days, I found myself slipping into a very dark (and somewhat different) emotional pit. Instead of just being ripped with acute anxieties and nameless dread, I felt hollowed out for periods of time. Empty. At times I simply stared into space without motivation. I just wanted to curl into a ball and let the world go someplace else. This mental state of mind would later become important when I found myself working with psychiatrists; for now, though, it was just one more layer of emotional suffering.

I told my counselor, Robert, that I didn't think I could continue on the job. "I've just given it everything I have to give. There's nothing left."

"That's the obsessive-compulsive disorder talking. You've never been able to delegate or keep your workload where it belongs."

"We've been over this before, haven't we? I have to be absorbed. I have to be busy."

"You don't *have* to do anything, you're making choices. And they haven't been good ones."

I knew he was right, but I simply didn't feel able to make the good choices. The Curse was ever active. Then he asked me, "Do you think you've been a good camp manager?"

After I thought for a few minutes, I said, "I guess so. I know how to train staff in a specific but nonauthoritarian way. I write lots of purchase orders, but I keep close track of spending. Every year we're always under budget. I have good relationships with all of our permanent staff. Our scheduling of groups is always accurate and timely. Visiting camp directors always appreciate my availability and responsiveness. So yes, I would say so."

"It sounds like you've found the perfect job."

"Maybe," I said quickly. "But I've also found the perfectly wrong job. The camp is so big with so much activity. There is always more work to be done. *Always.* And a lot of it comes after hours. Exhausting myself seems to be the best coping mechanism I know."

"I don't know what to tell you," said Robert. "You're driving yourself to a cinder. How much guilt do you feel when you don't work all those extra hours?"

"Plenty."

"You're a frightened, driven man, Jim. And I don't mean that as a put-down."

"I know. And you're right—I am frightened and driven. And I've been this way for a lot of years now."

"How much guilt would you feel if you left the job?"

"A lot. I have a loving, loyal wife and a loving son. Their lives would be just as disrupted as mine. I'm not much of a husband or a father."

"You're probably a lot better husband and father than you think, but you'd never give yourself credit for it."

"I know. Giving myself credit is not something I do." Even as I said these words, I remembered that I had coached Jason's youth soccer team each of the past two springs and his softball team as well. The facts said I was a pretty good father in spite of my acute emotional struggles. But another fact was that I couldn't participate in these activities without strong feelings of guilt. Every time I was gone from the camp, I couldn't help thinking of all the work there was that needed to be done.

Robert ended the session by advising me not to make a major decision when my emotional state was slipping into crisis mode. It was advice I knew well and even respected. But could I follow it? Would I be able to do that?

The answer turned out to be no. Warm spring days in April found me mowing, trimming, scraping, painting, and cleaning. When I thought about delegating, I realized that our full-time staff was just too small. In fact, I was too distracted and disoriented to make out work lists early in the morning. Staff members had to ask me what to do.

I was coaching Jason's softball team in the nearby village of Hudson, where his elementary school was located. We usually started practice or games about 5:00 p.m. My heart wasn't in it. I felt afraid, empty, and lonely. And I was *always* tired.

On several warm evenings after sunset, I made my way down the hill to the footbridge, where I stared vacantly at the moon and stars. The camp was so quiet in off-season. It broke my heart that I couldn't actually appreciate this remarkable beauty. Where was my peace? Where was my serenity? If the heavens couldn't lift me, what could?

But Toes was always with me. I let my legs dangle over the edge of the aging, rough planks. She sat upright beside me. "What should I do?" I asked her many times over. "If I left this job, what would I do instead?"

Sometimes the tears slid down my face. She never answered my questions, but she had the habit of leaning into me and pressing against my shoulder. Often, I got my face licked. I didn't doubt she understood my panicky dilemma. She couldn't use words, but she knew how to comfort. I put my arm around her, and her face was against my face. I knew she would sit there forever with me if need be. Why would she need to be anywhere else? Dogs don't need words; just us mixed-up, confused humans do. But we often don't know the words we want, so what good are they?

The tipping point came later in the spring. I was changing mattress covers outside of some of the basic cabins in one of our camping areas. This activity slammed me uncomfortably with the full recognition that we were preparing for another ultra-busy summer season.

I struggled with an especially stubborn mattress that seemed to resist capture in its new sleeve. I dropped it on the ground and sat with my head in my hands. I just didn't feel like I could go on with this; facing another frenetic workload the summer season promised was more than I could bear.

Toes was with me, lying in the grass nearby. She usually was, what with Jason in school (he was in fifth grade by this time) and Judie in town at the university for classes. I began to cry. The tears streamed down my face, and soon I was actually sobbing. Again, as if she could sense human sorrow or crisis, Toes moved to lie beside me. Pretty soon her head was in my lap. I scratched her between the ears while blowing my nose. Suffering though I was, I didn't feel alone. My dog perceived my despair and had come to offer comfort. I felt some. Suddenly, I just held her tight for what seemed like the longest time.

Then that afternoon came the final blow: the sewer line running from the main lodge was blocked again. All other staff were busy with jobs I'd assigned them, so rather than pull one of them off the work they were doing, I decided to take the job on myself. It hit me full in the face that this was my problem. It had been my problem for the last nine years. We had capable people, but I'd do the job myself. The least suitable person for the job—me—wouldn't ask others to be flexible.

I loaded the pickup with four rolls of cable in case the blockage was far down the line from the manhole by the lodge. I advanced and retreated the cable time and again for two hours without results. Toes ran off to greet the school bus, as she always did.

The blockage was extremely stubborn. I thought about stopping long enough to get something to eat in the dining hall but decided against it. I was determined to free this sewer line or die in the attempt. At that moment, I almost wished I would die right there on the spot. Someone would find my body, along with the pickup and the extra spools, and most importantly, I wouldn't have to confess the life-changing decision I had now reached to Judie. I couldn't go on.

It was nearly dark when I finally sent a cable thrust that broke the line free. I advanced and retreated it several times just to make sure. Exhausted and shaking, I rewound all the cable and loaded the truck. I had to stop and lean on the tailgate to catch my breath and let my pulse slow down. I felt terribly alone and lost.

I DECIDED to wait until the next morning to talk to Judie. I wanted Jason away at school before I initiated what I knew would be a terribly difficult conversation. It was a very long night of no sleep but plenty of inner consternation. Before dawn, after I put food down for Toes, I made out work schedules and posted them in the shop.

After the school bus left, I trimmed some bushes while waiting for Judie to get up and about. She had no early morning classes that day. As much as I wanted to wake her, I resisted. Finally, the two of us found seats on the couch with our coffee cups. Toes, as if sensing something important was taking place, squeezed in between us.

I didn't waste any time. "I can't do this anymore," I said. "I can't go on with this job."

The look on her face told me she was torn between anger and compassion. "I knew this day was coming," she finally said. "I just didn't know how soon."

I had no answer. I felt too much guilt and shame. I wasn't capable of managing my life or being a good husband or being a good father. The Curse was an affliction to last a lifetime. But there was a bottom-line question as prevalent as ever: *How much of this was my fault? How much blame belonged to me?*

"What will you do instead?" she finally asked.

"You could probably get me in as a teacher's aide at Raymond School," I mumbled, with my head bowed down. Raymond was the school for special needs students where Judie had spent a couple of years on staff.

"Probably. You'd be way overqualified, but they do like to get men when they can. But we'd be poor again, the pay is so low."

"Yeah," I agreed. "We'd be poor again. I'd have to get a second job."

"What job?"

"I have no idea. But I'd find something. I did in Urbana, and I can do it again." Toes turned sideways and lay her head in my lap, almost as if to say, "This plan might work."

The timing didn't seem right, but I said to Judie anyway, "In two summers and two semesters, you can be a registered nurse. You'll be able to get a real job with decent income. We won't be poor forever."

She looked away. "If that's supposed to make me feel better, it's not going to work."

One of those profoundly hard knots seized me; she might decide it's finally time to divorce me. If I was burned out by the job, why wouldn't she be burned out with the marriage? It was a logical but fearful thought. "I don't blame you if you hate me," I said. "No woman should have to put up with what you've done."

"I don't hate you," she snapped. "I hate the . . . the Curse. I hate the Curse. But sometimes it's hard to separate you from the illness."

"You can't help resenting me."

"No, I can't." Then it was time for her to drive to the university.

Of course I knew what she meant. I couldn't make the separation myself, as I had told Counselor Robert many times. I was alone in the house, somehow numb and afraid at the same time. My eyes burned from lack of sleep.

I made my way down to the footbridge with Toes alongside. What would I tell Jason? What would I tell my boss, Ralph, the new conference coordinator of camping? What would I tell the five people who made up the full-time camp staff, loyal colleagues all and good friends as well? How and where would I do all this?

As I asked her all these troubling questions aloud, Toes nuzzled in, leaning against me. She felt so firm. Despite all my shame and guilt and confusion, to her I was just plenty okay. She was devoted to me no matter what. At this moment and over the next few weeks, a dog would provide the few brief periods of comfort and reassurance without recrimination. In her eyes, there was nothing wrong with me.

That afternoon I drove to the conference office in Bloomington to tell Ralph of my decision. "Are you sure about this?" he asked.

"Yes, I'm sure." In fact, I wasn't sure about anything—past, present, or future. "I'm as sure as I can be."

"Have you thought this over? Talked it over with Judie?"

"Yes and yes," I said quickly.

He leaned back in his chair. "Well, all I can say is we'll certainly miss you. You've been a terrific camp manager."

"That's what I'm told but never really convinced. I never learned how to delegate. I've just burned myself out."

"That's a hidden danger of that job. One we've talked about before."

"Yes, we have."

Then Ralph said, "The Lord will bless you for it."

"Bless me for what?"

"All your hard work and dedication to the camp."

I got no satisfaction from this declaration. In fact, it made me angry. I had heard it before, usually from born-again, Evangelical Christian groups that had visited the camp if I relit a space heater in the middle of the night or replaced a blown fuse at four in the morning. *How will the Lord bless me? When will that happen? Would I become "normal" again? Would I no longer be overmatched by life? Would I ever feel* peace *or serenity?*

These were questions I might have asked Robert, but not Ralph. Before I left the office, Ralph assured me he could find my replacement before the summer season began, but he asked me if I would be willing to spend some time orienting the new person. I said I would, not that I wanted to.

In all the years I'd spent at East Bay, having lunch in the dining hall with the full-time staff had always been a pleasant break with food and fellowship, even though I never ate very much. I ate some soft stuff like pudding or mashed potatoes or soup. If the food required much actual chewing, I usually couldn't get it down.

Lunch on the following day seemed to be the best time to share my decision with my colleagues. It wasn't. All I did was throw a blanket of uncomfortable silence over the table. People were embarrassed because they didn't know what to say, especially in the company of others. In the days ahead, when I talked with them individually, they were better able to ask me about the decision. My answer was always the same: burnout. Each one shared their disappointment. They would miss me, Judie, Jason, and Toes.

Judie was distant during these days, mostly quiet, mostly keeping to herself. She spent more time in the university library (studying, she said) than she ever had done in the past. In the past, she'd done her studying at home. It was a clear indication of her need to be away from me at this crucial point in our lives. *Maybe she just doesn't want to be around me,* I often thought. And why would she? She knew how miserable I was, but she had paid her dues as the comforter with the shoulder to cry on—overpaid actually—for so many years.

To my surprise, she took it upon herself to inform Jason of my decision.

"What did you tell him?" I asked her one night when we were in bed.

"I told him the truth. That you had just driven yourself so hard on the job you had burnout."

"Did he know what that meant?"

"He seemed to. He's old enough now, and he's a pretty smart kid."

"What did he think of leaving the camp behind and moving into Bloomington-Normal?"

"That's the part he seemed to like. He'll be able to spend more time with his friends."

It made some sense. As unique and special as East Bay was, it could also be very confining (for me) and somewhat isolating (for our son). For a little while, I felt some gratification. Not that it lasted long. I knew that this would be another night of little, if any sleep. I didn't want to disturb Judie with my tossing and turning, so as soon as I was sure she was sound asleep, I went downstairs to spend the night with our Toes. On the couch.

Every year in the spring and fall, we had work groups, often called Adopt a Cabin, come from local congregations throughout the conference as our guests. The groups usually consisted of six to eight men with construction experience or similar expertise. Elmo, Jeff, and I would usually assign them to an appropriate camp job. Often, these groups would go to work on one of our cabins, putting on a new roof, installing interior siding like drywall or particle board, and sometimes even installing dropped ceilings. Sometimes they painted cabins or gatehouses or replaced dilapidated stairways.

A man named Marshall, who had led such work groups several times, had agreed to replace me as camp manager. I spent the better part of a week familiarizing him with camp facilities, equipment, office document procedures, and so on. Between the two of us, we interviewed and hired summer staff from the stack of college student applicants.

Through it all, I still felt guilt and plenty of shame, although that's not something I shared with Marshall or anybody else. We were leaving a unique situation with a unique set of human benefits that provided special enrichment opportunities for groups of all kinds, especially children. At times I was nearly overcome with regret and a keen sense of loss. Managing East Bay Camp could have been the perfect position for me for years to come, but the Curse and I had made it perfectly wrong. I was getting to know Marshall well enough to sense he would keep management in perspective.

In the late afternoons, I spent time playing catch with Jason (he was signed up to join a PONY League baseball team when we moved to town) or tossing the Frisbee with Toes in a low-level game that wasn't too demanding. She insisted on setting her limits, whether we liked it or not.

She usually tagged along wherever we went as I was orienting Marshall. He warmed up to her pretty good; he was a fellow dog lover who had two of his own.

The conference decided to pay me a severance package of $5,000. I think Ralph had convinced the board I had it coming. Maybe the Lord was "blessing me for it" after all.

With the help of Jeff and Jenny, we packed all our belongings into another U-Haul truck. We were moving again. Toes rode with me in the truck. I had a lump in my throat and was a little shaky at the wheel, but I was sure Toes was just ready to enjoy the ride. Judie and Jason rode in our little car, a jam-packed Plymouth Champ. What lay ahead? How intrusive would the Curse be now?

*Heaven goes by favor. If it went by merit, you
would stay out and your dog would go in.*
—Mark Twain

Toes: Part Four

WE FOUND a place to live in Normal, several blocks west of Illinois State University (ISU), where I had earned a master's degree some twenty years earlier and where Judie had been taking science courses to satisfy nursing school prerequisites.

It was a tacky apartment in a tacky complex. The reality of imminent poverty smacked us between the eyes when we paid our first month's rent, along with a month's deposit. All the years at East Bay, we had paid no housing costs.

My anxiety level escalated dramatically to a seven or eight on a ten-scale. I didn't sleep much or eat much after we moved in. Two blocks away was a dairy/convenience store. I slugged down a lot of milkshakes. Losing weight again was alarming because I soon landed a part-time job doing janitor work at the Normal Public Library in the evenings.

It was hard physical labor that included running a carpet-cleaning machine and a floor buffer. Losing weight meant losing strength. I was wearing belts with my blue jeans to hold them up. One night, driving home, I remembered with acute regret how I had once been a respected teacher at a respected college in Upstate New York, with pride, success, and a firm financial future. *Did that really happen? Was I ever really that person?* It seemed so remote as to be more like a dream than a reality.

I did coach Jason's PONY League baseball team to a championship that first summer away from camp; the coaching was another absorbing activity that provided some temporary relief. It was a special sharing opportunity for Jason and me in very difficult times. Unfortunately, as soon as practices or games were over, so it was with my sense of relief.

He was turning into a pretty good baseball player, although he was more captivated by his saxophone. Soon, the time would come when he chose music over athletics. He also made many good friends who lived close enough he could spend time together with them.

Judie was now enrolled in Mennonite School of Nursing in Bloomington. She studied hard, so I was now in charge of most of the housework (Jason helped out too) and much of the cooking. We had to plan meals carefully and buy cheap food at a cut-rate, warehouse-style grocery store. Lots of pasta and cereal and ring bologna.

Toes adjusted well to her new role as a city dog. No more running free and no more romping through the woods. Now she had to be content being walked on a leash along the neighborhood sidewalks. She didn't seem to mind; she had already made a partial move in that direction at East Bay after her gunshot episode and the drawn-out regimen of heartworm treatment. She wasn't young anymore either.

Neither was I. In my mid-forties and undernourished, I found myself fatigued and distracted most of the time. One such time during our first summer in that apartment, when I was beset daily with East Bay loss and disorientation, we had another dog crisis. I came home from the library late in the evening, shaky and exhausted. Instead of taking Toes outside (our new rule) for her evening elimination, I simply let her out on her own. Then I flopped on the couch.

I dozed a little bit off and on watching some old movie, when I heard a faint scratching at the front door. Alarmed, I got up to have a look. When I opened the door, there she was, standing still with her head hung low and blood dripping from her mouth. *Oh no*, I thought, as a surge of panic ripped me. *She's been hit by a car.* There wasn't a lot of traffic in the neighborhood, but enough to stick strictly to the leash rule.

She didn't seem inclined to step up into the apartment, so I nudged her backside enough that she could find enough footing to step inside. But then she simply stood in place. The dripping blood had to mean something. I quickly slid a newspaper under her mouth to absorb the drops. I didn't know where to touch her or try to move her; *she might have broken bones,* I thought. *Or serious internal bleeding.* Exhausted or not, I cursed myself for letting her outside unleashed.

Jason was gone, attending a sleepover at a friend's house. I was glad he didn't have to see this moment of suffering. Judie called Dr. Brunton's after-hours emergency number and arranged for his assistant to meet us at the office right away. Very carefully, Judie and I managed to roll Toes onto a bedsheet so she lay on her side. She didn't cry out in pain but she was panting hard, and her breathing was labored. *After all this loving creature has been through,* I couldn't help thinking, *was she now about to die because of my lazy moment of irresponsibility?*

Using the sheet as a large sling, we were able to get her into the back seat of the car. I drove fast to the vet's office, but along the way, we both expressed our fears that she might have serious internal bleeding that could be fatal. Brunton's assistant was a young woman with a gentle touch and genuine concern. The three of us managed to get her on her feet again. Toes did not cry out when the young woman rotated her shoulders and hips. "My guess is nothing's broken," she said. "But only x-rays will tell us for sure. We're also going to have to x-ray her torso to see if there's internal organ damage."

We would be leaving her overnight at the vet's office while these tests were run. On the drive back, I cursed myself (this time out loud) for my negligence, but Judie said I should give myself a break.

"Why should I give myself a break?" I asked. "This is all my fault."

"You were exhausted from the work at the library and not enough sleep or food."

"None of that takes away the guilt."

"You feel so much guilt you almost feed on it."

"Yes, that's what I do." It was past 11:00 p.m., and I knew the night would be a long one. And indeed it was—six hours of tossing and turning, my mind racing between fear and guilt.

The next morning, when Jason came home, we told him about Toes. "Is she going to die?" he asked right away.

"We don't know," Judie said. "We hope not."

The three of us drove to Brunton's office. He gave us the good news right away: "Nothing is broken, and there's no damage to her internal organs. She's going to be okay, but she's no doubt plenty sore from impact bruising. I'm going to send some pain medicine home with you. She's likely to be lethargic for a few days while she recovers. Make sure she's got plenty of water to drink, and let's hope she's got some appetite. Call me in a couple of days and let me know about that."

"What about that blood coming out of her mouth?" I asked.

"She probably got hit in the mouth. You'd bleed too if you got popped in the mouth." Then he smiled and added, "Do me a favor. Don't bring me this dog again in another crisis situation. She's had enough for this lifetime."

Truer words were never spoken. We didn't need the sheet this time to get her into the car. We got her onto her feet and then, as I supported her under the chest, we were able to guide/lift her into the back seat. Jason sat beside her, stroking her gently as we drove home.

For about a week, Toes lay on the floor for the most part, getting up to eat and drink but not much more. Her stiffness and soreness were obvious every time she moved about. She limped a good deal. But she seemed to get a little better as each day passed. She ate most of her food and drank plenty of water. When we took her out on the leash so she could eliminate, we could only coax her the thirty feet or so that stretched between our front door and a small patch of grass at the end of the building.

I spent most nights sleeping—or trying to—on the couch beside her. I couldn't begin to count how many restless, frightening nights I had spent sleeping on couches with dogs. And receiving comfort in the process.

I told her how sorry I was for my reckless decision. I told her she had gone through more disturbing crises than any dog should ever have to. Her answer came in the form of a tail that flopped up and down on the floor as she lay on her side; maybe she was able to discern the sincerity in my tone of voice. The tail seemed to be saying, "I forgive you. And thank you for all the loving care when I got shot and when I had to go through the heartworm treatment."

At least that's what I chose it to mean. I didn't fall asleep, but I felt comforted.

Eventually she got her strength back and we could walk her around the block. Then two blocks, then three. Jason did a good deal of this walking, for which I was grateful. I was always so tired. But we had our dog back. Again.

I made several job applications that summer, but they weren't jobs I wanted any part of, and none of them ever brought forth an offer. My best bet would be working at Raymond School as a teacher's aide, but the principal told me the hirings there would have to wait until August.

I had plenty of free time during the days, so I gritted my teeth and decided to try another round of writing. I sat on the back porch (it was only a small concrete slab) many mornings with my legal pad and clipboard. I still had my notes for a novel based on the young woman named Sue I had met while in the mental hospital years ago. She was a timid and frightened girl so overwhelmed by the difficulties of living she was essentially dysfunctional.

Mental health disorders are generally divided into two groups: affective disorders and cognitive disorders. Affective disorders, also known as mood disorders, include depression, bipolar disorder, and acute anxiety. Cognitive disorders, simply defined, represent "breaks from reality." Patients who suffer from cognitive disorders often have hallucinations, dementia, delusions, and/or amnesia. Schizophrenia is a good example of a cognitive disorder, perhaps the most common one.

I was (and am) a victim of several elements belonging to the affective cluster. Sue was unfortunate enough to have symptoms of depression along with panic disorder. She was very withdrawn but for some reason felt at least a little safe talking to me. I never knew why. When I was in the hospital, I was distracted and irritable, hoping in vain for some useful one-on-one counseling that rarely came.

At any rate, I thought I could construct an outline for a novel using the Sue character as a protagonist in a novel about a mental patient fighting through the suffering and discovering a level of strength she didn't know she possessed. The time would come, two or three years hence, when that novel would be published under the title *I Can Hear the Mourning Dove*, earn a good deal of critical acclaim, and even earn some decent income.

But all that was in a future I knew nothing about; I was only two summer months removed from East Bay. I got rattled and frustrated as I tried to flesh out the outline while terribly anxious, distracted, and unable to focus. I got angry at times and threw down the clipboard. I even broke at least one clipboard. So my writing sessions were usually short—maybe an hour or so at the most. But I did stay with the project nearly every morning, inching my way, one step forward and two steps back.

Each time I had one of my outbursts (usually involving plenty of out-loud cursing), Toes, who was usually lying near my feet, would look up and cock her head in apparent puzzlement, the way dogs do when they seem to be curious and would welcome some real information.

The slamming down of the clipboard usually found me leashing her and walking down to the dairy store so I could get another milkshake. Money was so scarce in our house at that time I had to be careful. Usually I had to scrape enough spare change together to buy that shake. There were some things in our kitchen I could eat, like soup, soft-boiled eggs, Jell-O, or a sort of sloppy, gruelish bowl I concocted of crushed graham crackers and milk. But it was never enough; little by little I kept losing weight. A loss of strength and stamina was always part of the bargain.

Then in the middle of August came the phone call from Raymond School. They wanted to hire me. This was good news, of course, but the offer also brought a healthy dose of trepidation. I had never worked with mentally handicapped (the terminology du jour at the time) students, so even though it was in a school setting, it would be unfamiliar work. Judie was a great help at this time, giving me a good deal of information about the students, teachers, programs, and what to expect.

My pay at Raymond School would only be about $6,000 per year, so I would also be keeping the evening job at the library. It was going to be a hard, physical grind, but somehow I would have to find a way to tough it out.

So the three of us were about to go off to school at the same time—Jason to the junior high, Judie to Mennonite for the fall semester, and me to my new job. Jason was able to borrow a saxophone from the high school, which was a blessing because we couldn't have afforded to buy or even rent one.

We desperately wanted to find the money somehow to buy him some back-to-school clothes, the kind his friends would be wearing. We had a little bit of the East Bay severance money in the bank, so we did the best we could. We couldn't match the kind of wardrobe many of his friends had, but I can't remember a time when he complained. We were reminded again and again what a good kid we had living in our home.

The harsh reality of poverty stressed us in many walks of life, but we reminded ourselves that in another year and a summer, Judie would graduate from nursing school, and nurses were in high demand. We just had to keep our eye on the prize.

After a month or so, I found that working at Raymond School was to my liking. I was working with the older students in a workshop classroom, which found students sealing vacuum cleaner belts in small plastic bags for retail sale. The school had a contract with the Eureka Company, and the work was designed to prepare students for jobs in sheltered workshops after graduation. The work was humdrum, but it kept me busy. I even found myself eating rather well in the school cafeteria.

I was recruited by the principal to coach the school basketball team. Some of the older students, although mentally challenged, were street-smart with athletic ability and a fearless attitude on the court. I taught them some strategies generally thought to be too sophisticated for special needs players to comprehend, but most of the players responded well and executed the game plan. We even won two state championships.

Even so, my ongoing pattern of acute anxiety, along with our stressful poverty dilemma, intensified a permanent condition of very low self-esteem. I gave myself little, if any, credit for any successes and could only feel the fear and the guilt.

THE SUMMER of 1988 was the second hottest on record in Central Illinois, and a severe drought came with it. Daytime highs routinely reached the upper nineties or even higher, while early morning lows bottomed out in the low eighties. The thirsty ground was rock hard and cracked, while lawns turned to brown brittle.

But for me (and my family), it was a year of major change unrelated to climate.

For the first time in our lives, Judie and I bought a house.

Jason entered high school, got his driver's license, hooked up with his first steady girlfriend, and started part-time work at a local McDonald's.

Judie began working as a nurse in early June. Not surprisingly, she chose psychiatric nursing as her specialty; she had been a de facto therapist for some fourteen years, and one of the local hospitals had a large psychiatric unit.

She had begun counseling sessions of her own shortly before she graduated from Mennonite. I was glad she had chosen to do so and, in fact, encouraged her in that direction. Still, I was worried because I had no doubt she talked with her counselor about divorcing me. As a full-time nurse, she would have enough income to become financially independent, and my drag on her life had been unremitting for a long, long time. I never asked her about this, though, because her counseling business was her own. Had she decided she'd had more of me than she could bear, I would have understood, even if the loss of my wife and son was a terrifying thought.

Once Judie began drawing regular paychecks, for the first time, I began regular psychiatric treatment. I could do this because Judie's benefit package included psychiatric coverage, and I needed to do it because that summer sent me crashing and burning in a disabling breakdown spiral every bit as overwhelming as the one that had afflicted me some fourteen years earlier in Middletown, New York.

Not surprisingly, buying a house staggered me, even though I could see the merit in doing so. Besides, Judie was enthused about going forward with it.

But it meant major change, which I had gone through plenty of times by now, always with intense fear and apprehension. My insides were ripped with both. My original breakdown had occurred without any apparent cause. Subsequent ones were caused by observable events or situations. But the original affliction was still part of the equation because I had never actually made a recovery. I was weakened and wounded, never really strong enough to adapt to conditions involving major change.

My questions regarding this house purchase were numerous and threatening. How could we do this with so little money? How could we make mortgage payments and make them on time? What would I do if some system in the house (plumbing, electrical, mechanical) broke down? I had learned some skills at East Bay, but what could I really fix? The apprehension spread in more directions than I could count, mainly because this house we were buying had been neglected and was in need of a great deal of work.

In May, our dear friends Sandi and Jon Hawthorne convinced us the time had come for us to understand the pride of home ownership. Sandi was a savvy realtor who was well connected in the community, while husband John was head basketball coach at Normal Community High School, the school Jason would enter in the fall.

Sandi showed us the house she thought we could afford to buy, even with a very small down payment by going through FHA financing. It was a small bungalow built in the 1940s on a deep lot on a low-traffic side street. Just behind its carport, strangely enough, was a tiny, neglected house about the size of an ordinary two-car garage. The house was only six blocks from the apartment where we were living. It was very close to the ISU campus. The house did not have central air conditioning or a window unit. I couldn't help thinking of the heat, the same heat we were enduring at the apartment.

The house had been occupied by college students previously, but now the neighborhood had been rezoned to single-family homes. College students renting a house usually ignore its upkeep at best and actually abuse it at worst.

Ugly, shapeless hackberry trees close to the back of the house spread dead and dying limbs onto the roof and seemed to shroud the property in a depressing cowl. Both the house and the tiny one behind it had widespread peeling and flaking paint.

None of the vegetation—including the mature trees—had been shaped or cared for. Inside, rooms and windows were very small. It was a dark, depressing house. The basement was a semi finished affair that included a laundry room, a tiny crude bathroom, a small bedroom, and even smaller "kitchen" with an old sink but no appliances. A larger central room surrounded the big furnace. It was obvious rental students had occupied this lower level as well.

"This is not unusual," Sandi said. "Landlords cram as many students into a house as they can. There's good money in it."

Inside the tiny house behind was enough trash and neglect to depress anyone. The bathroom was in the small kitchen. An old stove stood near a small refrigerator, but neither of these appliances was hooked up. It was clear nobody had lived in it for years.

"This is the worst house on the block," I said to Sandi.

"And that's exactly why you want to buy it," she said. "The worst house to buy is always the best one on the block." She went on to explain this strategy, but I wasn't listening. All I could see was work far beyond my capabilities. And we would have to take financial responsibility for all of it. *All* of it.

The one good thing was the price—$40,000. "Don't worry," Sandi said. "We'll come with an offer for less. This property owner wants to sell this place and do it fast."

"You won't be alone, Jim," said her husband, Jon. "We'll find people to help you."

"What am I supposed to do for a down payment?" I asked glumly.

"You said you have thirteen hundred dollars in the bank."

"Yes, but how could that ever be enough?"

"We'll make it be enough by going through the FHA process. You and Judie need to stop paying landlords for a place to live. They raise rents all the time. A mortgage stays the same. Now that Judie is earning a regular nursing salary, we can do this. I know this looks like a long pull, but once you've moved in, you'll be better off financially. Honest. And you'll have the pride of owning your own home."

I was so shaken I couldn't begin to understand the "pride" factor. But despite my fear and trepidation, Judie and I decided to try this.

Sandi was right about the mortgage. We qualified for an FHA loan. The question was, would the house qualify? FHA inspectors would have to approve it as well, and they were known for being very picky.

But the termite inspection came first, and what those investigators found was practically mortifying. The tiny house behind was a veritable termite playground. Exterminators tore away rotting drywall whose termite damage was so complete the sheetrock was scarcely more than tissue paper. The interior studs (four by fours, oddly enough) were laced with enough deep groove termite tubes to weaken most of them.

In what might presumably become our house, termite damage was limited to the basement ceiling, but it was profound; the ceiling was made of homasote, a common finish material in older homes, but the villains had reduced it to flimsy paper. The termite crew's boss showed me (in his gloved hand) a dozen or so of the writhing, destructive creatures. "You'll either need to install a new ceiling or simply clear away the debris and expose the cross beams. Luckily, they haven't been damaged at all. It's good wood."

These words, of course, gave me no comfort at all. As I watched the exterminator team drill deep into the ground around both buildings and start pumping in chemicals, my anxieties escalated nearly to the breaking point. "I have to go now," I said, heading up the basement stairs.

Our apartment had no air conditioning. At nights, Judie and Jason were using window fans. I moved downstairs to sleep with Toes in the living room, but she wisely wanted the kitchen's tile floor. I hooked up a fan to blow on us there then pulled cushions from the couch and lined them up next to her. It was lumpy and uneven, but it was better than trying to lie on a hard floor. Dogs are good at this but not those of us who walk around on two legs.

But of course, there wouldn't be any sleep—not for me at least. The staggering fears of this house project haunted me day and night. I might have stayed in bed with Judie, but I knew in this bewildered condition, I might wake her to cry on her shoulder again. At least one of us needed to sleep at night.

With Toes, I didn't feel any reluctance to share these darkest and profound fears. She was a good listener who never seemed to mind if I woke her up. I told her what we were doing and why the project terrified me so. She inched closer and flopped the tail up and down on the cool tile.

It was as if she understood the distress I was trying to communicate, and I knew she would never tire of hearing it. People who love dogs don't doubt the communication bond they share because they perceive their dog(s) as more human than canine. A loving family dog is never "just a dog." Such a dog can even connect and stabilize families whose lives take them in different directions because the love for—and devotion to—the dog is a shared and permanent common denominator.

*To his dog, every man is Napoleon; hence
the constant popularity of dogs.*
—Aldous Huxley

Toes: Part Five

THAT SUMMER of '88 found Toes to be the uniter of our family.
I was breaking down again, Judie was immersed in the adventure of
her first "real" job, while Jason was entering the independence-crav-
ing world of the teenager—new driver's license, ongoing requests to
use the family car, his first part-time job, baseball and summer band
practice. What we shared in common was our dog; Toes was the constant in each of our lives, the one who received love and returned it
with love of her own and steadfast loyalty.

She was fast becoming *my* dog. Although she had always been
the dog we wanted to grow up with a little boy, the siren call of teenage independence—as well as his summer activities—tended to limit
his contact with Toes, as well as his dog responsibilities. When he
had been a youngster, he was especially faithful to chores like feeding
and watering his dog; now the torch had been passed largely to me.
Not that I minded. Besides, I had gone through a similar pattern of
outgrowing our precious Shep when I entered high school so many,
many years earlier.

The long list of improvements brought forth by the FHA
inspectors was truly formidable. Both buildings had to be scraped and
repainted. All the windows (in both buildings) had to be re-glazed.
The crumbling front porch steps had to be replaced. Since the ground
around the main house sloped downward toward the foundation, all
four sides would have to be filled with dirt so that water would be
carried away from the building. All tree branches making contact
with the roof would have to be removed.

I was shaken to the core when I read the list. How could we possibly do all this work? I didn't know a thing about glazing windows. Anything requiring money would be out of our reach. Even though we had been approved for the loan, the house would not qualify until all this work was finished.

Sandi tried to calm me down. "There are no surprises on this list," she said. "We'll just have to work through one job at a time."

"We?"

"Yes, *we*. I keep telling you you won't be on your own here."

But at the start, I *was* on my own. Almost. On the first day, at about 5:00 a.m., I put food down for Toes, choked down part of a yogurt cup, then tried brushing my teeth but gagging throughout the process.

Then the two of us walked the six blocks to the daunting job site. "Our" house. I needed to leave the car at home for Judie. The temperature was nearly eighty-five degrees just before dawn, and I was bleary-eyed from lack of sleep. I was also losing weight again—it was one more worry, because I knew I needed to generate some real stamina over the days (and probably weeks) ahead.

We didn't need to leash Toes any longer; she walked patiently beside me as we moved along. It was safe because she never showed any interest in chasing rabbits or squirrels, and besides, she had now become accustomed to walking patiently beside any one of the three of us. She was now more than ten years old and seemed to have decided her running and jumping and exploration activities were over. And maybe, I often thought, she'd decided it was safer to embrace a more sedentary lifestyle; she'd lived through enough life-threatening crises. She still walked with a slight limp; the gunshot wound she'd suffered to that right front leg (it seemed so long ago) still took a toll.

It's hard for me to describe how important her companionship was that morning; the mental anguish I was going through was overpowering, and I thought I'd probably collapse if I were by myself.

In fact, this newest breakdown was beyond overpowering; it was truly dangerous. I began having regular suicidal thoughts again, only more of them and more often than I'd ever had in the past. Judie had a good job now. A "real" job. So she would be in an economic condition to support Jason and herself. If I were gone, it wouldn't really matter much, at least financially. Furthermore, I had loaded such a mental burden on my wife and son their lives might actually be better off. They might even be relieved.

But I didn't like any of the suicidal methods I was aware of, and I couldn't imagine traumatizing my family (including Toes) on such a crushing scale. In addition, I often thought I would die soon of natural causes; the adrenaline that had been coursing through my body on a daily basis for so many years had surely caused irreversible damage.

But as for suicide, I had vowed to Dick Dutton (and even to God Himself) fourteen years earlier that I would never give up. And I never did, no matter how strong the urge to take my own life.

I decided on that first morning to start by doing what I knew best—scraping and painting. I had done enough of it at East Bay to last a lifetime, but here was plenty more to do. The carport had shade and concrete, so I figured Toes would want to spend her time flopped there as another day promised to hit the high nineties, if not one hundred degrees. I put down a water bowl for her.

To get started, I started scraping the annex (that was what we had decided to call the tiny ex-house out behind). I could reach all the siding while standing flat footed. The house, on the other hand, had an attic, so there was a peaked roof; I would need to find an extension ladder somewhere.

And so it began. The irony (as always) was that this activity, absorbing and physical, gave me a place to throw my fears, anger, and bitterness at a time when I was too physically enervated to manage it. To my surprise, Toes came to join me despite the brutal heat. She lay next to my feet as I scraped away. I felt a small measure of comfort; without her companionship, my misery would be intensified by loneliness.

What a puny beginning, I thought, scraping a board at a time as the long list of eventual chores scrolled along my racing mind again and again like a spinning slideshow.

When I broke for lunch, I was drenched with sweat and terribly fatigued. I had a key to the house, and the utilities were hooked up, so I could get plenty of water for both of us. I got a milkshake at the dairy bar and a package of Twinkies; what I couldn't eat, I knew Toes would.

I knew I'd have to stop at three or four o'clock, because I'd have to get a little rest of some kind at home before evening came, and I'd be heading to the library to clean carpets and buff floors. It was a job I longed to quit because it now threatened to tax me beyond my capacity. But Judie had only started getting paychecks, and I received none from the school during summer months.

I got what rest I could at the apartment, stretching out on the floor with a fan blowing on me directly. I held my dog tight, like a little child with a comforting teddy bear. At times I dozed for a few minutes. I could usually eat some broth and Jell-O if I took my time before heading to the library.

ALTHOUGH I still wasn't sleeping or eating, things began to change as the days went by. Jason helped from time to time as his schedule allowed. He didn't have carpentry skills, but he did a good deal of scraping and painting.

And I found it was just as Sandi had promised; I wasn't on my own. One day when I was up on the extension ladder (it had appeared magically one morning), a man named Murray stopped by to say he was going to glaze the windows. In both buildings. I didn't know him, but he was very skilled.

He had them done by the end of the day and returned the next day to paint the firmed-up glazing. I never saw a drop of paint on window glass. He was obviously a skilled professional. He told me he was a member of Sandi's church; there would be no charge for the work. "It's the Lord's work," he said with a smile while sweat ran down his face and darkened his T-shirt. "And the Lord doesn't bill people."

Another day, I arrived to find a huge pile of fill dirt had been dumped on the side yard. The day after that, Sandi's husband, Jon, showed up with about twelve of his basketball players. Young and strong, some of them painted, while others worked through the blistering midday heat to fill all the low spots along the house's foundation, then tamped the dirt firmly into place. Before the day was done, they even spread grass seed on the fresh dirt and watered it all.

As gratifying as all this help was, it didn't have a mitigating effect on my symptoms. I was still a wreck. I was still choking down a Twinkie at lunch and combining it with another milkshake. My mind raced fearfully to the myriad of chores and upgrades this house and property would need even after we were cleared by FHA inspectors to move in. Acute generalized anxiety doesn't rest on any laurels, doesn't find a comfort zone in the present moment, is never satisfied with what has been done; its racing mind is always spinning toward a fearful future, a fresh new package of daunting obstacles.

The day came when FHA inspectors approved the improvements, and we were cleared to move in. Was I happy? No, because there were so many other needed improvements before this house could ever be a decent place to live.

And it was on that same night the library director (a kind and friendly man) had to let me go. Exhausted and shaky as usual, I tried to maneuver the floor buffer across some ceramic tile. Suddenly off balance, I swung the machine awkwardly when it spun out of control. It got tangled with a series of computer cords and pulled three computers off the main desk and onto the floor, where they crashed and shattered.

I sat on the floor and began to cry. *How did I get this way? How was all of this happening again?* I thought of suicide again, letting my dispirited mind travel over most of the usual methods and even some newer ones.

After I gained a sliver of composure, I called the library director, Robert, and told him to come and have a look. He was already in bed asleep. When he got there, it was close to midnight. He shook his head. "You can't go on with this job, Jim. You're too . . . too undernourished. Why are you so thin? What's going on?"

Any answer I might have given him would have been far more information than he wanted, so I just shook my head. I was not ready to speak for fear I would break down crying again.

When I got home, Judie took me to the hospital. "I haven't told you this, but I've been talking to one of our psychiatrists, Dr. Gordon, about working with you. He'd like to do that."

I was numb, staring into space. "You mean I'm going back to the puzzle house?"

"No, you're not going to be on my unit, that would be too awkward. You'll be Dr. Gordon's patient, but you'll be on a regular medical unit. He has ordered up some labs and some neurological testing. Over all these years, we've never bothered to find out if there might be something *physically* wrong with you."

"How long will I have to be in?"

"Two or three days. Long enough to run a full battery of tests."

"Can Toes come with me?"

"I know that's your attempt at humor, but you need to take this all very seriously. Dr. Gordon will meet with you there and probably administer some written tests. I'll get all the facts tomorrow."

"I did some written personality inventories back in the hospital in '74."

"Well, it won't hurt you to take them again, plus there will probably be some different ones."

I was amazed at what a take-charge person Judie was becoming. *Did I have another mother now?* Working on the psych unit, even if only for a few weeks, had exposed her to a wide range of mental disorders, treatment protocols, and outcomes. As glum and numb as I was, being admitted to the hospital with her leadership gave me some confidence. So did Dr. Gordon, even though he and I had never met. I trusted Judie to hook me up with a capable psychiatrist.

Over the next three days, I underwent a series of tests. Some were blood tests; others were neurological. I had an MRI. A specialist had me hopping up and down on one foot, then the other. I met Dr. Gordon, a laid-back man with a ready smile who gave me several written tests, including personality inventories and other measures of psychiatric history and symptoms.

When I came home, it was to the new house. Everything was moved in. Friends had made several trips with pickup trucks filled with furniture and household goods. Jason and Judie had already made some headway putting things away. Toes came to greet me in the carport with some of her old vigor, wagging her tail madly and reaching up with her front paws. I got three or four hours of restless sleep that night in our new bedroom, a very small room with a very small closet and two very small windows. *Could I ever learn to love this depressing place?*

A week later, I met with Gordon in his office. The first thing he told me was that all my neurological tests had come back normal. I found myself somewhat disappointed; I had hoped that an MRI would reveal a brain abnormality that could be treated.

"Of course," said Dr. Gordon, "an MRI can't analyze brain chemistry, which is where your problem probably lies."

"So what's wrong with me?" I asked.

"I've gone through all your psychological tests. I can't give you a single, definitive diagnosis. You have a cluster of symptoms—anxiety, obsessive-compulsive disorder, attention deficit disorder, and depression."

A cluster of symptoms? I asked myself. "I'm not depressed," I said immediately. "I've never had a history of depression. Just generalized anxiety."

"There's really no such thing as 'just anxiety,'" he explained. "Depression and anxiety are all a part of the same spectrum. Maybe you've never had symptoms of classic melancholy that renders you so lethargic you can't summon the will to get out of bed. But your tests indicate many of the standard symptoms of depression—irritability, lack of concentration, insomnia, poor appetite, and inability to enjoy life or find pleasure. Believe me, depression is a big part of who you are."

I had to chew on this new information for a while. "So what do we do?" I asked.

I expected him to start talking about psychoanalysis, but I was wrong. "We find the right medication," he said. "Right now you're not taking anything."

Immediately, I thought of Eva, my department chair's wife back at OCCC, who had said bluntly, "You have to take medicine. Medication is the only answer." *Had she been right all along?* Had I been a fool to reject this advice simply because I was afraid of turning into an addict?

"What's the right medication?" I asked.

He leaned back in his chair and smiled. "We don't know yet. What I am convinced of is that your brain is wired wrong. But mental patients are all different. When it comes to medication, there's no one-size-fits-all. Any honest psychiatrist will tell you it's essentially trial and error. I'm going to start you on some Prozac, one of the newer antidepressants that seems to work well for many patients. We'll see how that goes. It can take as long as a month to kick in, so that's when I want to see you again."

"A month?" Hearing this, I felt my spirits sag. "I won't be an addict, will I?"

"Not with Prozac. And I'm starting you on twenty milligrams, which is a low dose. But I'm also going to start you on some Xanax, which is an antianxiety drug. It's fast-acting, but has a short life. That fits the mechanism of addiction. With some patients, the body builds up a tolerance for it. It's grouped in with antianxiety medicines like Valium, Klonopin, and Ativan. Over time, we may work in the direction of one of those. I want you to take half a milligram of Xanax four times a day, every four hours. Then I want to see you again in a month."

"You said that before."

He leaned back again and smiled. "Okay, now I'm saying it twice."

When I got home, I quickly took the Prozac and the Xanax. I began unpacking boxes, when I suddenly felt a loosening of the knot inside my stomach. It was like a small sense of relief was spreading throughout my body.

"It's the Xanax," Judie explained. "It's fast-acting."

I felt a level of drowsiness as well, although it felt more restful than sleep-inducing. I couldn't believe it. *Could it be so easy?* Just finding the right pill? I felt enough relief to go to one of Jason's baseball games and was actually able to pay attention to it. I even got up and cheered when he hit a triple.

But no, it wasn't that easy. Although I was able to get a minor sense of relief from the Xanax and a little later some more from the Prozac, I had actually begun a seventeen-year journey with four different psychiatrists and many psychotropic drugs. It was an uneven journey that was gratifying at times, frustrating and discouraging at others. Often it felt like a maddening one-step-forward, two-steps-back proposition. Some drugs would provide help, while others would bring disorienting and disruptive side effects.

Over those many years, the drugs would change, dosages would change, combinations would change, and results would change. Sometimes relief would come but only for a short while. Other times the effects of the drugs would change according to situations and conditions in my life. Some made me more resilient, others less so.

Unwelcome side effects would eventually include spasms, extreme drowsiness, blurred vision, constipation, diarrhea, sweating, chills, nightmares, dizzy spells, and even, on some occasions, blackouts.

But all that was in a future I'd have to live through to know. On my second day with Xanax, a half hour or so after I took a pill, Judie, Jason, and I went to a nearby McDonald's. I was able to eat an entire hamburger. I felt like I had just won the lottery. The fries I couldn't finish I took home for Toes.

Over the next two years, I continued making progress. My two drugs helped me recover a modest level of emotional relief, although my anxieties still registered at a five or six (on a scale of ten), and I was still essentially a driven neurotic. I made it a point to schedule each event of each day rigidly. Whenever situations demanded that I had to make a change, I got knotted up inside again.

The meds seemed like a finger in the dike, holding back precariously a powerful surge on the other side that could spring new leaks at any time. I was nowhere near normal, not serene (ever), not at peace (ever).

But I was relatively functional. I was eating better and gaining weight, so I felt stronger. I was sleeping at least four hours per night intermittently most of the time. Toes always slept on the floor next to our bed, so during the periods when I was awake, I was able to reach down and scratch her head. She was always there, and that was a comfort. When a thunderstorm arose, though, she would dig madly to get under the bed. That was impossible because our bed had no frame. It was simply a mattress on top of box springs. It took her a while to figure this out, so she headed to the small closet and began scattering shoes around the bedroom. As usual, our attempts to comfort her were in vain. There would be no peace until the weather calmed down.

She also rested her chin on one of my feet whenever I was writing. It gratified me that I was able to write again, going back to my earlier outline and early chapters of my novel. The progress was slow; the attention deficit disorder disrupted my concentration often and made it difficult to move forward. I was always restless, irritated, and driven to get up and move around.

But move forward I did. In 1990, *I Can Hear the Mourning Dove* was published by Houghton-Mifflin, and with its release came several positive reviews, including those from the American Library Association. I had received a $12,000 advance, which seemed like a fortune to Judie and me. It was plenty of money to install a new furnace and central air conditioning system in the house. For several days I had that soaring feeling again, which would ultimately factor into the diagnosis portion of my mental illness.

Air conditioning the house was a major advancement in the never-ending series of projects designed to transform this house from a place to live to a *welcoming* place to live. Over the coming years, I found myself cutting back limbs from the out-of-control hackberry trees that shrouded the house, building a patio behind the house, building shutters for the windows, building and painting awnings for the west-side windows, installing additional kitchen cupboards, un-junking the annex, then knocking out its front wall and installing a garage door, planting a beautiful smoke tree in the front yard, making improvements to the basement bathroom, installing modern storm doors, building large flower boxes, and creating a lovely rose garden in the backyard. With the scraggly trees cut back, there was now enough sun there to make flower growing plausible. There were other projects as well, including replacing windows in the annex.

Judie and I installed a new tile floor in the kitchen. We also cut carpet remnants to fit the basement's large room and the bedroom with wall-to-wall carpeting.

I said to Judie at the time, "I guess this is what Sandi means by 'pride of home ownership.'"

Most of the work I did on my own, driven (of course) by an obsessive-compulsive's project mentality. It had to be done. It had to be done *now*. And it had to be done *fast*. There was no moving forward methodically, enjoying the process along the way.

Except for Toes. Whenever I was working, she was always by my side. On warm days (when I did most of this exterior work), I often took a break for a glass of water and sat on a picnic table I had built for the patio. She sat next to me. At times I got down and held my arms around her. I wanted to feel that warmth, the slope of her chest, the angle of her shoulders, and the pressing face against my face.

And I wanted to remember this—all of it, every smell, every touch. For she was getting old. Her muzzle was turning gray, and she moved slowly. At times she circled quite a bit (somewhat clumsily) before finding a comfortable position for lying down. As old as she was, I knew what all owners of aging dogs know: her time was coming. Maybe not this month or this year, but her time was coming. I would reach for her, and she wouldn't be there. I would long to hold her just once more, but it wouldn't be possible. I would step outside, but she wouldn't be next to me. I would sit at the typewriter (I still hadn't discovered computers or word processing), and her shoulder wouldn't be pressed against my ankle. *I wanted to remember.*

My schedule found me coming home from school in midafternoon, getting straight to work on one of the home improvement projects until suppertime, then collapsing. The discouraging fiasco at the library was only a distant memory. All activities involving Jason (mostly band activities or his part-time work at McDonald's), were prescheduled. We lived within easy walking distance of his high school but on occasion had to drive him to work and then pick him up late at night. Eventually, when he was a senior, we scraped enough money together to buy him a used car.

In the summers, I wrote in the mornings, then dived into one of the house projects in the afternoons. Jason's summertime sports, such as soccer or baseball were carefully scheduled; I didn't want to miss one of his games.

Judie was thriving at the hospital, gaining knowledge, judgment, and widespread respect on her unit.

Unfortunately for me, about the time *I Can Hear the Mourning Dove* was released, Xanax was no longer helping me. My body had built up a tolerance for it, even as Dr. Gordon frequently increased the dosage. I was now taking two milligrams every four hours, with little effect. It was a drug, as Dr. Gordon had reminded me, with the potential to activate the mechanism of addiction—fast-acting but short-lived relief. And two milligrams was as high as he was willing to go. There was no good reason for me to continue taking the drug.

Meanwhile, the Prozac was slowly but surely losing potency, providing only very mild relief if any at all. The Curse was now pushing back—and hard. When I talked to Dr. Gordon, he explained, "It's a sawtooth recovery." He moved his hand up and down in the air to simulate the jagged teeth on a big saw. "Your recovery is up and down, not constant in the direction of normalcy."

I was disappointed, as my symptoms had returned nearly full force. "It's very discouraging and disturbing," I said. "I've been going through this for sixteen years. I don't think I ever expect to have a recovery. But if I could only reach a point where I had manageable symptoms like I had a year ago or so."

"I know it's hard. Remember what I told you though about trial and error. It's a matter of finding the right medication, and that can take time."

This was too discouraging to respond to. I put my head in my hands with my elbows on my knees. "So what do we do now?" I mumbled.

"Let's increase the dosage of the Prozac. In two or three weeks, we'll see how that goes."

This was not the answer I wanted, but I couldn't think of a reason to argue with him. I knew he had a good heart.

It did not go well with the increased dosage of Prozac. In fact, it brought no therapeutic benefit at all. I was sliding steadily backward toward the original level of extreme anxiety that interfered with nearly every portion of my life. There was no pleasure, no peace, and no escape. Once again I endured those sleepless nights, the ones that were soooo long. I had trouble eating again and so began another round of weight loss.

During this time, Toes began to exhibit symptoms of failing health. Occasionally she seemed to fall for no reason, especially when I let her out the back door. Then she would recover her footing and was strong enough for me to walk her around the neighborhood. When we came home, she didn't come to greet us; she thumped the tail up and down but mostly stayed put in the living room in the prone position on the couch or floor.

But as long as we could go on the walks around the block, I felt confident her health was strong enough to carry her forward for a few more years.

But my (our) confidence turned out to be wishful thinking. Her condition deteriorated. She began stumbling down the short flight of stairs leading to the back door. On the landing, she struggled to get up, but her back legs seemed unable to cooperate. Dr. Brunton said she had a neuromuscular disorder that would get progressively worse. He gave her steroids to stall the inevitable while reminding us she was about fourteen years old now.

Judie and I had a teary conversation on one of our drives back from his office. We advised Jason of her condition one afternoon when he dropped by the house. He was now attending the local community college and had moved into a shabby apartment with a roommate; he felt like he needed the independence now that he had graduated high school. He was a bright kid and could have gone to a university, but the local JC was what we could afford. It saddened him to hear about Toes, but he took it in stride.

The fact that he did brought me an additional kind of sorrow. I wanted him to be more visibly disturbed than he was; she was his dog at the very outset when she first came home as a frightened puppy, but now the brave new world he occupied had moved him along the arc of life's journey. His mother and I were still the parents of a dog as well as a son, but he was an independent young man establishing his adult identity.

During one of the long, lonely nights after I had dozed off for a few minutes, I reached down and found an empty space where Toes usually slept. I got up and went to the living room. We always left a lamp on there, so I could see very well. What I saw was heartbreaking: She was positioned on her haunches with her front paws and head on the couch. She wanted to get up on the couch but couldn't; her back legs simply wouldn't work.

She turned to look at me with the saddest of eyes, the way dogs do when there's something on their mind and as if they long to share it. It was a look I knew well, not only from her, but from former dogs in our family as well as many dogs I'd observed while volunteering at the Humane Society. But the inability to speak doesn't matter; the eyes say it all.

That was the way it was at this moment in time. I lifted her gently up onto the couch and lay down beside her. I was miserable, and so was she. Her muzzle rested on my temple. I was swept back in time to the stone house outside of Middletown when I had lain with Nanook on a lonely couch so she could comfort me. Now, it was as if Toes and I were trying to comfort each other. We had spent plenty of time like this at East Bay when she had lived through life-threatening crises, holding each other as it seemed.

I began to cry, and soon the crying escalated to full-blown sobbing. *Why was there so much pain? Why was there so much suffering and sorrow? So much loss?*

Apparently my sobbing was loud enough to wake Judie, because she came to investigate. She sat on the floor and rubbed us both. My own emotional suffering combined with our loving dog's rapid health decline was taking another difficult toll on her.

A few days later, in January of 1992, we had her euthanized. For the next few days we were numb. We missed her terribly. In private moments, I shed tears and sometimes broke into uncontrollable sobbing. She had brought so much love and joy to us over so many years, in various locations and under various conditions. Her absence left a gaping hole in our lives.

We were terribly disoriented. She wasn't there to let out in the mornings. She wasn't there to greet us when we came home. She wasn't there to go for walks. She wasn't with me in the kitchen when I made the morning coffee. I thought back often to her running, jumping Frisbee days, her close connection with camp staff, her swimming with campers, her companionship when I was struggling through mental and physical exhaustion to qualify a neglected house for FHA approval, and other memories too numerous to count. For so many years, she had been friend, loyal companion, comforter, and valued family member.

And once again, I felt the desperate loneliness of an empty couch in the middle of an anxious, sleepless night. The long nights were just so much longer.

*If I have any belief about immortality, it
is that certain dogs I have known will go
to heaven, and very, very few persons.*
                                    —James Thurber

Squeak

IN APRIL, Judie and I adopted another dog, our first rescue dog. I
was doing volunteer dog walking at the Humane Society (when it fit
my prearranged schedule) and began warming up to a black Cocker
Spaniel from the first day she showed up at the shelter.

She came to the shelter with the name of Pipsqueak. Unlike
many of the other dogs, she didn't bark when I (or other people)
approached her cage. Instead, she pressed her shoulder to the mesh
so visitors could scratch the side of her neck and face. And she looked
at you with those hopeful, longing eyes. It wasn't long before I was
walking her each time I volunteered, then taking her into one of the
viewing rooms to sit with her. Always, her first move was to put front
paws onto my lap, with chin resting in between. I wanted to take her
home.

I felt guilty since Toes had only been gone four months, but this
little Cocker seduced me with her warm, calm affection. And my life,
whether roiled or not, had always been better if a dog was part of it.

Judie was skeptical but not for long. When she came with me
to view this dog, she too was charmed by its quiet affection. "Is she
old?" Judie asked me.

"Not according to her sheet," I said. "She's only two and a half.
And she's housebroken." And so it was that Pipsqueak became the
newest member of our family. It wasn't long before we had shortened
her name to Squeak.

When we took her to see Dr. Brunton, we asked if she was a purebred Cocker.

"No, she's got something else in her. For one thing, her muzzle is narrower and longer than what you'd find in a purebred." We didn't care, as she was an affectionate, loving dog from the start. As a matter of fact, we thought back to Fleance, our purebred Scottie, who had regrettably evolved from laid-back lap dog who loved to play tug-of-war, to aggressive and even vicious attack dog. I don't think we'd have been as confident had she been a purebred dog, although that was probably irrational.

Squeak would become a calm and quiet lap dog for the eleven years we were blessed to have her. She was never a ball or stick chaser, had little interest in Frisbees, didn't play tug-of-war with ropes or do any tricks. She almost never barked. She did have the winning habit of running to greet us whenever we came home, whimpering her joy as she pawed away at our knees.

She also loved going for walks (on a leash). She never showed much interest in chasing squirrels or rabbits and walked at a regular pace. It might have been possible to walk her without the leash, but I never took the chance. My new walking partner suited me fine; now in my fifties, I wasn't exercising much. I was no longer a jogger or runner, not a golfer, not a tennis player, and not a fitness gym participant. My exercise was essentially wrapped up in the physical labor involved with many of my home improvement projects, so walking was as beneficial for me as it was rewarding for our dog.

I often referred to Squeak as my "good luck" dog, as the next ten years would prove to be my most successful decade as an author. In 1993, I published *Dakota Dream* with Scholastic, even though I didn't have an agent. As a matter of fact, every book I've ever published I placed without an agent. *Dakota Dream,* which was marketed by Scholastic as a Young Adult (YA) or teen novel, also received several favorable reviews. The American Library Association included it on their Best Books for Young Adults (BBYA) list. It was adopted by many school libraries and classrooms across the country (as was *I Can Hear the Mourning Dove*) and still sits on many of those shelves yet today.

This second novel also brought with it a substantial advance, and sales were strong enough I actually received royalty checks over the next couple of years. Now that we had edged our way into the middle class financially, Judie and I agreed the time had come for me to quit my school job and devote myself to full-time writing.

It was at this time that my son, who was now an upperclassman in college, decided I needed to graduate from typewriter to computer. So we bought a computer, and he showed me the ropes of a word processing application. It turned out to be a major blessing for me and my career, as I'd always been something of a rewriting freak, and a word processing system enabled me to revise to my heart's content.

The first book I wrote on the computer turned out to be a blockbuster, at least with critics. *The Squared Circle*, published in late 1995 (again with Scholastic), was hailed as the best YA of the year and called the "finest basketball novel ever written" by one critic. Another outlet deemed it the best YA novel of the last quarter of the twentieth century. The irony was (and still is) that the book wasn't written for a YA or teen readership.

I received the largest advance I'd ever had, but the book's sales were only modest. I regarded it (and still do) as an adult novel. Its protagonist is a college student, and its other major character is a professor in her thirties. The book blends mythology (the Egyptian legend of Isis and Osiris) with basketball, so it has a symbolic level. And it is loaded with graphic locker room language. Many high school librarians refused to shelve it, so I guess I made my debut in the world of banned books. Many public libraries over the years have shelved it with adult fiction. Because it was what's often called an orphan book by the publishing industry (one foot in the YA section and the other in the adult department), its sales were doomed to fall short of what its critical acclaim had predicted.

I followed that with *The Flex of the Thumb* in 1996, *Blue Star Rapture* (Simon & Schuster) in 1998, *Plunking Reggie Jackson* (Simon & Schuster) in 2001, and *Old Hoss* (McFarland Publishing), a book I coauthored with good friend Don Raycraft in 2002. In 2003, I published *Faith Wish* with Holiday House, then came *Harvey Porter*

Does Dallas in 2004, a comic parody that was my first adventure in online publishing. Most of these books brought at least modest critical acclaim to go along with modest income. But it was a very productive decade.

It was productive despite the fact there were many days when I couldn't work much more than an hour. It always took a year or two for me to write a book because my inability to focus, combined with agitation and restlessness, often undermined my ability to actually make progress on a manuscript. At other times, when my symptoms were less acute, I sometimes worked throughout the morning as long as two weeks in a row. I could never actually *count on* anything— good days followed bad, and vice-versa. On bad days, I tended to grind away on the same page over and over without truly finding a way forward. My mind repeated itself maddeningly, with no useful outcome.

I've always wondered how many books I might have been able to write had I been blessed with a normal emotional balance and concentration capacity. And would the books have been better ones? Nevertheless, I gave myself credit (and still do) for my determination and—dare I say it?—courage.

The Flex of the Thumb deserves a paragraph. It was a comic novel I chipped away at from time to time over many years then usually set aside. My son, Jason, was the publisher. He was by this time a senior English major at the University of Illinois. He wanted to publish the book as a senior project, and his adviser, who was familiar with some of my work, consented. Jason went through the entire procedure of editing, securing Library of Congress copyright, ISBN number, taking bids from book manufacturers, finding an artist for cover art, finding a distributor, sending out review copies, etc. It was a long and complicated process. He even had to establish his own publishing company, which he named Pin Oak Press.

In the end, he got nine hours of A, and I made no money on the book. But it was a gratifying, bonding experience with my son. We are both still grateful we took this project on.

So what was going on with Squeak and the Curse during all this writing success?

The Curse was still an unwelcome, chronic affliction. At times it was debilitating although not actually disabling. At other times the symptoms were manageable enough I could work my way through them. But always my anxieties were prevalent enough to be discouraging. I now knew that I had a disorder that would last a lifetime; it would never go away. There was never going to be a recovery, sawtooth or otherwise.

Some nights I got as many as four or five hours of sleep; some nights less. My appetite was pretty good more often than not.

Dr. Gordon changed my medications often, sometimes adding a new one, other times increasing dosages. It was, as he had said from the outset, inevitably a trial-and-error journey.

Throughout the years, I took more psychotropic drugs than I can remember, but I do remember the tricyclic antidepressants like Triavil, Elavil, and Imipramine. I took some of the selective serotonin reuptake inhibitors (SSRIs), including Prozac and Zoloft. These two drugs are often prescribed as antiobsessive and antianxiety agents as well.

I took antianxiety medications, including Buspar, Klonopin, Valium, and Xanax. At one point when my anxiety level was particularly severe, Gordon put me on Zyprexa, a powerful antipsychotic drug often used in the treatment of schizophrenia. Its side effects were so profound I had trouble staying awake even when walking or mowing the lawn. When I did sleep at night, I was troubled with terrible nightmares that woke me up soaked with cold sweats.

I made an emergency appointment with Dr. Gordon and told him about these troubling side effects. "Then we need to take you off of it. We work to find something better, something that does work."

The day before, I had done some dog walking at the Humane Society, when a small brown terrier rescue had been brought to the shelter. The poor creature was matted, emaciated, and terrified. There were imprints of chain links on his shoulders. His suffering had haunted me overnight.

One day I said to Gordon, "You know, no matter how bad you have it, somebody else has worse problems."

Gordon paused before answering, leaning back in his chair. "I suppose that's true."

"I've suffered a lot, for a lot of years, but somehow I've maintained my physical health. I don't know how, what with adrenaline pumping through my body all the time."

"Your central nervous system has made an adjustment. But I've never seen a case of generalized anxiety as long lasting as yours. At least not one so acute."

I had heard this before, of course, and it never brought anything other than discouragement.

"There are people who are dying of cancer," I said. "We all know them. I usually watch the evening news. There are people starving to death all over the planet. There are little children in war zones who are blown to bits. The world is full of suffering worse than mine."

"Does knowing this bring you any relief?"

"No."

"Then why bring it up?"

"Because of the dogs at the shelter and the therapy dogs I've worked with."

"And? Tell me about it."

"Sometimes I work with a pet therapy group. We take gentle dogs to visit patients in nursing homes. I see all the suffering there, the loneliness, the vacant stares, the people whose hope is completely gone."

"You once told me you used to be a religious man."

"That's true. I was at one time, but not now. There's simply too much suffering to justify belief in a loving god. Are you a religious man?"

Dr. Gordon smiled before he answered, "I don't know if I'm religious, but I consider myself a spiritual person. I'm unchurched. There, how about that?"

I wondered for a few moments if he had just described me as well as himself. But I changed the subject: "Are you going to recommend any medication changes?"

"Well, we obviously have to discontinue the Zyprexa."

"So what will take its place?"

"For right now, nothing. Let's get all of that out of your system. We'll continue with the Klonopin but increase the dosage. I think you've said it sometimes brings you relief."

"Yes, but nothing seems to last. Relief is always temporary, whether it's a matter of weeks or months. I long for something that lasts."

"And that's why we have to keep working away."

Other antidepressants I can remember taking were Effexor and Remeron, a drug also used in the treatment of attention deficit hyperactive disorder (ADHD). I have used brand names here rather than the generic names because I think they may be more recognizable for readers than the generics.

During this time, I was not seeing a counselor or participating in any group therapy. I had hitched my wagon to medication and was sticking with it because a good deal of the time I had manageable symptoms. Through all the ups and downs, I was convinced (and still am) that without the therapeutic impact of medication, the Curse would overwhelm me and render me miserable and dysfunctional. It was never going to go away, and my central nervous system was incapable of outlasting it. Its lifespan would be my lifespan.

When my symptoms were severe, I had to hope a new medication (or combination) would serve to alleviate them. When that didn't happen, I had learned to suck it up and tough it out. Not a very comfortable way to live, but however bad the Curse might seem, I always found a way to get through it.

An important part of the way was Squeak. She was always a comfort; her loving, affectionate personality made for warm snuggling. She had the endearing habit of pressing her shoulder and face against my chest (anybody's chest for that matter) pretty much the same as she had done up against her cage while at the Humane Society. When times were bad, she was always there, close and pressing, as if she understood I was suffering and wanted to help.

I was beginning to have a lot of back pain. Sometimes in the evenings, I lay flat on my back on the floor while watching TV. Without fail, Squeak would climb up to stretch out on my chest and belly. She weighed about thirty pounds, half as much as Toes, so I could take the weight. Having this pressing phenomenon on top and bottom actually brought some relief from the back pain. I never talked to a doctor about the back pain. I was in my fifties now and still doing plenty of hard physical labor, so I just wrote it off as a concession to Father Time.

IN 1998, we bought a much nicer house in a charming historic district in Normal, Bloomington's twin city. The house was built in 1912 but had been kept up and improved across the many decades. Selling and buying property brought me plenty of restless nights and high-anxiety days, but nothing close to my meltdown ten years earlier. This new house required no improvements whatsoever, and because we'd saved my advances carefully, we were able to make a substantial down payment. After we moved in, I made double mortgage payments every month we lived there. Judie and I were always frugal and careful with money. That can happen when you've lived through periods of abject poverty.

Our new house was part of an old and hilly subdivision that featured curving streets, enormous shade trees, and many houses in the arts-and-crafts tradition. The neighborhood looked (by design) like an English village. It couldn't have been more perfect for dog walking.

It also brought me back as close to home as I could ever hope to get. The house was only about three blocks away from the big old house we'd lived in when I was a high school student. It was also about three blocks away from the campus of Illinois Wesleyan University (IWU), my undergraduate alma mater. I had graduated there thirty-four years earlier. Athletic facilities were so close I could walk to any game I wanted to see, no matter the sport.

I had regrets about selling our old house and moving out. Saying goodbye wasn't easy. It was in no way comparable to our new home, nor was its neighborhood. But we had spent ten years of very hard work and plenty of money improving it. It was also the first home we'd ever owned and in part a testament to my survival. Consequently, we loved the house despite its many shortcomings and always would.

Our new home had a lovely—though small—screened-in front porch perfectly suited for summer evenings leisure time. Often I would sit there in the evening listening to Cardinals baseball on the radio while holding Squeak in my lap. It was also an ideal spot for drinking coffee and reading the morning paper.

In the spring of 2002, Squeak developed a urinary tract infection; she was suddenly peeing in the carpet then running away quickly from the spot. When I took her for walks, she stopped every twenty to thirty feet (or so it seemed) to squirt. She was visibly uncomfortable and lethargic. When we took her to see Dr. Brunton, he gave her some antibiotics and a piece of foreboding news: "These kinds of infections are common to the breed and can eventually involve the bladder and kidneys."

We didn't have an answer for that, so he added, "I don't mean to scare you, but she is twelve years old or so, and she's always been in good health."

Judie and I drove home not knowing what to make of his comments. *Were we on a dark road here, one leading to ongoing health problems?* We tried not to think about it, and anyway, as Judie said, "That's nothing for us to worry about now. We need to get her well, keep an eye on her, and go from there."

Okay then, I thought. I always tried to take her assessments seriously because after all, she was the balanced member of the family. That night on the porch, Squeak peed on my lap. She seemed so startled she scrambled her way down to the floor. I wasn't mad; I just felt bad for her.

In a day or two, the antibiotics cleared up the infection, and she was good to go again. When I took her for walks, she didn't stop often to eliminate, and she had the spring back in her step. I thought to myself, *Maybe the infection is just a one-time event, and her good health will be permanently restored.*

But I was wrong. A few months later, she had another round of the infection. She needed to squirt every five minutes or so, even when she had a dry run. Again, she was clearly uncomfortable and lethargic. Another trip to Dr. Brunton brought her home with another round of antibiotics.

She never pooped in the house, but she had a frequent need to spray the carpet. Actually, it's better if a dog poops in the house because you can find the result and pick it up. Wet spots in a brown-and-beige carpet can't really be seen. We never chastised her or brought forth any punishment because we knew her illness made this behavior beyond her control. She was no doubt as upset about it—if not more so—than we were. She would look up at us with those sad eyes characteristic of dogs that are in trouble and yearning for words.

When the calendar turned over to 2003, Squeak's episodes of urinary tract infections had become so frequent Dr. Brunton had her on antibiotics and steroids on an ongoing basis. We were reminded of his earlier words of warning, words that now seemed to be coming true. Judie and I both worried about her on a daily basis, wondering when the next episode would show up. Sometimes her episodes would be on hold for a month, other times only for a week or so. We were going through the early grieving process pet owners experience when they come to grips with the fact that their loving friend's time has come or is coming soon.

During a visit to Brunton in early March, he told us we should begin preparing ourselves; Squeak's infection had no doubt spread to her bladder and kidneys. She was a pretty sick dog and not likely to get better. We took her home that day with heavy hearts. "She's sick so much of the time," I said. "What quality of life can she be having and for how long?"

"I know," Judie said. "One of these days, and it won't be long, we're going to have to let her go. Anything else would just be selfish." We were both right. Her lethargy was by this time so chronic that keeping her alive was more of a sentence than putting her to sleep would be. Neither one of us was in denial any longer.

So we were both resigned to the inevitable, but our reluctance to let her go caused us to say "Maybe tomorrow . . . maybe tomorrow . . . maybe tomorrow." Until one night in the later part of March, when I was restless and unable to sleep, I went downstairs to pick her up (she was either unable or unwilling to try and climb the staircase by this time). The clock said 2:00 a.m.

It was a warm night, warm enough for me to sit on the porch and lift her into my lap. She squeezed herself in with her head under my chin, the way she always liked to do. I held her tight. *I wanted to remember.* I knew that her life was about to end, but she didn't; somehow the disconnect seemed cruel. She might be suffering from a terminal illness, but perhaps her not knowing was a blessing, maybe even a measure of freedom.

Our quiet little street was utterly silent. Then she peed on my leg again, but this time made no move to escape or adjust. I began crying, not out loud but silently, tears sliding down my face and into the corners of my mouth. The tears that slid around the edge of my jaw and onto my neck she actually licked away. I put words in her mouth: "Don't cry. I need to go. It's the only thing that works." Probably my overreach, but at that moment, I was convinced those words would have expressed her actual thoughts. I ignored the pee on my thigh, which was turning from warm to cool. I continued to hold her tight. *I wanted to remember.*

The next morning, we had her euthanized. I didn't have the courage to watch, but Judie held Squeak in her arms until the drug did its work, and the little black Cocker's head slumped. She had taken her last breath. It was only then that I went into the exam room (execution chamber that day), where Judie and I stroked her for several minutes as she lay still on her side.

On the drive home, we reminisced about the eleven years Squeak had shared our home and our lives. She had never been an exciting dog that raced after Frisbees or leaped high to catch them in midair. She had never been shot with a gun. She never got lost in a snowstorm or underwent a personality change that altered her demeanor. She was what she was: a vital member of the family, a constant companion, a steadfast, loving lap dog who was always front and center with warmth, affection, and comfort.

For quite a while afterward, life seemed empty and sad. She wasn't leaning against my ankle when I worked at my desk. She wasn't waiting at the front door to slip into her collar and go outside. Our laps were empty. My chest was empty when I lay on the floor in the evenings to try and find a position to relieve back pain.

When we came home, she didn't come running to greet us, whimpering out those little notes of joy. My restless nights were more disturbed; I often sat on the front porch in the dark with tears sliding down my face. This was the pain dog owners contract for when they bring a pet into their lives. It's what you signed up for but choose to ignore because the day of reckoning seemed too far away to have any relevance. And that's a good thing. Otherwise, we would simply crawl into shells.

Besides, she had brought eleven years of joy and love into our lives. We had all those memories safely tucked away in our hearts. It was gratifying to know we had brought an unwanted, homeless dog into our family and gave her a safe, loving home.

We got a handwritten letter from Dr. Brunton the week after Squeak was euthanized. I'm sorry to say I've lost the letter. I had the best of intentions to keep it in a safe place. But I can remember parts of it well: "I hope you'll be able to take comfort from the fact you 'rescued' Squeak and gave her a loving home for eleven years. It's because of you she had a good life, and I'm sure she felt ever safest in your hands. You brightened a small corner of the world with your patience, love, and kindness."

I said to Judie, "How many vets would take the time to write a letter like this?"

"I don't think very many."

"Neither do I." I read the heartwarming letter every day for two weeks, but never with dry eyes.

Dogs got personality. Personality goes a long way.
—Quentin Tarantino

Beau

HIS NAME WAS BEAU.

He was a thirteen-pound Bichon Frise, the smallest dog we'd ever brought into the family circle.

And a time would come when he would save my life.

I discovered him one day in June, about three months after we'd lost our Squeak. I found him in the usual way, while volunteering at the Humane Society. He was white, with large brown eyes. His curly hair was somewhat matted. And although the shelter manager told me he was a member of an active breed, he was subdued at the time because he was recovering from the surgery that had neutered him a couple of days earlier.

He came close for snuggling in the grassy area outside the shelter. At first I thought he was a poodle, but a closer look said no. I asked the shelter manager why he'd been relinquished, and she told me his previous owners had to give him up when their landlord adopted a "no pets" policy.

I asked her about the nature of the breed. "I'm no expert," she said, "but they're thought to be very smart and spirited. They're also hypoallergenic, so they don't shed."

"How old is he?"

"Two and a half, the sheet says."

"Is he a purebred dog?"

"As far as we can tell, but we can't ever be certain. You're hooked, aren't you?"

I had to admit I was. "Don't take too long to make up your mind," she warned me. "He won't be here long."

That afternoon, when Judie got off work, I took her out to the shelter. We brought Beau out into the grass and sat on the ground. He walked slowly to her and sat in her lap. "He's hypoallergenic," I said, "which means he doesn't shed."

"I know what hypoallergenic means. Are you sure you're ready for another dog so soon? It's only been three months."

"I'm not sure, are you?"

"No," she said, but while she said it, she was stroking the little guy curled up in her lap.

"I think I'd feel a little guilty," I said, "this soon after we lost Squeak. I still miss her a lot of the time."

"So do I," she said, "but guilt doesn't do any good, and it's not a reason for making this decision."

"Maybe not, but it sure seems like one. I'd sure like to bring this little guy home, though."

Then Judie said, "If we really want him, I think Squeak would tell us to take him home. She would want another homeless dog to have the same opportunity she had."

It was touching in a way, how she was putting words into the mouth of a dog now at rest in doggie heaven. But it seemed to make sense. Judie always made sense. And we were dog people; we would learn to love this little Beau and give him a safe home.

THREE DAYS LATER, after the vet had cleared him for adoption, I brought him home (Judie was working at the hospital). It didn't take long for me to realize that our new family member was quite different from our previous one. He went plunging through the house, sniffing every corner of every room. He raced up the stairs to check out the bedrooms and bathroom. When he came back down, he looked up at me as though in anticipation. "What's up?" he seemed to be asking. "What's on the agenda for today?"

I took him out on the porch, where he immediately jumped up and landed on one of the windowsills. I was amazed that this very small dog could even do this; the sills were a good thirty inches above the floor, and he was very small. The leap looked like something only a cat could manage.

The porch was made of painted bricks and concrete masonry work, so the sills were about eight inches wide. Moving back and forth, he scanned the neighborhood; he needed to know what was going on in the big, wide world. His porch needs couldn't have been more different from those of Squeak, who was always content to sit quietly in a lap.

Within only a few minutes, a squirrel ventured into our yard. Beau's reaction revealed another dramatic behavioral difference; he began barking like crazy, running back and forth along the sill, then dropping to the floor and racing madly around the small porch to see if there might be a better viewing location. Finding none, he scrambled his way back up onto the sill; the squirrel was still there, so he kept the barking going.

I picked him up and put him in my lap, but I had to restrain him; he was squirming to get back to that lookout position. After a while, I put him down, but he immediately made the leap to the sill. The squirrel was apparently gone, as the barking stopped, but he was alert to any outside movement; he was clearly on patrol.

So this little guy was territorial. Not since Fleance had we had a dog with this characteristic. And as time went by, we discovered that Beau had protective instincts that showed up in unusual ways. He never did realize he was too small to be imposing or threatening. That's one of the wonders of dogs. Like people, they are all different, with distinctly individual personalities and temperaments.

I had read an online article about Bichons that warned prospective buyers or adopters that they were needy dogs and active; they were high-maintenance creatures. This information made me somewhat uncomfortable. What if Judie and I had bitten off a little more than we could chew? What if we couldn't give this little fellow the kind of high-octane home he needed?

"Beau," I asked him, "are you going to be a problem child? Are you going to be more than we can handle?" At the sound of my voice, he turned away from the window to look at me. He cocked his head as if to say, "Who, me?"

His coat was scruffy and somewhat matted. The online pictures of Bichons showed dogs with fluffy, puffed-up coats. I took him down to the basement sink and proceeded to give him a bath with some of Squeak's leftover shampoo. He didn't seem to enjoy this undertaking at all—he squirmed but didn't thrash. When he was soaked to the skin, I could see how small he truly was. I could nearly circle his rib cage with my two hands.

After I toweled him off, his coat was still flat and matted. He was clean, but he didn't look anything like the dogs in the pictures. I could only conclude that those were photos of show dogs that had been professionally groomed. Judie and I decided that night we'd get his hair cut short all over. Neither one of us cared if he didn't look like one of the fluffy show dogs. After all, it was June, and we wanted him to be comfortable in the hot weather.

That night I went to bed before Judie did. That was not unusual; my broken sleep habits left me tired—or even exhausted—by late afternoons or early evenings. As soon as I sat on the edge of the bed, Beau jumped up to join me. It was an endearing maneuver, but it also stirred my anxieties; we'd never had a dog that chose to share our bed at night, and I wasn't sure what to make of it. What if he didn't know the difference between night and day? What if his active nature meant he'd be up and about the house during the night? If so, it would be one more obstacle to sleeping, something I certainly didn't need.

But as it turned out, it wasn't a problem. He stretched out next to me when the light went out and lay still. He shifted positions a few times, but not nearly as often as I did. But when Judie came to bed (I was still half awake), we learned something else about our new dog: He growled in what sounded like a menacing fashion and even approached her with a snarl. *Oh no*, I thought. *What the hell is this?*

Judie was understandably apprehensive (as was I), but it turned out we had no cause to be. When the little guy reached her, he did an about-face and began pawing and licking her. The ostensibly angry growling turned out to be a prelude to a show of affection. It seemed very peculiar, but from that point forward, Beau was essentially *my* dog. He deemed himself my protector, I guess. Anytime he was in my lap or next to me on a recliner, he growled the low growl that crescendoed to a full bark if anyone approached me. Sometimes it scared people who were not familiar with him, or young children, because it did sound menacing. Whenever someone knocked at our front door, he charged the door with loud barking, then pawed away at the intruder, seeking affection.

After a while, most everyone who spent time in our house (including Jason and family) figured out this was a show of protective instinct that quickly ran out of gas. *I'm just letting you know I'm in charge here, and you need to respect that.* In all the twelve years we had him, he never bit or snapped at anyone. He did lick a lot of faces.

Beau did know the difference between night and day. He lay calmly in bed most of the time throughout the night. Anytime either one of us got up to use the bathroom, he stood up at the foot of the bed, watchfully waiting for our return. Occasionally, he wanted to burrow himself beneath the sheets to curl up between us. After an hour or so, though, he came climbing out to get back on top.

Two days after we brought him home, we took Beau to see Dr. Brunton. As soon as we got him inside the office, though, he began to shake and tremble and scrambled frantically to try and get back outside. We had never had a dog previously that reacted this way in a vet's office. He was obviously very scared, and it made us feel bad. I had to pick him up. After Brunton examined him, he said, "It's nothing to worry about. Many dogs and cats have vet office anxiety, happens all the time. He seems in good health, and he's had all his shots, so there's really nothing for me to do."

We asked him if he thought Beau was a purebred Bichon. "As far as I can tell, he is. If there's something else in there, I couldn't guess what it might be."

Hearing this gave us no sense of pride; we just wanted a healthy dog that we could make happy in our home. It did, however, cause us a little concern. We told him the story of our purebred Scottie, Fleance, and the sorrow that came with his abrupt personality change.

But Brunton was already shaking his head. "Scotties are aggressive by nature. It doesn't take much to set them off. With this little guy, you're looking at a completely different breed with typically loving and affectionate natures. That's not something you need to worry about."

A couple of days later, when we were both away from the house several hours, Beau pooped on the carpet. He came running to greet me as soon as I got inside the door, barking his enthusiasm and pawing rapidly at my knees before I discovered the poop. I raised my voice and said, "No, no, Beau!"

Immediately he fled to a corner of the living room and curled up into a ball, cowering in fear. He obviously knew what his transgression was and was expecting physical punishment.

But there wasn't going to be any. He was ashamed and afraid. I was ashamed for overreacting, and in such a tired, thoughtless way. Because he was as unhappy about what he'd done as I was, I resisted the urge to pick him up and stick his nose in it.

Judie and I had housebroken dogs before, usually the old-fashioned way with loud disapproval accompanied by sticking the dog's nose in the excrement. But over the years, my work in Humane Society shelters had brought me in contact with professional dog trainers. I knew the better—and less traumatic—method was with patience and kindness, not a stick or a rolled-up newspaper.

At this moment, our new family member knew what he'd done wasn't acceptable, and his fear of a cuffing or a slapping was evident. No punishment would serve a purpose, and his trembling fear tugged at my heart. I picked him up, and we sat on the couch. "We'll work through this," I told him in a lowered voice. I tried to be soothing. "I don't want you to be afraid, little guy. No one here is going to hurt you." He soon calmed down.

The carpet was mostly brown anyway, and the small pile was firm. No damage done. I remembered his sheet at the shelter had said he was *mostly* housebroken, unless he was left alone too long. When I told Judie about the episode, she frowned. "Oh, I hope his people didn't beat him or abuse him."

"So do I," I said. "But his reaction makes you wonder." Judie and I realized this was an issue we could manage without too much difficulty. We could control how long he was left alone in the house and gradually increase the intervals. She might have had a timecard to punch, but I didn't. Even though I was a hidebound neurotic, I did have the freedom to set my own schedule. In the coming weeks, we would have three or four more episodes, but that was about it.

His sheet had also said he liked to play ball and tug of war. We still had Squeak's rope toy (the one she showed little interest in), so I took it out of storage to see how Beau might react to it. Well, he reacted with enthusiasm and energy. I tossed the toy across the living room, and he sped after it. Once he got it in his mouth, he slammed it around on the floor rapidly back and forth, growling that growl of his all the time. When I got hold of one end of it and tugged, he pulled back hard, shaking his head while growling. The growling was just part of the game. When I was able to actually pull it free, he jumped up on his back legs and pawed the air with his front legs. *Do it again!* he seemed to say. *Throw it again!*

I threw it again. And again. And again. Each time he ran it down and maintained an urgent growl as he slammed it repeatedly on the floor. It was clear he'd never tire of the game. We had ourselves a fun-loving, high-energy dog who loved to play.

The first time I showed Judie this action, she laughed out loud. It was entertaining to watch; eventually she tossed the rope a few times herself, but her interest faded more quickly than mine. She said to me, "His sheet at the shelter said he also liked to play ball. What do you suppose that means?"

"Maybe he likes to chase balls," I said. "The question is, does he bring them back? If he doesn't, then the game would be fun for him only. I'll have to find out."

The next afternoon, I did find out. I got a tennis ball and took Beau to the Illinois Wesleyan practice football field, just a couple of blocks away. The first time I threw the ball down the field, this little dog astonished me; he exploded with an incredible burst of speed and ran like the wind. As soon as he got it in his mouth, he turned and came back at a slow trot.

He was coy about giving the ball up, but as soon as he did, he was off like a flash again, even before I had a chance to cock my arm. He assumed that somewhere down the field the ball would bounce in front of him. I had to crank up my arm because if I threw the ball less than thirty yards, it would fall behind him. So each time, I threw

JAMES BENNETT

it as high and far as I could, then watched him leap to snare it on a high bounce or at least try to. Then he trotted back with the ball in his mouth. Eventually he would drop it on the ground, although he always made me walk ten to fifteen feet to pick it up.

The only way I could end this game was by putting him on his leash before he dropped the ball. *He* was certainly not going to end it.

He was a good walking dog from the very first day we brought him home. He moved at a relatively brisk pace but not straining on the leash. We walked and walked throughout the neighborhood, uphill and down, nearly every day. He behaved himself well—until he saw a squirrel or a rabbit, that is. Then he would bark and jump, pulling the leash taut. Given the chance, he would have sped after them. I have no idea what he might have done had he ever actually caught one. But this impulse to chase reminded Judie and me that we'd always have to keep him leashed outdoors. Our quiet little street had little traffic, but some of the cross streets had plenty.

We didn't have him long before we found out how smart Beau was. He had quite the vocabulary and seemed to pick it up quickly. Whenever I came home, after he rushed me with enthusiastic dancing on his back legs and barking out his joy, I would often ask him, "Where's your rope, Beau?" He would then make his rounds, moving swiftly from room to room until he brought it forth with a spring in his step that seemed like pride. When I asked him, "Where's your ball, Beau?" he scurried through the same search. He knew the difference between the two. Of course, as Judie pointed out, he might have learned those distinctions from his previous owners. I always preferred to think he learned his vocabulary from us.

In any case, it didn't take us long to learn to love this little dog and cherish the fun that came with him. Fun had been largely lacking from my life for the past thirty years. Most of the time I was too strung out from the Curse to make room for it. Most of the fun I had experienced had been connected with our canine family members Toes (and now) Beau in particular.

Beau's arrival coincided with a particularly good period in my mental condition. I seemed to be doing pretty well on relatively large dosages of Buspar, along with relatively small doses of Klonopin three or four times daily. I was sleeping better and eating better. I was still running at least a five on the anxiety scale, which would have been terrifying for most people, but I had long since resigned myself to this level of discomfort as something I could work through. Or fight through. Life was as good as it was going to get, at least in terms of mental health.

Faith Wish, one of my successful YA novels, was published in the fall of that year (2003). It took almost two years to write, including revisions, and was receiving strong notices from publishing industry journals and publications.

I've always recalled that summer and fall fondly; frequently Beau and I played tug of war and nearly every day I took him to the practice field to play fetch the tennis ball. It was fun. *He* was fun. I was volunteering at the shelter as well as with the dog therapy group in local nursing homes.

In addition to that, I was working with a co-author for the first time, good friend Don Raycraft, on a fictional biography of Old Hoss Radbourn, a Bloomington native and the greatest big-league pitcher of the nineteenth century. That was fun too—brainstorming together on how to fill the gaps. Radbourn's baseball life and a few of his biographical facts were available, but many more were not.

Judie and I spent more time with friends; we were generating some actual social life, a fact that gratified me for her sake more than my own. For far too long my mental condition had curbed this very important part of life. Even though having a chronic mental illness wasn't my fault, and even though I understood this in my mind, I still felt plenty of guilt for the manner in which the Curse had caused her to suffer uncertainty, bewilderment, and difficult lifestyle adjustments. But my improvement led to *our* improvement.

BUT WHEN DECEMBER CAME, just two weeks before Christmas, Judie lost her job.

State funding for the hospital was cut dramatically, which led to a number of layoffs. Some of the nurses on her unit who got the pink slip were those with longer years of service; they were more expensive. Judie was one of those. Christmas in 2003 wasn't going to generate much seasonal joy in our house. The job loss was even more stunning because she had had the job since 1986—seventeen years.

For several days we more or less sat around, staring into space in disbelief. It didn't seem possible. Now what were we supposed to do? The money I had made from book advances had been put to work in investments, so we had that to draw on, but for how long? Besides that, these investments were intended to establish a bona fide nest egg for retirement, not be dribbled away over time to pay electric bills and buy groceries.

Now it was Judie's turn to feel guilty; she was the one who lost a job and put us in a difficult position. Like me, she understood none of this was her fault. But also like me, she nevertheless found it hard to shake the guilt. I tried to comfort her even as her tears fell. The whole thing was just so unfair. Sometimes when I was hugging her, Beau got into the act. He barked his disapproval at being left out of this human peer bonding and pawed his way up our legs. Or insisted on burrowing his way in between us in bed.

I could feel my anxieties/depression stirring to a less comfortable level as Judie contacted other agencies in town that had mental health and/or substance abuse programs, but I was still in a better place than I usually was. Judie's job seeking efforts resulted in dead ends, so she had her share of anxiety as well. But she was always stable; she still slept well at night. Her ability to weather crises without coming unglued had always been a huge part of our family survival and togetherness.

At the end of January in 2004, we drove to Key Largo in Florida, to visit Bruce and Winni Earle, our dear friends from way back in Middletown, New York. Over thirty years' time we had kept this friendship alive even though we lived so far apart. We had occasional summer visits together, but the consistent get-together was Super Bowl week in the Florida Keys. Watching the big game while sitting seaside at a tiki bar in short sleeves was always a highlight.

Like me, Bruce was a former English teacher; he was four years older than I, and his calm and confident demeanor always comforted me. He knew all about my breakdown in Middletown and long-term mental illness that followed; we had discussed it many times. He was always a good and empathetic listener.

He was important on this particular visit, reassuring Judie and me that her job hunt would eventually be successful. He had no particulars in mind, but his confidence that "life finds a way" for good people felt convincing. None of this was tied to religious belief; he always had confidence in his ability to work things out without the intervention of a higher being.

We had Beau with us on this trip, and we were a bit apprehensive, as the Earles had a five-year-old Rottweiler named Cassie. As a rule, Rottweilers don't get along well with other dogs, but our concerns weren't warranted, as it turned out. The two dogs got along famously and even tried to play together in the small living room. Cassie was so much larger than Beau that she flattened him from time to time, but he was so much quicker and more agile, she couldn't usually keep up.

On the visit, my splintered nocturnal habits usually found me up and out of bed by 4:00 a.m., long before anyone else was stirring. This was the most uneasy part of the day for me, although I surprised myself by my lack of acute anxieties. I was bearing up better than I expected, given the latest crisis Judie and I were up against. I guess it was the comfort and reassurance our special friends provided.

In the dark, I walked Beau a few blocks to the corner gas station/convenience store on Highway 1, where I bought a large coffee and the *Miami Herald*. I would read it on the porch beneath poor lighting while waiting for the world to wake up.

One morning we came across a slow-moving armadillo along the way, and Beau practically strangled himself on the leash in his urgent need to chase it. He was barking like crazy, until the peculiar creature slipped away into a hedgerow. And since our hosts lived in a neighborhood that preserved all possible trees (gumbo-limbos were most common), there were squirrels aplenty. Walks with Beau were not uneventful.

On the drive home, we stayed overnight in a hotel in Naples, a picturesque small city on the Gulf Coast, where the splendid white sand beaches are preserved as public places. By city ordinance, neither hotels nor opulent mansions can stake out private beaches to make them off-limits to the general public.

We had been charmed by Naples before on previous trips. The next morning, as I was up and moving around the hotel lobby before the world came to life. With Beau as my lone companion, I used the hotel computer to do an Internet search. To my surprise, I came across a mental health hospital named the David Lawrence Center, in Naples. According to the map, it was located outside the city proper, some ten to twelve miles from the city center. But it had a Naples address.

When we were on the road again, I told Judie of my discovery. She said, "Are you thinking what I think you're thinking?"

It was hard for me to believe I was. Another major move involving major adjustments. How could I possibly be entertaining anything so bold, so far beyond my comfort zone? But inside, I was having that *soaring* feeling again. "Maybe," I finally said. It was the *soaring* feeling, the brief periods of euphoria that would lead later psychiatrists to diagnose me as bipolar (manic depressive).

"You're thinking I could get a job at this David Lawrence Center and we would move to Florida?"

Now that she had said it out loud, it did seem preposterous. I had a thirty-year history of being unable to adjust to new circumstances or behave with spontaneity. "I was just thinking, that's all. Maybe I'm just charmed by Naples."

"We don't know anything about this David Lawrence Center."

"We know it's a mental health facility that must have psychiatric nurses on its staff."

"That's not enough. That's not enough information. Besides, what do we really know about Naples, other than it has a charming downtown area?"

Of course she was right. The very thought was crazy. "We would be leaving our home and our friends," she pointed out. "The world we know. The home we love. The neighborhood we love. It's your comfort zone. It's your safe place."

"I know." I had started on a new novel called *Fresh Killed*, whose protagonist was a teenage boy suffering from polio during the Korean War. "But as long as I've got the computer, I can write wherever we live."

"I'd have to know a lot more about the David Lawrence Center, and I'd have to know a lot more about you. Buspar and Klonopin are holding you steady right now, but how many times have we seen your medications lose their effectiveness?"

"More times than I like to remember," I said honestly. "But we'd only be about two hours away from Bruce and Winnie. Straight across the Everglades on Highway 41 to Key Largo."

But it turned out I wasn't the only one romanticizing. Judie was too. After another month or so of hitting brick walls as she tried to find work at other mental health facilities in communities close to Bloomington, she called me inside one day around St. Patrick's Day. We had had a wet snowfall the night before, and I was outside throwing snowballs down the alley for Beau to chase. Just like Nanook and Toes before him, he pawed them to pieces as soon as he ran them down. It wasn't quite as much fun as chasing the tennis ball on the practice field, but it was a satisfactory winter alternative.

Judie told me she had contacted the David Lawrence Center, and they were willing to interview her over the phone. "It sounds like a good operation down there," she said. "The unit sounds well established with a good history."

"You've changed your mind?" I asked.

"Not completely, but maybe it's an option worth exploring. You're sixty-two now, and I'm fifty-eight, maybe we owe ourselves one last adventure."

She surprised me. I hadn't given the idea much thought since we'd returned home, but I wondered if this "one last adventure" concept might be worth trying. But I said, "It sounds exciting, but I'm not sure if I could step that far outside my comfort zone."

"I wonder the same thing," she said. "I think you have to talk it over with Dr. Gordon. I'd like to know what he says."

I talked it over with Dr. Gordon the following week, just after Judie had had a preliminary interview with the David Lawrence

CEO. "This sounds awfully bold," Gordon said. "Are you confident you can handle it?"

I was honest: "I'm never altogether confident about anything in life."

"You've had writing success for several years."

"I know, but my confidence only comes in fits and starts. I've had my feet held close to the fire too many times."

"How do you feel when you think about this move?"

"Anxious at times, but at other times I have the soaring feeling inside. I don't know how else to describe it."

"That's manic," he said immediately.

"Manic? Am I bipolar now? Is that what you're saying?"

"No. I'm saying it's just another piece of who you are. You know my position as a psychiatrist. Mood disorders form a spectrum, not cubicles. Like I've told you before, there are no clear-cut diagnoses. You have a cluster of symptoms, and we've worked a long time on a trial-and-error basis to find the right medical protocol for you."

"Once you called it a flavor of a lot of things."

"That too. Same difference. If you move to Florida, what mental health support system would you have? Do you know anybody in Naples?"

"No, but I live with a psychiatric nurse, and if Judie got that job, she'd be in a network of mental health professionals."

Then he leaned back in his chair and smoothed his bald spot. "Jim, why do you want to move to Florida?"

"Part of it is opportunity. Judie had a good interview with the CEO of that clinic, and she's scheduled for a follow-up. Career wise for her, it looks promising."

"And what's the other part?"

I thought for a few moments, then thought I got it right: "I'd like to challenge myself. Fear has dominated my life for thirty years now. I'd like to prove to myself that I can step outside the safe zone and make things work. I'd like to prove I'm not overmatched by life. Before I die, I'd like to know that."

Dr. Gordon just nodded. Because he didn't speak, I sensed he probably had doubts. It didn't make me comfortable or confident.

About the middle of March, Judie was hired by David Lawrence, with a projected start time of mid-May. We would have two months to sell our house and buy one in Naples. Sometimes the very thought of what seemed like an audacious move caused me to tremble; at other times it gave me the soaring (manic) feeling. I'd never had a brush with bipolar disorder before (that I knew of), and it caused a blend of skyrocketing enthusiasm that was actually painful due to its intensity. Sometimes we can experience pleasure so intense it actually hurts. Even for people who are normal.

We were going to move to Naples, Florida. When our dear friend Sandi the realtor put the For Sale sign in the front yard, I felt a sweep of regret. It was a lovely home in a lovely neighborhood. The reality of what we were doing smacked me between the eyes.

Somewhat shaken, I sat on the porch with Beau in my lap one spring morning and said to him, "Beau, you're going to be a Florida dog." He just cocked his head in a puzzled manner.

A dog is the only thing that can mend
the crack in your broken heart.

—Judy Desmond

Beau: Part Two

THE DISASTER that was Florida didn't begin that way.

Naples, Florida, is not a large city. Its actual population hovers around thirty thousand people. Judie and I had not known this. And we soon discovered that even the most modest home within the city limits would likely cost more than a million dollars. Up and down Gulf Shore Boulevard, hugging the white sand beaches were miles of opulent mansions ranging in price from $10 to 25 million. Many of these palaces sat empty for long portions of the year, as their owners tended to own other luxury homes around the world.

The center of town, that which had charmed us, would prove to be largely off-limits. Several blocks of tony shops and upscale restaurants blended with real estate offices and elegant hotels. The area economy was driven by tourism, real estate activity, and a large financial management sector.

Beyond the city limits were miles and miles of private gated golfing communities with luxurious condominiums starting at roughly $1 million per unit. It didn't take us long to figure out that Collier County was in effect a third-world economy, made up of unspeakable wealth (much of it absentee) alongside an enormous population of the unthinkably poor. "There's not much in the middle," our realtor remarked. Many of the poor were illegals. When you went shopping, it would be beneficial if you had at least a minimum of the Spanish tongue.

We were strangers in a strange land who had not taken the time to investigate the nature of this city or the far-flung affluence surrounding it, nor had we found a way to establish human (or business) contacts with people who lived there. We were on our own and, in many instances, in over our heads. In a relatively short period of time, this culture shock would contribute to our feelings of isolation and disorientation.

However, against nearly all odds, we found a house we could (barely) afford to buy, at $180,000. Since I had been making monthly double mortgage payments on our Normal home, we were able to make a sizeable down payment. Prices for homes in the Naples area had begun to skyrocket; had we tried to buy the house six months later, it would have been well out of our price range.

It was a very well-kept, if modest ranch-style home with attached one-car garage, located about four blocks west of Highway 41 in an obscure subdivision some eight miles southeast of Naples proper. Strictly speaking, it was located in unincorporated Collier County, but it still had a Naples address. We moved in the middle of May.

Built with typical CBS (concrete block stucco) South Florida construction materials and painted coral color, the house sat on a large double lot with chest-high chain link fencing on three sides. No fencing in front. The large backyard, probably fifty feet deep and one hundred feet wide, created plenty of space for Beau and me to play pitch and catch.

The house had a large master bedroom and two other small ones. The large back porch (called a lanai in South Florida) ran nearly the entire length of the house; it was screened in from ground level to the edge of its metal roof. Only two-thirds of it had concrete flooring; the other portion was loose gravel.

A few feet outside that portion was a palm tree that bore plenty of fruit. It took a day or two to figure out that tree would activate Beau; it attracted plenty of squirrels. When one of those visitors made its way into the tree, Beau would charge, barking frantically, while scattering gravel and yearning to get outside the porch (lanai).

There was also a healthy mango tree, so one of our earliest Florida pleasures was eating fresh mangos.

The neighborhood was working class, with modest homes that were mostly well cared for. The subdivision, however, was largely unfinished. There were no sidewalks or curbs or drainage systems. The narrow blacktops crumbled like cake at the edges, where they tapered down into substantial ditches known in Naples as swales. There was a large one about fifty feet from our front door.

About a month after we moved in, the tropical model of predictable afternoon downpours set in, usually about two or three o'clock. Sometimes for twenty minutes, other times somewhat longer. It didn't take long before the swales were full of standing water, generating a stale and fetid odor that would prove to last clear into the late fall, well after the rainy season tapered off. Cranes and egrets stalked these waters, stabbing for tadpoles or other snacks.

Despite these unattractive elements, since there was very little traffic in the neighborhood, I was able to take Beau for long walks, usually in the early part of the morning. Everything went smoothly unless we encountered a squirrel (frequently), snake (infrequently), or a lumbering armadillo (rarely). South Florida seemed to have lots of squirrels but almost no rabbits.

Our new house was not conveniently situated for Judie's work. The David Lawrence Center was located some fourteen miles to the north, also positioned in unincorporated Collier County but bearing a Naples address. Each week, nurses were scheduled to work three twelve-hour shifts, with four days off. If I had some compelling reason to need the car on a day she was working, we set off at seven in the morning, and I went back to fetch her about eight in the evenings. Sometimes the twelve-hour days lasted thirteen hours, as the nurses scrambled to complete all of that day's paperwork.

To alleviate the stress of driving her to work and then driving back to pick her up at night, I bought myself an adult tricycle with a basket in front. This way, I wouldn't need the car on the days she was working. I was able to pedal my way to the convenience store located alongside Highway 41 (also known as the Tamiami Trail, since it links Tampa with Miami) and a small strip mall with a family restaurant four blocks beyond. I enjoyed eating there while reading the newspaper, and I got to know the waitresses well enough to work at improving my very basic Spanish.

Other than that, I had no contact with Naples people. I spent the long days at home alone with Beau. We walked, and we played ball. I resumed work on the outline for the new novel and started planting bougainvillea shrubs in the front yard. The first time I turned over a shovel, I discovered what Floridians take for granted: The state doesn't have soil; it has sand.

Judie began to get accustomed to the David Lawrence Center, discovering early on the clinic was the area dumping ground for all patients on public assistance, many of whom were actually substance abusers rather than mental patients, although the line between the two afflictions is often blurred. It was hard work (and somewhat dangerous) because many of the patients were violent.

It didn't help her state of mind that early on, the clinic began calling her in to work a fourth day each week. "We're just short staffed" was the usual reason given. Short staffed or not, the clinic was reneging on its terms of employment. Some weeks it was worse: a fellow nurse might call and ask her to fill in for a day. Judie always had difficulty saying no. So some of the weeks included five twelve-hour shifts. It meant more money, but the stress of so many hours in such a difficult work environment exhausted her, physically as well as mentally.

In short, the David Lawrence Center was poorly managed and not what she (we) bargained for.

AND THEN came August. The year 2004 would eventually come to be known as the Year of the Four Hurricanes, with four category fours and fives assaulting the state during a six-week period from mid-August to late September.

It started August 13 with Hurricane Charley, a powerful category four when it made landfall. Two days prior, county officials issued a mandatory evacuation notice for all residents living west of Highway 41. That meant us. Homeowners throughout the area were covering windows with plywood, but planning to ignore the evacuation order.

Later, I found out that "mandatory evacuation" simply meant if you stayed in your house, you wouldn't get arrested, but you would be on your own. No essential services like police, fire, or ambulance would respond to a call for help.

Most of our neighbors (after boarding up their windows or sliding hurricane shutters into place) made it plain they would ignore the evacuation order. They were longtime Florida residents who would simply hunker down inside their homes and ride out the storm.

We, however, were not Florida veterans. We would be following the evacuation order. Realizing our house had no hurricane shutters, I felt anxieties beginning to claw at my stomach.

For reasons I still can't comprehend, the reality of hurricanes overwhelmed me. Maybe it was just a confrontation with a frightening situation far beyond my control; I've never been sure. But I knew from years of experience that threatening or complicating situations had the potential to push me over the edge, since I was always compromised and vulnerable even on my "best" days.

I found myself shaking as we loaded our computer and personal file drawers into the car, along with the hurricane box we had prepared shortly after moving into our new house. It included flashlights, spare batteries, a battery-operated radio, some canned food, and bottles of water, among other things. I put some mangos in the car, a few bowls, and Beau's bag of food, but I was still shaking.

The deadly threat of hurricanes was one more South Florida fact of life we hadn't planned on.

We had made reservations at an economy hotel inside Naples city limits, on the east side (barely) of Highway 41. With Beau in Judie's lap, we drove there the afternoon of the twelfth, just as the winds began increasing, bending palm trees and shaking traffic signals.

We spent a frightful night. Judie slept some, but I didn't sleep a wink. It wasn't long before the hotel lost its power. Taking Beau out to eliminate was nearly impossible. We were on the third floor, so the best I could do was take him out on the walkway in the howling wind and lashing rain and let him go on the concrete. As small as he was, the wind blew him off his feet several times. Both of us got drenched from head to toe. Once back inside, I toweled us both off the best I could. Then we wrapped up in blankets.

The storm didn't seem to frighten him. Once he was dried off, he seemed peppy and energized like it was time to play. Somehow, somewhere, I guess I wasn't too surprised; he'd always ignored thunderstorms and, in fact, seemed to like watching them from his perch on the porch back in Normal.

Shaking in one of the blankets, and watching from the open door, I could see the hotel pool down below snapping with whitecaps, while the palm trees surrounding it were bent nearly double. Finally, after what seemed like an eternity, the first light of dawn appeared. The winds and rain were still strong but beginning to diminish. I took Beau out again and tried to shield him with a blanket. But we both got soaked again. I simply kicked his pile of poop over the side.

I hadn't thought to bring a change of clothes. I tried to eat a mango but could only choke down a couple of bites. When full daylight came, I told Judie we needed to drive back home. "I have to see our house," I said. "I need to know if it's okay."

"We should probably wait a little longer," she answered.

"I can't. I just can't. I have to know." As I spoke, I feared that I was headed for another complete breakdown, and the thought terrified me. As we loaded our things in the car, I couldn't help noticing that nearby buildings were dark from lack of power.

Driving home was tricky. It was early in the morning with a light rain continuing to fall and the wind still coming in occasional gusts. Several of the roads were flooded. When most people think of hurricanes, they think of the obvious wind damage but often overlook the devastation of flooding, which can be an even bigger problem.

Police had closed off streets that were flooded and/or dangerous due to downed power lines, so we had to drive through a maze of side streets in neighborhoods unfamiliar to both of us. Eventually, we blundered our way back to Highway 41, which was open, but traffic signals were damaged and completely knocked down in some cases. Drivers simply took their turns. There wasn't much traffic. Commercial buildings and shopping centers were dark on both sides.

I noticed roofs blown off or partially so the farther south and east we went. The sight made my heart sink. Judie said, "I hope our beautiful new house is okay."

It was. When we finally got there, we found the house in excellent shape. It wasn't damaged in any way. The same was true for our neighbors' homes. But our entire neighborhood was without power. Our yard was soggy but not flooded, and the rain had stopped. At least I could take Beau outside on his leash.

The power outage lasted several days and extended beyond our immediate neighborhood to all the stores, restaurants, and gas stations beyond. We had the small portable radio to listen to; occasionally news reports identified areas of the county where electricity had been restored. Each day, the morning newspaper, the *Naples Daily News,* included maps that included the same information.

It was hot, so we took the mattress off the bed and put it down next to the open front door; the screen door let in the breezes that came and went. But the daily sun brought the stifling heat and humidity so characteristic of South Florida. I found myself unable to sleep as intense anxieties tore away at my stomach. I wanted to blame it on the heat and humidity, but I knew better.

I tried to talk myself out of this dangerous downward spiral. *You had a storm,* I told myself. *You lost electrical power, but your home wasn't damaged. One of these days, everyone will have power again. You'll have your air conditioning back. Your computer will work again. You'll be able to watch TV. Stores and restaurants will be open. Life will return to normal.*

It didn't work. I was curled up into a ball at night and part of each day. I couldn't eat anything. I thought I might have been able to eat some cereal or pudding, but the milk was spoiled, and grocery stores were still closed. Judie got accustomed to the conditions and slept just fine. Beau drank a lot of water (we had plenty of bottles of it as part of our hurricane preparedness), but otherwise it was simply "life goes on" as far as he was concerned. I wanted to play ball with him, but I was so shaken I couldn't summon the energy. The best I could do was play tug-of-war with him and his rope toy on the bed, but even that never lasted long.

Judie was driving to work some of these days. The David Lawrence Center had emergency generators. In fact, some of the homes on our block had them too; you could hear the engines running day and night. Then some of them went silent. A neighbor told me he had run out of gasoline and gas stations with no power couldn't pump any.

My wife was worried about me. She was going to work at a mental health facility and then coming home to another one. We tried to persuade ourselves that what I was going through would just be temporary; it would pass. I tried pretending that I was feeling better, to see if I could alleviate some of her worry. She could see through it, of course. It was terribly discouraging to think I was going through another round of the Curse squared; I didn't think it could ever happen again.

When Judie was gone, I curled up on the mattress and hugged Beau to death. I tried explaining the anxiety/depression to him. He didn't need the words. He understood that something was wrong and that I needed him for comfort and reassurance. Anyone who knows dogs knows how this works, all logic to the contrary.

The first day our section of the county had power restored, we drove to the restaurant we liked so much for a late breakfast. It was very gratifying to get a hot cup of coffee, something we'd gone without for several days. I ordered a bowl of oatmeal but could only force down a couple of bites. We went to the store and bought a few groceries; I made sure we got plenty of applesauce, pudding, and bottles of chocolate-flavored Ensure.

Frantically, I made phone calls to companies advertising hurricane shutter installation. I got their names and numbers from the yellow pages. Since I didn't know the area well, some of the companies I reached were too far away to service Naples residents. The ones that agreed to do the work had (not surprisingly) long waiting lists. In most cases, we'd have to wait at least three to four weeks. I said to Judie, "Let's hope there won't be more hurricanes this season."

"Yes," she said. "Let's hope for that. But we know now how important they are, so pick one company and get us on the waiting list."

"I don't know anything about any of the companies."

"Well, there's probably no way to figure that out, so just pick one." I did, but the company was in Bonita Springs to the north, and the best they could do was three to four weeks out. My heart was in my mouth. This entire experience caused me to think back to our wonderful dog Toes, who had been terrified by thunderstorms, but once the storm was over, it was as if it had never happened. Why couldn't I be like that? *Why?*

I was running out of my psych meds (not that they were doing much good) but didn't have a prescribing physician. Judie tried to hook me up with a semiretired psychiatrist at her clinic; he was taking a few private patients, but since he was also on staff part-time, the David Lawrence CEO ruled it would be a conflict of interest if he were to work with me.

I was doubling my intake of Klonopin without a doctor's approval but getting only mild relief for half an hour or so. In desperation, we called Dr. Gordon back in Bloomington to ask (beg would be more like it) for a new prescription. He agreed, but only this once, he said. He insisted I find psychiatric help in my new community.

One of Judie's colleagues recommended a doctor in Naples who agreed to take me on, but we had trouble working together, partly because I had such an extensive history and far more knowledge of psychotropic drugs and treatment protocols than most patients. He was brusque and terse. I can't even remember his name. He simply prescribed the drugs I had been taking and warned me not to take more of either one than what was prescribed. He didn't give me much reason for optimism.

The psych meds didn't bring any relief. I started smoking again, usually while pacing. I could no longer take Beau for walks; physically, I was too shaken and weak. All I could do was take him out in the front yard to eliminate. I was rapidly losing weight again, so I told Judie we needed to buy a bathroom scale. On days when she was at work, I found myself crying again. I was alone and afraid.

Beau's company never meant more to me. Several times a day I talked to him while holding him in my lap. I told him about the Curse. I told him about Nanook and the comfort she had brought when I'd had the first major breakdown. I told him about Toes, who had been such a crucial presence in my life when I'd had another one. He cocked his head and listened; I knew he couldn't understand the words, but I knew my tone of voice was never lost on him. His little body was warm and comforting as we sat on the living room recliner with the TV on but neither one of us really watching.

Every day, I tried to work at least a little on the book outline I had started. Each day, it didn't happen; my anxiety level was so profound I was unable to sit still or concentrate. I just slumped in my chair in front of the computer, Beau wrapped around one of my ankles.

HURRICANE FRANCES, another strong category four, hit Collier County on September 4. But my terror escalated well in advance of that date; every morning for at least ten days running, the morning paper had a colored graphic, a map of Florida with the cone of the hurricane superimposed. The cone represented the predicted path of the storm, with a dotted line dead center forecasting the precise location of its deadly impact. Naples was squarely in the center of Frances's cone. Occasionally, meteorologists would adjust the cone, a little north or a little south, and that was what I always hoped to see each time I tore open the newspaper. But the predicted path of Frances never altered, and she was gathering category four strength as she moved daily toward South Florida.

I shook with fear and apprehension as we entered September. On September 3, county officials again issued a mandatory evacuation order. Once again, mostly because our shutters hadn't yet been installed, we decided to obey the evacuation order. Once again, although they were boarding up again, most of our neighbors chose to ignore it. I made reservations at the same hotel. This time, though, Judie had to pack workplace clothing, as she was scheduled to work on September 5. And this time, I arranged for Beau to stay with our vet, who had a large sheltered area and was quite willing to board his clients' pets during hurricanes.

On the afternoon of September 3, as we drove along Highway 41 headed northwest toward Naples city limits, the strengthening winds buffeted the car, bent the palm trees, swayed the traffic signals, and scattered debris. It started to rain, not hard at first, but a reminder (as if we needed one) of what was on the way. Many of the houses, as well as some commercial buildings, had the now familiar blue tarps covering their roofs. These were roofs that had sustained damage from Hurricane Charley; the temporary tarps were usually provided by FEMA. Unnerved though I was, I said to Judie, "Our roof didn't have any damage. We were lucky."

"Yes, we were lucky. I hope we're lucky again."

"I'm worried about Beau," I said. "The poor little guy is going to have to ride out this storm in a strange place, under cramped and scary conditions. Just going to a vet's office for any reason has always frightened him."

"At least he'll be safe," she answered. "He's better off there than with us."

I knew she was right, but I still worried about him. Of course, at that point in my life, nearly everything that happened could set me off, no matter how small or inconsequential.

It was another miserable night at the hotel, with howling winds and horizontal rain knocking the facility's power out before midnight. The hotel didn't have a generator but did have a few battery-powered lights in the lobby. I longed to share my fears with Judie but instead just curled myself into a ball and shook with fear. She needed to get the sleep she could since she'd be working the next day.

By 7:00 a.m. on the fifth, we loaded the car again as the winds and rain diminished. Some roads were closed due to flooding, but we managed to maneuver our way by suggestion and guessing to the David Lawrence Center. "I'm worried about you," she said, as she got out of the car. "You're going to have to pick me up tonight after eight."

"I know. It'll give me something to do. Right now I have to get Beau and check on the house."

"Please call me and let me know if there was any damage."

"I will." Due to flooding, I had to take a couple of alternate roads to get back to our part of the area. I was so worried about Beau I fetched him before I bothered to check on the house. He was straining at the leash to get out of the vet's office, but the secretary told me he had done just fine.

As it turned out, the house had done just fine too, although we were without power again. The streets in our neighborhood were not flooded, although I had to skirt the car around some downed trees and power lines. Downed power lines created a significant danger where police cruisers were often stationed. But our neighborhood was well off the beaten path, and it was still early in the morning.

Hurricane Frances had lost some steam while passing across the Florida peninsula and was downgraded to a category three. Once it reached the warm waters of the Gulf, however, it recovered its energy and headed north toward the Gulf Coast states of Louisiana and Mississippi. Eventually it would cause major damage in those locations. We learned over time that Florida Hurricanes often followed this changing level of force, which made the level of destruction difficult to predict.

But such long-range inconsistencies aside, there was always significant property damage, flooding, and power outages. No hurricane left our little corner of the world unscathed. And in my case, the crippling anxieties and depression associated with them spiraled me into perhaps the worst breakdown of my life.

I took Beau into the house, curled up on the bed, and held him tight against my chest. I told him I was sorry we'd left him at the vet's, but I also told him how much worse it would have been for him at the hotel. I liked to think he understood, because, despite the obvious advantage for him, I felt guilty.

No one could know it, but the Year of the Four Hurricanes was only getting started; the 2004 Atlantic hurricane season would become the costliest in Florida's history. Its title, however, would turn out to be short-lived, as 2005 would prove to be even worse.

For me, the next twelve to fourteen months would be a devastating nightmare of the Curse gone wild. During that period of time, I would face crushing loneliness, go sleepless through nights that never seemed to end, longing for daybreak but knowing it would bring light but no relief. I had to go without help (other than Judie's patient ear) or hope, would lose so much weight I would become scarcely more than skin and bone, long for death, and eventually collapse.

Without Beau, I would have died, and willingly.

Dogs leave paw prints on our lives and our souls.
—Ashly Lorenzana

Beau: Part Three

THREE DAYS after Frances, workers came to our house and installed the hurricane shutters on our windows and doors, at a cost of $4,500. Judie and I were both pleased with the work; the shutters were strong metal accordion style, operated manually, but easily opened and closed. The locking mechanisms were simple to operate. "It's a lot of money," she said. "But it will increase the value of our home."

She was right. We also agreed to close the shutters up and hunker down in our own home if another hurricane came, even in case of a mandatory evacuation order.

We didn't have to wait long. Hurricane Ivan was well developed in the Atlantic about a week after Frances. It hit Collier County on September 16, twelve days after Frances, as a strong category three. A week before it made landfall, I got the shakes every day as I eyeballed the cone in the morning paper. Judie urged me to stop looking at that graphic since it roiled my guts every time I did. But I couldn't resist; that graphic was the flame, and I was the moth.

Sometimes Naples was dead center in the cone, other times on its outer edges. But the cone, although usually reliable, was never 100 percent accurate. Hurricanes are too dynamic to lend themselves to perfect predictions.

A day before Ivan hit, I took Beau to the vet facility to shelter him there. Eventually, that would become standard procedure. But I felt so guilty knowing how much anxiety he experienced at the vet's office. *Any* vet's office. We bought him a thunder shirt to try and alleviate some of his apprehension, but it didn't do any good. When

I told Judie how guilty I felt, she answered with her usual rational balance: "He's safer there. Besides, if we had him here, you'd have to take him outside in a storm so powerful it's life-threatening." I tried to borrow some of her composure, but it was futile; I was too tied up in knots.

Judie was not scheduled to work that day. The two of us huddled together in the house as the high winds and strong rains of Ivan rattled the newly installed shutters. There was one loud bang that turned out to be someone's clay flowerpot sailing through the air before colliding against one of the bedroom shutters. Already, the shutters paid a dividend.

We did not lose power during that storm, a blessing we hadn't dared hope for.

The following afternoon, when winds were diminished and rain was scarcely more than a drizzle, I stepped outside to examine the storm's aftermath. The street was flooded, and the swale was overflowing; water had crept up the slope of our front yard, some thirty feet from the front door. I couldn't see any damage to the house, but a half dozen mangos had been blown off the tree and scattered freely about the backyard.

The lanai showed no sign of damage. This would be the case in all nine hurricanes we lived through in '04 and '05. It always amazed me; if there were any part of our home that seemed utterly vulnerable to powerful storms, it should have been that back porch. It had a flimsy fiberglass roof. The wooden supports that held the screens in place were one-by-three pine boards, scarcely more than furring strips. One of my neighbors told me later it wasn't unusual. The screens simply let the winds whistle right through; they didn't establish any resistance. It seemed as logical as any other explanation, although it didn't address the question of the roof.

I drove to the vet's to get Beau. As usual, trees and limbs were down, but I was able to maneuver my way around them and get to 41. There were more blue tarp roofs in our neighborhood and up and down 41. People always checked the roof after a major storm, as roof damage was common and complicated to deal with.

Highway 41 was, and would continue to be, the main line of our existence in this new world. Shopping centers, grocery stores, banks, strip malls, restaurants, and convenience stores/gas stations stood along both sides of the highway, all the way to the Naples city limits, where upscale elegance took over.

Beau was straining madly at his leash when one of the technicians brought him out. He was dry, but he was shaking. So was I. The difference was that as soon as we got back home, he would have forgotten all about the experience, while I would have been driven ever deeper into the black hole.

Judie and I took turns holding him as soon as he entered the house. He was all perky and energized and ready to play. The best I could do was tug-of-war with his rope. He growled that menacing growl as he pulled and tugged then slammed the rope proudly around the living room as soon as he got it away from me. He was happy. *Storm? What storm?*

Hurricane Jeanne blasted its way through the county ten days later as a strong category four. This time, though, Judie was at work, so I was alone in the house. I got into bed and pulled the sheet up over my head as the shutters rattled in the powerhouse winds. Then the power went out, and the house was ever so dark. I got a flashlight and turned on the portable radio, hoping to get a piece of good news. There wasn't any.

Because Judie had the car and wouldn't be back home until possibly the next morning, I curled up and trembled with crushing anxieties. Several times I nearly vomited. I couldn't help remembering Dr. Gordon's cautionary question when I told him about our decision to move to Florida: "Are you sure you're ready for this?" I thought I was, but face-to-face with another round of crippling breakdown that had now completely disabled me, my discouragement was off the charts.

An unexpected October event moved me to tears. A local Franciscan Church was celebrating St. Francis of Assisi's Feast day by holding a Blessing of the Pets. Judie convinced me we should take Beau there and have him blessed. The whole idea was foreign to me, but it seemed like something worth doing. I treasured him and wanted this blessing, as odd as it might seem.

When we got to the church, we found a dozen or so people already in the pews with dogs of all sizes on a leash or their cats in their laps. The dogs were often straining to sniff each other but were by and large well behaved. One by one, the animals were taken to the altar, where a friar wearing a brown robe cinched by a white cord said a prayer and even sprinkled the pet with holy water.

When our turn came, I held Beau in my arms as the friar began by scratching him between the ears and asking for his name. I saved the program bulletin, so I still have the prayer offered by the friar: "Blessed are you, Lord God, maker of all living creatures. We ask you to bless this pet. By the power of your love, enable it to live according to your plan. May we always praise you for all your beauty in creation. Blessed are you, Lord our God, in all your creatures. Amen."

And then he sprinkled Beau's head with a few drops of water from the holy font. The sprinkling didn't frighten Beau, but it did get his attention. He cocked his head in a puzzled manner at the friar and then at me. By this time, my tears were flowing freely. I was so terribly vulnerable this spiritual act of validation reinforced my elevation of this small dog, my constant companion and support, to near personhood. At that point in time, Beau was no longer "just" a dog.

On the drive home, Judie was behind the wheel while I held him in my lap. This special moment in this quiet church provided a day's worth of vacation from the wretchedness that had haunted me nearly every minute of every day and night.

IN THE WEEKS that followed, I curled up with Beau in bed. If I turned on my side, he burrowed into the hollow of my back to press against me. His sympathy couldn't have been plainer. I'm sure he missed the fun we'd had back in Normal, the long walks, the ball games. He knew something was wrong, even if he didn't have the intellectual capacity to ask what it might be.

The psychiatrist I was seeing simply continued me on the same meds, even though I told him they weren't bringing any relief. Our sessions were simple fifteen-minute med management appointments. He always began by asking if I was doing any better.

"No" was always my answer.

"Well, we'll hope for the best. Maybe now that the hurricane season is over, you'll begin to feel better."

It seemed logical and was the only sliver of hope I could try to clutch. But I didn't get any better. On the days when Judie was working, I paced and smoked, moved restlessly from bedroom to kitchen to back porch to living room, restless and agitated and terrified. Wherever I went, Beau followed. He sat with me in the recliner, pressing his little face against my neck. Often the tears flowed (mine, not his). And then it was time for more pacing.

Every now and then I sat at the computer. I printed out the portion of the outline I had completed for the new book. But attention deficit disorder on overdrive prevented me from adding any direction or structure. I sensed the outline was out of sequence but really couldn't figure how or why. I can remember sitting on the back porch in November, using scissors to cut and rearrange sections, then paper clipping the pieces together. But these efforts accomplished nothing.

It was a crushing feeling to accept that even though I was a successful author who had written several critically acclaimed books, I couldn't even construct early stages of a coherent outline. And my agitation and restlessness limited me to not more than thirty minutes per session. One day, gripped with frustration, I threw the clipboard across the concrete floor. It broke in half. Thinking this might be a new kind of game, Beau jumped down to chase it, but once he sniffed the plastic, lost interest.

I drank Ensure several times a day and tried eating applesauce. One night when Judie came home, she had some ice cream and chocolate syrup. She whipped up a milkshake for me in the blender, even though she had just finished working a thirteen-hour day. It was a compelling moment because it underscored her unwavering devotion to me at a time when I felt like an unworthy parasite, little more than a barnacle on the hull of the whole world. I didn't matter. If I were dead, what would it matter? What would be the difference?

But from that point forward, I made my own milkshakes. By Christmas, though, I had lost thirty pounds and was down to 150. Judie urged me to see a doctor. "I am seeing a doctor," I reminded her. "My shrink is a doctor."

When Beau and I were home alone, we sat on the back porch for longer periods of time, just because we could. It was supposed to be one of the most gratifying aspects of Florida living—warm winters. But it was hurricanes—actually a single hurricane—that had sent me headlong into another incapacitating breakdown. One so severe I was not able to enjoy the other side of South Florida's coin, warm-weather winters.

Unable to sit still on the porch for longer than fifteen minutes, I usually smoked a cigarette halfway down while Beau charged at the squirrels that had the temerity to hunt for fruit on his palm tree. One day a good-sized iguana lumbered past the porch, and when he spotted it, he was so agitated I thought he was going to tear away the screening to get after the exotic creature.

I tried to take some pleasure during those winter months from the high level of success the University of Illinois basketball team was having. The Illini were going undefeated for the entire season and were ranked no. 1 in the nation, week after week. They were on ESPN often, so I got to watch them play several times. Even our Florida newspaper ran features on the team. But the pleasure was always equivocal and short-lived. Once the game was over, I was tossed back into the depths.

In January of 2005, we contacted the local chapter of NAMI (National Alliance on Mental Illness) to see if I could get some counseling. They hooked me up with a woman named Brenda, who had her MSW and a pretty substantial client list. She was a creative listener, and I welcomed the chance to vent to a professional about my suffering, but it took nearly the entire month for me to summarize thirty years of a chronic mental disorder. I saw her weekly for about a month, but then she moved to Utah.

Before she left, however, she recommended a different psychiatrist, a man named Dr. Elliot. He was willing to take me on as a new patient. Judie was glad because she was convinced (as was I) that the man I was seeing was not creative or helpful.

The first day I saw him, he diagnosed me as bipolar. I was shocked and mystified because I had never had this diagnosis before. He seemed very sure of himself, but I didn't really believe him. I told him I had never had any classic manic episodes; I was never hyper verbal, had never gone on any manic flings that caused me to live risky or max out credit cards.

He replied that my "soaring" feelings (although I hadn't had any such moments for months) were clear signs of preliminary mania. He also said, "What about your decision to move to Florida? Wasn't that risk-taking behavior? That's a pretty big deal, wouldn't you say?"

"Yes, but that was a joint decision I made with my wife."

"But weren't you the one that talked her into it?"

"I wouldn't say that. I might have been first to suggest the idea, but I can't remember pressuring her."

"And all of this disabling anxiety you speak of—I'm seeing it more as depression."

I remembered Dr. Gordon's maxim that anxiety and depression were all part of the same spectrum. As much as I doubted Elliot's diagnosis, a part of me wanted to believe it. I had talked to—and known—many bipolar people over the years, and many had said that once they started taking Lithium, it worked "almost like magic." Maybe, I thought, if this psychiatrist was correct, I could be "set free" in the same way.

"I want you to stop taking the Klonopin," he said. "You've been taking the maximum dosage for quite a while now, and it's not helping you. You've built up a tolerance for it, and probably long ago."

"What about the Wellbutrin?" I asked.

"Let's stay with it, but I want to start you on Lithium as well."

I was almost eager now. "When can I expect some relief from it?"

"You'll have to be patient about that," he said. "It will take a little time."

"How patient?" I asked. I had been told to be patient so many times over the years I dreaded hearing it.

"We'll see in about a month. If there's no progress, we'll increase the dosage. But you have to keep taking the Wellbutrin as well. If you do get some relief from the Lithium, don't jump to the conclusion that you can take it alone. That day may come, but we'll deal with that when the time comes."

By late March, Illinois had marched clear to the national title game against North Carolina, but they lost in a very close game. Beau was always with me when I watched these games, and I treasured his warm little body and unconditional love. But I also longed for human companionship, some friend to share the game with.

By this time, I had lost twenty more pounds. I was still going sleepless, night after terrifying night. I was no longer able to pedal my tricycle the four blocks to the convenience store to buy a soft drink. I shook so much I was dropping silverware and kitchen utensils to the floor. I often fell off-balance when fixing my blender milkshakes, and my hands trembled each time I tried to light a cigarette. More than once I burned my fingers.

I didn't have any clothes that fit. Anytime I went to a store with Judie, I had to use one of the motorized carts at least part of the time. Sometimes all the time. It was embarrassing and frightening.

Fearing that my entire body was atrophying at an alarming rate, I sometimes walked around the living room / dining room area in circles, pretending that I was engaging in actual "exercise." Sometimes I ran the vacuum cleaner for the same purpose. I went to my knees one day in tears, the vacuum still in my hand. *Could I be any more dysfunctional? Could the suffering be any worse?* Beau got up on his hind legs and pushed his face into mine.

I let go of the handle and held him to my chest. I had been taking Lithium now for several weeks, with no result, positive or negative. I might just as well have been taking raisins. I decided I was right (I was not bipolar), and Dr. Elliot was wrong. My belief in psychiatry was plummeting, and I had now lost all hope. Nevertheless, I called Dr. Elliot to see if we could increase the dosage. He endorsed the idea.

More and more, Judie was filling in for nurses that needed a day off for one reason or another, leaving me home alone again. And exhausting her. I spent most of those days in bed, thinking that if I just curled up and didn't try to eat or drink, I would simply die. It was absurd, of course, but I thought it might be a painless and natural way to commit suicide. But it couldn't possibly work because I couldn't complete the process in a single day, as Judie would always come home from work.

I had plenty more suicidal ideation. Maybe I could just sit in the car with the engine running and the garage door closed. But if the car was home, it meant Judie would be home as well; I was too weak to drive her back and forth to work. There was a bathtub in the smaller bathroom. I could just sit in a tub of warm water and slit my wrists. I had plenty of Klonopin pills left in the cupboard, even though I was no longer taking the drug. I could take the whole bottle and wash it down with water. Somehow, I just wanted to die. Eternal rest seemed the only real path to freedom from pain and suffering.

But there was always Beau. When Judie left for work at seven in the morning, and I went back to bed and curled up on my side, the little guy was always there, pressing into the hollow of my back. Sometimes he had his rope toy with him, no doubt wondering if some fog might be lifted and we could play again. But in any case, he was always there, pressing in with that force that seemed purposeful and urgent. I could imagine him saying, "We're not giving up. We're not going to quit."

He loved me. In spite of everything, his love and compassion was ever present. No matter how bad I felt, how hopeless, I understood he needed me. If I were dead, who would feed him? Give him water? Who could possibly love him as well as I? Who else could possibly share that love by holding him tight like I could? Take him outside to eliminate? If I were dead, he would be helpless and miserable.

I sketched out a timetable in my brain: 6-10-2-6-10. Every day I would haul my ass out of bed no matter what and take him out into the yard at those times. He could have waited longer than four-hour intervals, but I owed him something in return for all the love and support. As lonely as it all might seem, I was never alone. He was saving my life. At that point in time, the two of us were as securely bonded as man and dog can ever be.

I had two other reasons for needing to stay alive. I didn't want to die in Florida. If I had to die, I wanted to do so back home in Illinois, where I had friends. If I died in Florida, no one would miss me. No one would care. In addition, and more importantly, if I were no longer alive, Judie would have to place Beau at the Humane Society or some other rescue shelter; her work schedule would prevent her from being able to care for him. I couldn't bear the thought of our special little loving guy removed from our family circle.

None of this was lost on Judie. She knew how dysfunctional I was and for what length of time. She too felt helpless, and the stress of her workplace only intensified her own anxieties and concerns. One day in late spring, our son Jason called (unbeknownst to me) to see if he and wife Dayna could come down for a visit and enjoy the Naples beaches. With tears running down her face (she told me later), she had to advise him not to come since my condition was so dire and her work schedule so unpredictable.

She knew that I was not capable of hosting them if she happened to be away at work. When she told me about this phone conversation later, she let me know that Jason was sorry I was so sick and asked if there was anything he could do to help. There wasn't. I wasn't even up to carrying on phone conversations. I did read e-mails (I got very few) but sometimes didn't even answer them.

Many times I told Judie how sorry I was that she was suffering this way, how useless I felt and how unworthy of her love and devotion. Her answer was always the same: "I can't stop loving you because you're sick. I will always hate the Curse, but it won't ever stop me from loving you." Two people loved me no matter what: Judie and Beau.

The hurricane season came again, with sweltering heat and humidity. Daily downpours filled the neighborhood swales with stinking, brackish water. Before it ended, 2005 would surpass the previous year for hurricane frequency and damage. There would be five major hurricanes raking South Florida, beginning with Dennis on July 10 and concluding with Wilma on October 24. Storms that late in the fall were rare, as Atlantic basin waters had usually cooled by then. All five storms were strong category fours or fives that brought major damage. The blue tarp phenomenon proliferated across Collier County.

Throughout that four-month period, I was paralyzed in panic mode.

The hurricane season routine in our home was always the same: the daily mounting of apprehension from newspaper cone watching, taking Beau to Dr. Randall's vet hospital hours before the storm hit, huddling behind the rattling hurricane shutters (whether I was alone or with Judie), dealing with power outages for a day or two, if not longer, throwing away spoiled food, and then getting Beau and bringing him home.

Each time the power went out, we could hear the emergency generators grinding away up and down our street. Most houses didn't have one, but those that did were noisy. Judie and I had often discussed buying one, but they were expensive, and they only had the capacity to run two or three systems in your home. Lights, refrigerator, air conditioning, fans, selected room sockets, water pumps, pick two.

And each time, good fortune smiled on us; our house was spared major damage. Up and down the street, damage was uneven. Some homes had shattered windows or decorative shutters blown away. Some had serious roof damage. Some had uprooted trees colliding with them.

Others, like ours, were left unharmed. Hurricane Wilma did bring strong flooding; water made its way up the front yard to our stoop and filled all the low places in the backyard. It also blew downspouts off the house and uprooted our mango tree. It might have fallen on our back porch and crushed it, but as our good luck would have it, the tree fell in the opposite direction.

I was now down to 120 pounds and scarcely able to leave the house.

MY COLLAPSE came about a week after Wilma. I awoke to find myself in the Naples Community hospital emergency room. I had monitors and electrodes all over me, it seemed.

With an ER doctor next to her, Judie asked me, "You don't remember any of this?"

"Any of what?" My vision was blurry.

"You don't remember collapsing on the lanai?"

"No. What are you talking about?"

"Do you remember your ride in the ambulance that got you here?"

I didn't know what they were talking about. I was confused and fuzzy. I got the summary from Judie. Apparently, unable to sleep and restless, I had gotten out of bed shortly after midnight and went to sit on the lanai. I had collapsed unconscious, falling onto the concrete and taking the chair down with me. I had called for help several times, eventually waking Judie up. She found me prone on the concrete, with Beau sitting near my head, pushing his front paws up and down and wagging his tail.

She had called 911 immediately. It had taken about half an hour for the ambulance to arrive and then nearly that long to drive me to the hospital. "At first I thought you were dead," Judie told me. "But you had a pulse. Then I thought for sure you would die before you got to the ER."

I had a hard time comprehending any of this; I was dizzy and disoriented. The story seemed preposterous, but there wouldn't be a reason for anyone to lie to me. "What's wrong with me?" I asked.

"We don't know," said the doctor. "So far, all we know is that you collapsed and fell unconscious. We'll have to run tests."

I was in the hospital for six days. I had test after test—blood tests, neurological tests, a brain scan, an MRI, even an angiogram. The hospital food didn't work for me, but one kind nurse brought me all the applesauce and pudding she could commandeer from the cafeteria. I also got lots of chocolate milk. I couldn't sleep during the nights, so I left the TV running with low volume to see if that would help. It didn't. Restless in bed, I turned over from side to side constantly, often unhooking an electrode, which sounded an alarm at the nurse's station. A brusque nurse came in during the night once to hook me up again. "You need to lie still," she said. "You're in the hospital now."

"You can go straight to hell," I told her.

The second day I was in the hospital, Judie came to visit. "How's Beau doing?" I asked.

"He's doing fine."

"Because we have to think of him too at a time like this."

"He's doing just fine, but I'm sure he misses you. Do you remember those problems you were having three or four days ago?"

I did remember. A couple of days before the collapse, I was having blurred vision; I noticed it mostly when watching television. I was also having episodes of lightheadedness and dizziness. We thought they might be side effects from medication, so we called Dr. Elliot's office a couple of times, but the office never returned the calls. "I remember," I said. "We thought they might be side effects."

"Well," she said, "I talked to one of the doctors at David Lawrence, and he said the combination of meds you've been taking often produce those side effects. It can be a dangerous combination. It's possible your collapse was caused by the interaction of drugs you've been taking."

"Elliot should have called me back," I said. "He had two days."

"Well, anyway, he didn't, and here you are. You're not taking them now, are you?"

"No. I don't think I'm taking any psych meds. They give me something in the morning and something at night. They're probably just sleeping pills."

"I'm going to find out," Judie said.

"I've got to get out of here," I said.

"When all the testing is done, then they'll probably discharge you. The tests could be important."

"Just get me out of here."

None of the tests revealed anything abnormal. One of the doctors told me, "It's possible your entire central nervous system simply shut down. You only weigh 120 pounds. What's your ideal weight?"

"About 180," I told him.

"Hmmmm. We have to do something about that. What do you usually eat?"

I told him, and he said, "Okay, keep drinking those milkshakes. If you have to, force yourself. It's not exactly health food, but it does put a lot of calories in you."

By the fifth day, my restlessness was so acute I was up and walking around the corridors, using the handrail, but trying to show the nurses how strong I was. In fact, I was still weak and unsteady, but I was trying to put on a good show.

The following day, one of the doctors asked me if I felt ready to go home. I told him yes with no hesitation. "You need to eat more and get stronger," he said. "I also think you need to find a new psychiatrist. The combination of meds you were taking may have put you in here."

"Do you have anyone in mind?" I asked him.

"Actually, yes," he said, as he pulled his wallet from his back pocket. He handed me a business card of a shrink named Vivian Patel. "She's Indian, but she has perfect English. She's also a little younger and seems to be on the cutting edge."

"Do you know any of her patients?" I asked.

"I know two of them. They are very satisfied with her."

It seemed like good advice, although I dreaded the thought of starting over with a new doctor, trying to summarize my thirty-year battle with mental illness. There always seemed to be far more history than I could remember or explain coherently. Even so, the thought of a new doctor gave me a flicker of hope; somewhere on the planet, there had to be someone who could lead me out of the current wilderness.

The next day, Judie took me home. "All your tests were normal," she said. "There's nothing wrong with you." I guess she thought humor was appropriate.

"Yeah, that's true," I said sarcastically. "There's nothing wrong with me."

When we got to the house, Beau greeted me with unrestrained enthusiasm. He jumped up and down on my legs, whimpering and yipping his joy. I got down on my knees so he could lick my face. "You're always here, little guy," I said to him. "You're always here."

I picked him up and stumbled my way onto the lanai. I sat in one of the chairs and held him in my lap. I noticed the mango tree was upright again, held in place with stakes and ropes. "What happened here?" I asked Judie.

"The man who mows the lawn brought a little tractor over and pushed it back up. He said he didn't know if the roots would completely take hold again, though. At least I think that's what he was saying. He was speaking more Spanish than English."

"I don't care what the damn tree does," I answered. "I'm home, and I've got my Beau."

"Yes, and there's nothing wrong with you."

"Yeah, we can't forget that. There's nothing the matter with me."

Dogs do speak, but only to those who know how
to listen. Your dog makes you a better person.
—Kaylee Lenai McGinness

Beau: Part Four

DR. PATEL was as advertised. A petite woman in her thirties, she and her husband had moved to Naples only recently; consequently, she was taking new patients. She was an upbeat person who smiled a lot. When I first met with her, I'd been home from the hospital about two weeks. She told me she had all the test results. She also told me our introductory session would be an hour long, while subsequent visits would be thirty minutes.

Once again, I was seated in the office of a health-care professional who needed to know my story. I did the best I could, but I was agitated and restless. There was so much to tell I found myself wandering off topic again and again. "You have attention deficit disorder, don't you?" she said.

"Yeah, that too."

She said to me, "So you've been going through this very difficult time for more than a year now?"

"Yes."

"That's a lot of suffering."

"Yes, it is."

"Do you have any idea why that first hurricane upset you so much?"

"Not really. I only know that after my first major breakdown, those thirty-plus years ago, I'm always vulnerable. Dr. Gordon said I would probably have that condition the rest of my life. My body, my central nervous system, has a mind of its own when unexpected, difficult situations come up. I lose all control."

"You told me you used to have good days. What's a good day like?"

"On a good day, I still have strong symptoms, but they're manageable."

"How strong?"

"Usually about five or six on a ten scale. I'm never serene or truly peaceful. It's like a pot that always simmers but doesn't boil over."

"That's a lot of suffering," she said again.

"Yes, it is," I said again. "Can you help me?"

"I'll certainly do my best." Then she asked me why I had chosen to change psychiatrists. I told her about my unfortunate experience with the side effects just prior to my collapse. "I also disagreed with his diagnosis. He told me I'm bipolar. I don't believe that."

She didn't comment on that. I didn't expect her to; doctors don't judge other colleagues, at least in response to patients. She wanted to start me on Effexor, an antidepressant I'd never tried before. But she warned me I'd have to take it incrementally, increasing the dosage every two weeks for six weeks. She also warned me the drug might take that long to kick in.

I slumped in my chair. "Don't be discouraged," she said.

How could I not be discouraged? How many times had I heard these same words? Again, I was looking at a prolonged trial-and-error experiment: six weeks on a medication that might never kick in.

Then she said, "But let's add something that's faster-acting, a med that can bring you temporary relief in the meantime. Have you ever tried Xanax?"

"Yes, but I built up a tolerance for it. I was addicted. It no longer helped."

"Valium?"

"Same thing."

"Klonopin?"

"Same thing." I felt like I was wearing her out, but there was no point in misleading her.

"Ativan?"

"No, I've never taken it."

So I started taking Effexor and Ativan, a common antianxiety agent. Dr. Patel told me I could take the Ativan as needed, but not more than four times daily. I took it four times every day, but it never provided any relief.

Neither did Effexor, even after six weeks, even after I'd reached the strongest dosage level. Another drug regimen that produced no results. My only source of comfort came from Beau; I was still spending countless hours curled up in bed holding him. At those times (when Judie was working), he was all I had. And I was all he had.

The lack of relief from the two drugs was another crushing development. In desperation, I called Dr. Patel on the phone.

"You're not getting any relief at all?"

"No," I said dully.

"Do you think you need to go into the hospital?"

No," I said firmly.

My next appointment with Dr. Patel came about two weeks before Christmas. She said she wanted to start me on Seroquel. It was a drug I'd never heard of. "It's one of the atypical antipsychotics," she said. "It's a very powerful drug, but after all this time and all you've been through, I think it's time we got more aggressive."

"You think I'm psychotic?" I asked. I could only think of Dr. Gordon's "cluster of symptoms" diagnosis. "I don't have hallucinations or dementia. I've always been diagnosed with a mood disorder with a lot of different elements."

"I don't think you're a schizophrenic or anything like that," she said. "I will just repeat myself and say we need to be more aggressive."

When I told Judie about the Seroquel, she raised her eyebrows. "On the unit, that's considered one of the major tranquilizers like Haldol or Thorazine. That sounds a little over the top."

At this point in my miserable life, I didn't really care if it sounded over the top. I was ready to try anything. "Dr. Patel thinks we have to be more aggressive," I replied.

The psychiatrist was right. In a week's time, I was feeling better. Not recovered or well, but better. Suddenly I found myself sleeping up to two or three hours per night. We went to breakfast one morning at the favorite restaurant; I ate a complete bowl of oatmeal and a couple slices of bacon. I couldn't believe it. For the moment, I was almost overjoyed. A few nights later (Christmas Eve, actually), we went to Pizza Hut. I ate two slices of pizza and washed the food down with a soft drink. I could eat again!

The anxieties were still strong but not disabling. When the calendar turned over to 2006, I was walking Beau clear to the corner and back. I reported all this to Dr. Patel, who was encouraged. "It's a good start," she said. "Now let's increase the dosage and see if we can make you even better."

This strategy also worked. I felt better, ate better, slept better, and had more energy. I felt so blessed and relieved I often found myself in tears. By March, I had gained twenty pounds and was feeling strong enough to ride the tricycle to the restaurant for a hearty breakfast on mornings when Judie was working. I could take Beau on walks of up to eight blocks or even longer. Sometimes I even took him into the backyard and tossed his tennis ball so he could chase it.

I still had strong anxieties a good deal of the time, but I was no longer hopeless; I was confident I could work through them. As a matter of fact, on some days, I drove Judie to work and picked her up in the evening. I always had Beau with me; he liked to snoop around on the David Lawrence campus. I still had periods of surging anxiety/depression, but now I was getting temporary relief from the Ativan, usually two to three hours. For the most part, my symptoms were more or less manageable.

I contacted the librarian at a nearby high school to see about tutoring students who needed extra help. Shortly after we had moved to Naples, she had somehow found out about my arrival in her neighborhood. She was familiar with my books and wanted to know if I would consider an author visit to her school. But her call came after Hurricane Charley and the meltdown it had triggered. I had politely declined the invitation, feeling terribly discouraged. I had made dozens of author visits to high schools in Illinois but was so shaken at the time she invited me I didn't believe I could manage it.

This time, I was ready. I made an author visit in April, speaking to several English classes whose teachers were familiar with at least one of my books. I even got paid a thousand bucks for that day, although I would gladly have met with classes free of charge. Simply having the capability to meet students and teachers—and actually *enjoy* the experience—was worth far more than the money to me. I had the soaring feeling that day, but I welcomed it. If bipolar was one of my flavors, then so be it. The euphoric feelings were eventually uncomfortable but never escalated into a danger zone in terms of my behavior.

After that, I began tutoring at-risk students one-on-one at the school, on a volunteer basis. I enjoyed the kids, and I think they enjoyed me. To make our lives simpler in terms of transportation, we bought a used car, an old banger of a Ford, for me to use driving back and forth to the school. The school was about three miles from our home, too far for cycling. It also meant Judie could drive back and forth to work every day without having to worry about what mobility I might have.

Deep into May, the preliminary signs of summer appeared. Occasional heavy afternoon rains left water standing in the swales. Judie and Dr. Patel were concerned about how I might react to another hurricane season. So was I, although even though I was worried, I didn't have those disabling feelings of terror clutching at my stomach. I felt like I could handle worry.

It turned out I didn't even need to worry. In a complete Atlantic basin about-face, there were no hurricanes at all. The year 2006 was the first year since 2001 that no hurricanes made landfall in the United States. There were several tropical storms that brought significant rain to Caribbean locations and South Florida. That was it. No evacuation orders or advisories, no need for cone watching, no need for hurricane shutters, and most important, no need to park Beau in the vet's fortress.

But by late summer, Judie was having ongoing difficulties in the workplace. There was turnover at the top and instability at the clinic. Her hours were unreliable and unpredictable. Often, changes in scheduling were stressful; she (we) couldn't count on much effective leadership. She told me more than once how stressed out the nursing staff was. I tried to comfort her by saying sooner or later the clinic's leadership would stabilize and provide reliable scheduling. I don't think those efforts did her much good, but my emotional progress did. It was one major concern—probably the biggest—that was lifted from her shoulders.

In the fall, I had regained forty pounds, and I was plenty strong to take Beau on the long walks he loved so much. At that time, I started working with a remarkable young man from Haiti named Randy, who was a student at the nearby high school. He was a member of a basic senior level class that had adopted one of my YA novels, *Dakota Dream*, for classroom use. He was one of the most gifted athletes I'd ever seen; he was a star on the track and football teams, but his reading level was scarcely above fourth grade. It wasn't surprising, because he hadn't moved to Florida until the ninth grade. His native language was Creole.

While the class read the book and discussed it, I worked with Randy in a separate room. We took turns reading pages. It kept him on his toes without wearing him out. He was being heavily recruited for football by the University of Florida, one of the nation's top teams, but I couldn't imagine there would be a college textbook on the planet he could hope to read.

No matter. What the university did or wanted to do wasn't my business. Randy was good-natured and affable; I enjoyed the time I spent with him. The final day of *Dakota Dream*'s unit, I spent the period dialoguing with the class and answering their questions about the book. I was doing this work as a volunteer, but I was still happy to do it. To be *able* to do it.

By October, I was feeling strong enough I decided to have another go at my book outline, to see if I could get it in workable order. But I found that no matter how I tried, or how often, my inability to concentrate or focus long enough usually left me at square one. It frustrated me. It wasn't as if I was actually trying to *write* a book, just compose a functional outline.

I told Beau, who was usually curled up at my feet whenever I was at the computer, I felt like the long periods of incapacitating breakdowns had taken a toll I didn't count on: I was somehow impaired by brain damage. I hoped that wasn't true. I didn't want to believe I could no longer be a successful writer. But the thought suggested a disturbing possibility I couldn't help brooding over.

Also in October, we were blessed with the birth of our first grandchild. Jason called to tell us of the arrival of Sailor Grace Bennett, a healthy eight-pound girl. Judie and I were both moved but not quite sure what to do to greet this child since we were so far away. We talked it over and decided maybe around Christmas we could fly up to Wisconsin and enjoy this new little person. "She won't be a newborn any longer," Judie said. "She'll have some personality and be ready for snuggling." We called Jason, and he agreed it sounded like a good plan. He also told us he was learning the art of diaper changing. He was already sending us pictures online that he had taken with his smartphone. She looked like what she was: a newborn baby.

Judie and I were excited by this new development but not quite sure how to perceive ourselves as grandparents. We were certainly old enough (I had begun taking early Social Security benefits), but it was still a new world we weren't accustomed to. What we knew for sure was that our son was a good man who had always been a good husband and would now be a good father as well.

But shortly afterward, on a gloomy day in late November, just after Thanksgiving, Judie came home from work downcast. It was likely, she told me, that David Lawrence would be laying off some staff. "There's a state grant they're not going to get renewed."

"When?" I asked.

"The grant runs out at the end of the year. And it's a big one. It's almost certain layoffs are coming."

"It's probably another example of mismanagement at the top by your administration," I said, not really knowing what I was talking about. It was my clumsy attempt to comfort her, as if placing blame might have that effect. But she was worried, and so was I. Because she earned a higher salary than some of the younger, less experienced nurses, she might be one of those employees at risk.

It turned out she was. She came home from work one day in December in tears; she'd received notice that day that she was one of the nurses being laid off. I held her and tried to console her, but my heart was in my mouth. We both felt frightened and disoriented.

The entire Florida "adventure" had not gone well. I had been much too sick for much too long, and Judie's workplace had turned out to be a mostly negative experience; there was simply too much mismanagement and lack of clear direction and leadership. Promises made about working hours were often broken, which meant the ongoing stress of unpredictable and often dishonest scheduling.

And she had struggled through it all while trying to bear up under the burden of my chronic (and needy) illness. We were both standing up next to the kitchen table, holding each other. Beau yipped about it and got up on his back legs; he was being left out and letting us know he wasn't pleased. I picked him up so all three of us could embrace.

For a couple of days we were numb, wondering what to do. Neither one of us had any job-related connections in this strange part of the world or even social connections, for that matter. What I was doing at the high school was volunteer work. There was a community college not far from the high school, but I had been away from teaching for so long it wasn't plausible I could ever get a job there. Even if I did, my scattered consciousness would make me dysfunctional on the job.

Furthermore, Judie's work at the David Lawrence Center hadn't connected her to any network of other mental health facilities in the county.

On the third day, when Beau and I got back home from our morning walk, I thought I had the answer. It was bold but also sensible: "We have to go home," I told my wife.

"I know," she said, with tears sliding and Beau licking them away.

"We have to go home where we belong." Immediately we recognized how complicated a move back to Illinois would be. There would be stress and confusion. But we were also feeling a sense of relief. My symptoms, thanks to the Seroquel, were usually manageable; I was no longer a burden to my wife. In addition, although being laid off from a job was always traumatic, Judie couldn't hide a sense of relief. The David Lawrence Center had generated much more stress than reward. Her good work with patients had never been gratifying enough to overcome the anxiety delivered by a badly managed workplace.

And so it was. We knew we had to go home where we belonged, just like that awful dog day afternoon in Middletown, New York, some thirty-two years earlier. But home was where the heart was, and we needed that heart back.

*There is no faith which has never yet been
broken, except that of a truly faithful dog.*
—Konrad Lorenz

Beau: Part Five

THE MOVING VAN pulled up in front of our new condo in Bloomington near the end of January 2007. The move had been remarkably easy, although since it was another radical change, I felt plenty of anxiety and stress throughout the process. Our dear realtor friend, Sandi, had identified the small home as the right move for us. And so it was. It was a ground-level duplex in a small courtyard of similar homes. It had an attached two-car garage. It was an ideal dwelling for two people advancing in age.

The complex was far away from our prior neighborhood, the one with such English village charm. It was also far away from the center of the community, in a part of Bloomington where homes were newer, trees were smaller, and character was largely missing. Nevertheless, it was, as Hemingway might have had it, a "clean, well-lighted place." Houses were large and well-tended middle-class properties.

The neighborhood had plenty of sidewalks in good condition, so taking Beau for walks was a pleasant, if not vintage, experience. I might have felt a certain deprivation, but I'm sure Beau was utterly satisfied. He had to get reacquainted with snow, though, as sometimes those small legs could barely lift his torso out of the white stuff.

We were favored by fortune with the sale of the Florida house. It sold quickly, and home values had risen so dramatically in Collier County during our two-and-a-half-year sojourn it sold for nearly twice as much money as we had bought it for. As a consequence, we suddenly were living in a paid-off home, while our nest egg savings had increased significantly. We had a financial buffer zone; earning income was not urgent. We could pick and choose what might work.

In addition, I was still receiving Social Security checks, while Judie had found part-time employment at a local family services institution that specialized in teaching and housing children of all ages with developmental disabilities and significant emotional difficulties. She often worked with impaired teenagers by taking them on community enrichment activities. The trips included activities as simple as going out to movies or even just going out for lunch. The pay didn't amount to much, but the work was much easier and far less stressful than her work in Florida. It was what she felt she could handle.

An old friend, Ed Pyne, was publisher/editor of *The Normalite,* a local community weekly newspaper. He asked me if I'd consider writing a weekly column for him. I said yes immediately. Even though my concentration for longer projects (books, for example) had been compromised, writing was still in my blood. I could handle weekly projects of a thousand words, give or take.

I was also tutoring special education students at Bloomington High School on a volunteer basis. Even without any money, it was still gratifying. I think the kids liked me, and I know I liked them.

Through all this, my mental health was fairly stable. I still had bad days, because our lives had been turned upside down again, and getting reoriented activated some acute anxieties. But at worst, I was the simmering pot, not the pot boiling over. I renewed my relationship with Dr. Gordon, who was pleased that Seroquel had made such a difference in my life. He increased the evening dosage a little bit after I explained to him that best nights brought me only four or five hours of sleep. "Let's see if we can do a little bit better than that," he said. "Keep me posted."

About the same time, Jason, Dayna, and our new granddaughter, approximately six months old, came to visit. She was a beautiful baby who was developing plenty of personality. She reacted to silly stuff with smiles and giggles. The first time I held her in my arms, I pondered how this tiny creature was blended with my own life; she was flesh and blood obviously, and so I hoped (even prayed) her psyche would develop in the years to come with little of my genetic code manifest. I felt like I loved her but wasn't exactly sure what that meant. When so much of your life is given over to merely surviving, it can have an uncoupling effect on basic emotional connections with others.

Judie had no such double vision; she loved the baby unconditionally and passionately from the first moment she saw her. Beau was curious about this new little person, coming close to investigate, then licking her face. Sailor pulled away and made a face like she'd just taken a huge bite out of an onion.

Sometimes, on nice days, I frequently found myself taking Beau and driving to the old neighborhood. I wanted him to be able to play his favorite game again on the Illinois Wesleyan practice field, where it had all begun. As I had done some three years earlier, I threw the ball high and far, twenty, thirty, forty yards or more and watched him turn on that burst of speed to catch it and grab it. Often, he grabbed it out of midair on a high bounce. And then he would come trotting back to me, eventually dropping the ball close to where I was standing. It was never right at my feet. And each time I picked it up, he was off with an amazing burst of speed before I even cocked my arm.

He seemed to be saying, "This is more like it. Where have we been?" At times, I even put him on the leash and walked him around some of the blocks we used to walk. Occasionally, I stared into space with substantial regrets. We had chosen to leave this unique, charming neighborhood for a Florida misadventure that had scorched me (Judie as well) in a profoundly disabling chain of events that had nearly cost me my life.

IN 2010, the teacher who had been using me regularly as a volunteer retired, and for some reason I could never fathom, other teachers and/or librarians did not contact me for help with at-risk or underachieving students. It was a mystery; I even called the principal and made it plain that I was still available and ready to help. But no cry for help ever came. It hurt; it felt like rejection. I even offered all the local high schools free classroom author visits (the kind that had once earned me $1,500 to $2,000 per day), but I never got a response. This discouraged and mystified me.

Consequently, I was beginning to spend much more time home alone. And I soon got stung with another kind of rejection: book rejection. I finally unraveled the outline that had frustrated me for so long, which allowed me to finally finish actually writing the book. It was a YA novel called *Fresh Killed.* I thought it was quite good, and based on my previous success with YA fiction, I trusted my judgment.

A couple of years later, about 2013, I also finished another YA novel based on an experience I'd had in the eighth grade, when a rape-murder occurred in our small town, sending the village into an identity-crisis frenzy that resulted in vigilante justice. It was also a basketball novel. Its title was *Double Team*, and it had a 1957 setting. I also thought this book was quite good.

But the editors I sent them to turned them down. *Fresh Killed* was (is) set in the early 1950s; its protagonist was (is) a teenage boy stricken with polio during the period of time when the nation was at war in Korea and terrified by the polio epidemic. Most editors told me they liked the quality of the books, but since they were essentially historical novels, they weren't the kind of fiction editors were looking for.

The rejections were crushing; I hadn't had a book rejected since the late 1980s. Although I had to work slowly, due to my deteriorating powers of concentration, both books were the product of much hard and careful work over long periods of time (approximately two years apiece). I didn't have a literary agent at the time, so I was submitting these books directly to editors, just as I'd always done in the past. I was also discovering that the publishing world had changed: many editors would only examine manuscripts submitted by agents. My attempts to find a good agent didn't work very well either.

I was still writing the weekly newspaper column and doing good work, but I found myself starting to withdraw. I moved away from articles that included interviewing, so that was a people connection that dried up. In addition, many of my old friends had died or moved away to other states (Florida mainly). Even though my symptoms were manageable, by and large, I often felt deeply depressed. My entire central nervous system had sustained such damage over so many years that my people instincts were impaired. I was shy. I didn't feel capable of initiating contact. I wasn't a joiner. I wasn't a golfer or a card player. I didn't bowl or play tennis.

I had Beau, whose steadfast love and companionship meant a great deal to me every day. Many times I told him, "Beau, go get your ball." He would run from room to room until he located it, then come prancing proudly with that well-worn tennis ball in his mouth. He was my best friend. In Florida, not counting Judie, he had been my only friend.

Then off we would go in the car until we were standing on that goal line at the old practice field in the old neighborhood. Across the way in the actual football stadium, games of lacrosse or soccer were in progress. We ignored all that and played *our* game. When we got tired, we would sit on the grass. He always sat flush against me on his haunches, while I scratched his face or between his ears. I always had a bottle of water so he could get a drink. Actually, we both drank from the same bottle. Sometimes, we sat like that for as long as thirty minutes.

When she turned sixty-two, Judie retired and began collecting early Social Security. She had had an unfortunate incident with one of her teenage clients, who went out of control at a fast-food restaurant, threatening not just her safety but those of other patrons. Eventually, the young man was back under control, but Judie recognized she was no longer physically able to subdue an out-of-control teenager. Her own safety, as well as that of the client, would be at risk in case of similar future incidents.

But even though she was receiving Social Security benefits, she was not old enough for Medicare. Her health-care premiums and the cost of prescription drugs were very high. By this time, both of us had developed some significant health issues, and the cost of health care became a draining financial burden. We still struggled through, doing our best to avoid dipping into the nest egg to pay ordinary bills. Some months we failed to cover costs. My income from writing columns was very small.

We had to watch our money carefully, so Judie and I limited our visits to athletic events, concerts, or other public presentations to the ones free of charge, for the most part. These financial exigencies cost me several sleepless nights as well as occasional bad days. Dr. Gordon increased my Seroquel by a little more; I was now taking a fairly large dosage. My finger was still squarely in the dyke.

Judie and I made occasional trips to Wisconsin to visit Jason and his family. We now had two grandchildren. Finnegan was born in 2011, so Sailor now had a little brother. Sometimes they drove down to visit us. For me, the visits were always bittersweet. As special as it was to share our lives with these two little ones (and their parents), I was never in a comfort zone. I didn't know how to enjoy life and hadn't for some forty years. I didn't know what it meant to have fun.

Having fun would have meant letting my guard down, which I didn't know how to do, although several counselors had urged me to overcome this roadblock. But the counselors had never experienced mental breakdowns or known a life often dysfunctional and out of control. They didn't understand the safety net (whether illusory or otherwise) of a guarded existence.

Enjoying the grandchildren was no problem for Judie. She relished their company unequivocally, overjoyed to hold and interact with these flesh-and-blood little people. I think her enjoyment was enhanced because back at home, she often longed for social and spiritual interaction but was somewhat incapacitated because of a withdrawn and depressed husband.

But she did find outlets with friends that didn't need my involvement. She also joined some groups with intimate friends and began going to church regularly. Eventually I (sort of) joined her by involving myself in an adult Sunday school class made up of kindred religious souls who ranged from freewheeling Christians to confirmed agnostics. It was a simpatico fit for me.

Nights when I had trouble sleeping (still a relatively common occurrence), Beau would creep into my back or slip under the covers. Since he was getting up in age, I often worried about his mortality. How much longer would he live, now that he was twelve or thirteen years old? How much longer would that life be a good life? Now in my seventies, I had the same thoughts about myself.

When I did, I always hoped I would die before he passed away. A life without the little guy whose love and loyalty had sustained me through some of the darkest periods of my life, whose companionship filled the larger part of every day, sounded depressingly empty. More than once, I told him this: "Beau, please don't die before I do. It's okay now, Judie is free to take care of you. I may be gone, but she'll still be here to love you and care for you." He looked and me and cocked his head.

Since I could feel old age undermining many of my physical capabilities, I thought my chances of dying first were good. In addition, I now had some serious health issues, including multiple melanoma surgeries and stage three kidney disease, not to mention the ever-present Curse. I didn't welcome these threatening health conditions, but they played a part in my belief (wish, actually) that I wouldn't live long enough to witness Beau's death.

I did not get my wish.

FRIDAY, APRIL 20, 2015, became the day I can never forget. But then, I've never even tried. I got up at the usual time, between 4:30 and 5:00 a.m., went into the kitchen to start the coffeepot, and get Beau's leash. But I looked around, and he wasn't there; he hadn't followed me into the kitchen. This was unheard of. So I went back to the bedroom and found him standing near the edge of the bed, staring down at the floor. His stiff front legs told me he was afraid to jump down, as he always did the moment I got out of bed, and his head was wobbling.

Something was very wrong. He didn't trust his body to make that leap. I was concerned and confused. My stomach knotted up instantly. When I picked him up to set him on the floor, he began thrashing. Once on the floor, he began walking toward the bedroom door, but he was wobbling from side to side; he collided with the doorjamb before he staggered into the hallway.

I knew immediately that something was terribly wrong. I was so shaken I woke Judie up so she could see what was going on. The poor little dog wobbled and fell as he tried to navigate the hallway. He got to his feet, took a few tentative steps, then fell again. It seemed as if he had lost control of his body.

Judie and I were so alarmed we called Dr. Brunton's emergency number. He told us he could meet us at the office at seven. I wished it could have been earlier as I wasn't sure what to do with the poor little guy for two hours. Judie said what I thought but was afraid to say: "It looks like he's had a stroke."

"Don't even think that," I told her.

"We might not want to say it out loud, but that's what it looks like."

I picked him up to take him outside, but he was thrashing so madly his head collided with my chin, hard. By this time I was feeling truly distraught—how many times had I picked him up and held him? Hundreds? Thousands? But in this case, it seemed as if he was feeling a free fall panic if his feet were not actually safely on the ground. I rushed out to the yard in order to get him there before I dropped him. When I put him down, he fell to his side, tried to get up, fell again, then stumbled in wild circles until he fell on his back. Watching his disoriented struggling brought me a heartbreaking, helpless feeling.

He regained his footing and took a few clumsy sideways steps before he took a long pee. Then he crouched as well as he could to take a poop. I was surprised he could even do these things. He walked crooked and fell more than once on his way back to the front stoop. He put his front legs up, but the back legs stayed on the sidewalk. He needed help to take that eight-inch step up. So I boosted him. We had to follow the same procedure when he got to the doorway, where Judie was holding the door open wide; he got the front feet up but was either unable to lift the back end up or afraid to try. I boosted him again.

He couldn't manage his food or water dish. His balance was too compromised, and his head wobbled too much. Judie hit on the idea of putting his food on a very shallow dinner plate and his water as well. She put them down on the living room carpet to better hold them in place. Lying on his side, Beau was able to eat a good portion of his food, but he could only do it by licking one of the pellets at a time. It was tedious, but he managed. The same with his water dish.

We drove him to the vet's office to make sure we'd get there no later than seven. On the way, I said, "If he had a stroke, it had to come in the middle of the night. Just yesterday I was walking him around the neighborhood, and he was fine."

"It could have even happened in his sleep," she said. Beau was lying still in the back seat. Judie and I were alarmed and afraid. "In fact," I said, "I've taken him on two other walks as recently as last week."

"I know."

Our little dog squirmed madly when Dr. Brunton, after watching him try and walk, lifted him onto the exam table. "He's panicked," the doctor said. "If he's not making contact with the ground, he feels completely out of control and terrified."

"Do you think he's had a stroke?" Judie asked. I was afraid to say the words.

"We can't rule that out. In fact, that's more probable than possible. But let's don't rush to judgment, and let's don't assume the worst. There is a possibility it's an inner ear issue. I'm going to send him home with some medicine that could address that issue and some steroids as well. Then I want you to bring him back in on Monday morning."

I may have spent worse weekends in my life, but at that point in time, I couldn't think of one. Following Dr. Brunton's advice, I used a long winter scarf as a sling to help Beau in and out of the house. I looped it under his chest and belly so he could feel something firm beneath his feet. He seemed to feel grounded, so it worked pretty well. But once I took the sling away, he invariably stumbled in circles and fell backward before regaining his footing. "I think that happens," Judie said, as the two of us watched together, "because he's trying so hard to find a position for peeing and pooping." It sounded sensible. But it was so hard to watch.

Once or twice, he managed to lift himself up onto the stoop; it gave us a sliver of hope. Judie gave him his pills every day. Maybe he would get better. *Maybe he would get better.*

We felt we couldn't let him sleep in the bed at night for fear he would fall off. He seemed somewhat mystified at this change of routine, looking up at me with his wobbling head while falling against the bed frame. "No, Beau," I said sadly, "you have to stay down." For me, every night was restless and mostly sleepless; I got up numerous times to see where he was and what he might be doing. Most times I found him asleep against a pile of dirty laundry or the base of a recliner. He seemed peaceful enough. Maybe he would get better. *Maybe he would recover.*

I often lay next to him on the floor as he licked the individual pellets from the dinner plate and licked down some water the same way.

When we took him back to Dr. Brunton on Monday, we had to be honest: he was not getting better. Wrapped in his favorite blanket (one we'd received from the Humane Society years earlier) Judie held him as he shivered in the exam room. Dr. Brunton decided to take him off the inner ear medication but stick with the steroids. He was very honest with us. "We could transport him to the University of Illinois veterinary hospital for a series of tests like brain scans, but it would cost a lot of money and probably only confirm what seems obvious: a stroke."

"What should we do at home?" I asked.

"Just keep doing what you're doing. Let's see what happens over the next few days. Dogs and cats do recover from strokes, just like some people do."

We continued doing what we were doing, but there was no progress. In fact, he seemed to get worse as the days passed. He wobbled and fell consistently as he tried to walk from place to place. Judie and I knew what day was coming, and it looked like it was coming right soon. But we didn't talk about it. My moments of hope, which were few and far between, came when I saw him sleeping or resting in the prone position. He seemed comfortable, as if nothing was wrong. And I was extremely grateful he could somehow find a portion of peace in this very difficult time.

Sometimes I lay beside him on the floor. I usually held him firmly, the back of his head tucked beneath my chin, his back against my chest and my arm around him. Sometimes we lay face-to-face, and I pressed his face against my cheek. *I wanted to remember.*

One afternoon when Judie was gone, I helped him out into the front yard so he could eliminate. He circled and spun and fell then took care of business. I marveled at the fact that never—not even once—during these days had he had an accident in the house. It was as if he was determined to abide by the rules of the house, no matter what. It seemed like courage as well as an ode to duty.

Once inside, as we lay face-to-face on the carpet, I gave him two or three of his very small dog treats, which he managed to eat. I stroked his head and neck as we looked into each other's eyes. You can only guess what a dog is thinking, but his/her eyes can be a pretty clear window into the soul. I was looking directly into Beau's deep brown eyes, where a longing revealed his soul. The eyes seemed to be saying, "Please."

I felt tears forming; some of them slid down the side of my face and into the carpet. So many times I had needed his help, and now he needed mine. I remembered vividly the countless times in Florida when I was yearning for death, but somehow his pressing love and understanding provided enough comfort and hope to keep me from ending my life.

Now it was he who was suffering and afraid. Now it was he who had no "quality" of life. The eyes seemed to say once more, "Please."

I knew what we had to do to grant him peace. Taking more steroids and waiting day after day for some sign—even if only a small one—would have been selfish and even cruel. And no matter how hard the decision to pull the trigger, I could never allow myself to contribute to his suffering. I held him tight and tucked that little face snug up against my chin. *I wanted to remember.*

The next morning, April 27, we had Beau euthanized. Judie and I drove him to the vet's office in silence. We knew what was coming, but the words would only get in the way. Once again, she held him in the exam room, shivering in his favorite soft blanket. He had always shivered at the vet's or at the boarding place, but this time I indulged the unlikely and unproductive thought that the little guy knew what was coming. *He knows he has come here to die,* I thought, not believing it for a moment, and not forgetting how his behavior was standard in this place. I dismissed this gratuitous theatre from my mind. But my tears were already forming, and I knew I needed to make my way to the waiting room. "I'll put the catheter in," I heard Dr. Brunton say on my way out.

So once again, just as it had played out when we'd had Squeak put to sleep, Judie held Beau tight in her arms until he slumped and lay still. She came out to tell me, "He's gone now. Come and tell him goodbye."

I went into the exam room where his little body lay still on its side on the exam table. Dr. Brunton had left so we could be alone with him. I stroked his warm body from head to tail for quite a while, not daring to speak for fear I would break down in sobs. My tears had already formed.

"He didn't suffer," I finally said quietly. It was a question.

"Not at all," Judie said. "He didn't tremble or twitch or anything. His head just slumped into my arm."

"Did you say anything to him?"

"Yes, I said, 'We will always, always love you, Beau.'"

Then my tears were too many, so I couldn't speak anymore. "I think right now he's thanking us," she said.

I nodded. She was always so much stronger. I got out my handkerchief, wiped my eyes, and blew my nose. Once again, I started stroking that small, warm body of the loving companion who had been such a crucial part of my life the past twelve years.

I BUILT a shrine to Beau in the bedroom, on one of the dressers. I put his cremains inside the little clay pot that had always held his dog treats. I put the lock of his white hair and the plaster of paris footprint beside the pot, as well as his many dog tags, his tennis ball, two rope toys, his little blue winter coat, and a single food pellet I found by accident in the carpet. I taped about ten photographs to the dresser mirror, showing him in all ages and stages and different locations.

The loneliness and loss were present at every turn. I could only sleep in fits and starts. When I got up in the morning to make the coffee, he wasn't there. When I sat at the computer, he wasn't there. When I felt the urge to take him for a walk, his leash was in the usual place, but he wasn't. When I got up in the middle of the night to use the bathroom, his spot on the covers of the bed was empty. When I came home, he wasn't there to greet me with that exuberant tail-wagging enthusiasm. When I sat on our screened-in porch to read the morning paper, he wasn't there. When I sat in the recliner watching a ball game, he wasn't there squeezing his way in beside me.

For weeks, I spent parts of every day in tears. As those weeks went by, I tried to restrict the crying jags to moments alone. I didn't want to keep burdening Judie with my sorrow, as she was making a normal adjustment to the loss of a loved one. My grief was so intense, for so long, I wasn't even moving out of stage one of Kubler-Ross's five stages model.

I took several of Beau's items to the Humane Society. Although I saved the blanket he loved the most, I took several others to the shelter, as well as a Humane Society of the United States (HSUS) tote bag that held his remaining bag of dog food, his leftover doggie treats, and one of those cone collars dogs have to wear after surgery or medical treatments to their bodies. I keep the one blanket on top of the bedspread, remembering each night how he dug at it and fluffed it to suit him.

I kept his leash (with his collar attached) and left it looped over the umbrella stand next to the front door. I still have it. About three months after his death, on a warm July day, I put the leash in my pocket and walked the neighborhood route we had walked so many, many times. I let his collar hang some six inches or so outside my pocket. Doing this only made me cry.

About the same time, I peeled the label off a pill bottle and put just a few of his ashes inside. Then I drove to the old practice field, where I buried the bottle about four or five inches deep. I sat on the grass and gazed across the field, remembering all those times he had taken off at breakneck speed watching for the tennis ball to land and bounce. I was sobbing uncontrollably, grateful there was nobody else around.

I got a thoughtful letter from a dear friend, who had tucked an anonymous document inside the envelope called A Dog's Prayer. The last paragraph touched me deeply, so I cut it out and stuck it on the refrigerator door. I still look at it every morning and visualize again the traumatic moment in late April of '15 when Judie held the shivering little guy in his blanket in the exam room. Love and loss together.

The final paragraph of the prayer reads: "And, beloved master, when the great Master saw fit to deprive me of my health, you did not turn away from me. Rather, you held me gently in your arms as skilled hands granted me the merciful boon of eternal rest—and I left you knowing with the last breath I drew, my fate was ever safest in your hands." The truth herein reassures me but at the same time brings sorrow.

I still stop to gaze at Beau's shrine every morning when I get up and every night when I go to bed. I know it's not normal, but I don't know if it's unhealthy or *how* unhealthy. Even though I have lost parents, a sister, more friends than I can count, and even other loving, precious family dogs, I have never known grief so intense or long-lived. In the cases of those other losses, my grief has been normal, if I apply the Kubler-Ross model of the five stages of grief. It's risky business to calculate grief on any formula, but usually by the end of six months, I'd made an adjustment. In Beau's case, I'm still stuck in stage one—denial.

In some mental health circles, including the psychiatrist's Bible, the most recent version of the Diagnostic & Statistical Manual (DSM), "complicated grief" is listed as an authentic mental disorder. Just what I need. Another mental disorder. This one doesn't prevent me from functioning, but I have no doubt I will grieve the loss of Beau until the day I die. If that's perverse, so be it, but maybe it means I've been blessed with the uniquely enriching, joyous experience of total union with another being.

Judie and I have been dogless now for more than two years. Neither one of us is ready yet for another four-legged family member. Or in my case, when Beau is actually gone, when the day comes that he's truly gone. This is what being stuck in stage one is like, the essence of complicated grief.

If there are no dogs in Heaven, then when
I die I want to go where they went.
—Will Rogers

A Life Without Dogs?

AFTER SOME 38 consecutive years of having a loving canine as part of the family (not to mention the ones that came earlier), Judie and I have accepted the fact we can't in good conscience adopt another dog. Well into our seventies, we're too old, with too many limiting physical health issues. We couldn't give a dog the exercise it needs, and there's a good chance it would outlive us. We have no plan B. After we were gone, would the dog simply have to go back to a shelter?

So many of them have enriched our lives with their steadfast loyalty, love, trust, affection, and fun that life without one seems like a life with a gaping hole. When we visit the Humane Society, we often see a pooch or two we'd like to make our own. But in truth, I haven't made an adjustment to the loss of Beau. I would want a sequel. Or to be even more honest, I would want *him* back. If only death allowed for second chances.

Although more than two years have passed, I feel like I'm still stuck in stage one. Denial. I still have tears when I look at his shrine. I know my life will never be the same again. Part of my enduring sense of loss is the guilt I feel. Couldn't we have waited a little longer? Couldn't we have opened up the checkbook and put him through a series of x-rays, brain scans, and other neurological tests? But then I remember his eyes—those pleading brown eyes that seemed to ask "Please" as we lay together on the carpet. So I try to be comforted by the fact we put *his* interests ahead of our own. We released him from suffering when the time was right and granted him the peace of eternal rest.

EVEN THOUGH I am vigilant about taking my psych meds, I still have restless nights followed by days of discouraging fatigue. And even though the pot doesn't boil over, I still have days of fairly acute anxiety/depression. I understand that there will be days like this for the rest of my life. It's a comfort knowing that Seroquel and Klonopin can hold the Curse in check, but it's also a little scary when I stop to think those pills are all that stand between me and very likely another round of disabling mental crisis.

Writing is still difficult because of concentration and focus issues. I often travel the same terrain again and again in my mind while wanting to move forward with an outline or a book project. But I don't give up; I refuse to accept the notion that I can no longer be a successful author. If writing a complete manuscript is a heavy lift, so be it.

I do manage to write an effective newspaper column each week. Several of the columns have been about dogs, and I share some of them here.

Our son, Jason, now in his forties, is happily married, with two wonderful young children of his own. He has a good job with a large corporation. He is an excellent employee, husband, and father, whose ability to multitask seems to have no limits. Jason has never experienced the Curse, even on a superficial level. The genes he inherited from his mother seem to prevail. For that I am eternally grateful.

Normalite Dog Columns
By James W. Bennett

"Toto" was Really "Terry"

THE STORY GOES that circa 1935, while he was away on vacation, MGM studio head

Louis B. Mayer instructed his studio people to "Drop the fat one." He meant Judy Garland, but the folks back home let Deanna Durbin go instead. In the blink of an eye, she signed with Universal.

Durbin and Garland were MGM'S winsome ingénues, a pair of singing teenage beauties destined for stardom. According to MGM Days, "When Mayer found out that Judy Garland was still at the studio and Deanna was gone, he was very upset."

Maybe so, maybe not. The story probably has a 50/50 rating on the apocryphal meter, as do many of the Hollywood tales and rumors associated with Garland and Durbin, MGM and Universal studios.

My interest in Durbin has always been keen, but gap filled because of her early departure from Hollywood. But already I digress.

THE CAPTIVATING little dog we know as Toto, primarily due to her major part in 1939's *The Wizard of Oz*, was a Cairn Terrier named Terry who appeared in many movies between the years 1934 and 1945.

Had this dog been quick to housebreak, she probably never would have had a movie career. Willard Carroll, author of *I, Toto*, a book new to our local libraries, reports it this way: "Exasperated with their own failed attempts, her Pasadena owners deposited her at the Carl Spitz Hollywood Dog Training School, located in North Hollywood."

Many of Spitz's dogs—including St. Bernards and Great Danes—were players in Hollywood movies.

As a dog lover and movie buff, I had to check this book out. Carroll writes much of it as an "autobiography," as if the dog herself were telling her own story. Cute stuff, but no barrier to a wealth of movie information.

Spitz trained and directed Toto (Terry), at age one, in her first silver screen appearance as Shirley Temple's dog "Rags" in *Bright Eyes* (1934). She appeared in 6 other films before her 1939 signature role with Garland, alongside stars like Ida Lupino, Fredric March, Walter Brennan, Mickey Rooney, and Spencer Tracy.

Terry had roles in ten other major motion pictures after "Wizard." Her final role was in *Easy to Look At* in 1945. She died shortly after and was buried at the Spitz training compound.

AS YOU'D EXPECT, the book contains a lot of information about Garland and Toto in "Wizard" production. You might not expect, however, to discover that the iconic production wasn't the first attempt to bring the 1900 L. Frank Baum novel to stage or screen. Not by a long shot.

The full title of Baum's novel, by the way, is *The Wonderful Wizard of Oz*.

A 1902 Broadway production, *The Wizard of Oz*, came first. Then according to Carroll, "*The Wonderful Wizard of Oz*, a 1910 one-reel silent film adaptation was produced by William Selig. The 1925 Larry Semon vehicle left out the dog. The 1933 Ted Esebaugh animated short portrayed Dorothy with her dog, Toto, as a partner in the complete journey."

Toto's "autobiography" revisits many of the 1939 Technicolor movie's production fits and starts, from scripts revised and junked to director Victor Fleming's sudden departure to take over another movie also mired in numerous production snafus. It was called *Gone With the Wind*.

The cute canine had a starring role in "Wizard," and it created challenges for Spitz. She appeared in nearly every scene, had to bark 44 times on cue, and had to sit still on that metal tractor seat throughout Garland's rendition of "Over the Rainbow."

THERE ARE MANY stories that link Durbin to the role of Dorothy, none of them verifiable and none thoroughly explored in *I, Toto*. Some have it that she turned down the role. Others say MGM executives wanted her for the part, but Universal wouldn't "loan" her back to the studio that gave her her start. We'll probably never know the "real" story.

Durbin was the singer that Judy Garland could only dream of becoming. Garland was a very good singer; Durbin was a great singer. Her classically-trained lyric soprano voice put her in a comfort zone with spellbinding operatic arias or popular standards. All by the age of 17.

Her first two movies for Universal, *Three Smart Girls* (1937) and *One Hundred Men and a Girl* (1938) were blockbusters that thrust her into international stardom and saved the studio from bankruptcy, according to most film history sources. She made these films at ages 16 and 17.

Durbin, who died in April of this year at age 91, "Retired from the movies at age 28 and never looked back despite appeals from directors, studios, and fans," according to *USA Today's* April obituary article. From the date of her silver screen retirement until the time of her death, she lived privately in a small village outside of Paris. That's nearly 65 years. We can only assume she was happy.

She was the highest-paid actress of her era. According to the newspaper obituary article, "She made *Can't Help Singing*, her first and only Technicolor film, in 1944. Her other films were in black and white because studio executives said it was too expensive to have Deanna Durbin and color film in the same movie."

It's too bad "Toto" never got to work with her or hear her sing. He probably could have held his perch on a tractor seat all day long.

I, Toto, is a quick, fun read I recommend for any aficionado of Hollywood history. It would appeal to adolescents as well.

Dogs Vs. Cats? I'll Take the Canines

RECENTLY, I was driving an older man than I to a doctor's appointment. We were driving on Clinton Boulevard in Bloomington when I slowed down to avoid hitting a dog that had wandered onto the street. "Whadja do that for?" he grumbled. "The only good dog is a dead dog."

We'll call him Harold. He's a small minded, provincial curmudgeon but I stayed the course in the direction of his appointment. I did push back a bit: "Try telling that to blind people," I said, "Or cops in charge of canine units." He just "harumphed" at me.

He and his wife are cat lovers; they always have two or three roaming inside their home. I don't know why they have so many; neither he nor his wife pay them much attention as far as I can see, but his jarring remark took the age-old dog vs. cat argument to extremes.

I was talking to an old friend the other day who was extolling the virtues of his adult son's newest cat. He started by saying, "I know you don't like cats, but—"

"Not true," I interrupted. "I like cats, I just like dogs better. My wife and I have had cats for pets in the past." I think my position on the dog v. cat argument is far more prevalent than Harold's "dead dog" school of thought.

In the comic movie *Meet the Parents*, Ben Stiller says to his future father-in-law, a cat lover played by Robert De Niro, "I like cats okay, I just like dogs better."

"I'm sorry to hear that, Greg, that you're attached to such an emotionally shallow animal."

This is the usual claim by cat lovers, that dogs long for the affection and attention of their owners. They are "needy," while cats are independent.

DOG LOVERS (myself included) have to concede that claim. Dogs require more time and energy in terms of house training, for one thing, and need to be taken outdoors or walked on a leash frequently each day. You can't go away for a weekend and leave them alone with a litter box and a big feed bowl.

It is this independence that impresses many cat owners; it seems like strength of character. You may be fond of them but they don't really seem to need you (or anybody else for that matter). But not in all cases; there are some cats that like to share their owner's affection; lap dogs are common, but there are lap cats as well.

On the other hand, dogs are far more likely to seek you out on a regular basis and cherish your affection. Their loyalty is usually warm and unequivocal. They want to "be" with you and feel your approval. For these reasons they seem more "human" than their feline counterparts.

IN ANY CASE, Harold's heartless remark, although not new or original, stayed with me for a couple of days. I almost wished I'd have dropped him off at the corner and told him he could walk the rest of the way. Using his walker.

Had he been younger (and healthier) I would have given him a laundry list of items extolling the virtues of "man's best friend." For here's the thing: Dogs not only seem more human, they can be trained to take on human responsibility and do so consistently and reliably. The list, which would have featured a series of rhetorical questions, would have sounded something like this:

When is the last time you saw a seeing-eye cat leading a blind person safely across a busy intersection or along the corridors of a crowded mall?

When is the last time you saw a hunting cat first pointing out the game, then retrieving the fallen prey?

When is the last time you saw a feline unit deployed by the police to subdue an aggressive criminal suspect? Or leading the chase to track down a kidnap victim?

When is the last time you saw a drug-sniffing cat ferreting out contraband in airports, schools, or a dope dealer's house?

When is the last time you saw a bomb-sniffing cat risking its life to locate hidden explosives in a forward combat area, in many cases saving the lives of U.S. GIs? For that matter, when is the last time you saw such a cat lose its life in service to its country? Or receive a medal for combat heroism?

When is the last time you saw a trained cat charging to the rescue of a stranded skier on a snowy mountain slope?

When is the last time you saw a trained cat herding sheep or cattle?

THE LIST could be longer, of course, for even the sheep can be useful and functional, often put to work by government entities to keep the grass closely cropped in certain municipal problem areas.

Although some people take this disagreement seriously, dogs vs. cats is an argument that can't be "won" or "lost." What works is pretty simple: There are dog lovers and cat lovers. What doesn't work on any level involving human sensibilities is "the only good dog is a dead one" mentality. The next time Harold asks me for a ride I may just turn him down.

"He's Not a Dog, He's a Soldier."

A SEPTEMBER 2 feature by conservative columnist Jonah Goldberg (USA Today) left me angry enough to throttle somebody in the Pentagon. But who?

The good news was Goldberg got through a complete column without leveling an attack on President Obama. I wonder how much that hurt.

The bad news was his report that "retired" military dogs are often left behind when troops return home, leaving them "to languish in shelters—or worse." We are left then with the scenario of loyal military canines who risk life and limb sniffing out mines and IEDs, abandoned as strays in dysfunctional, dangerous locations like Afghanistan.

I told a fellow dog lover this practice was deplorable. "It's worse than that," he snapped. "It's evil."

According to Goldberg, here's where the problem lies: "Once they are too old, too shell-shocked, or simply not needed, the dogs are automatically declared equipment that can be left behind like a latrine tent. The military sometimes says they are 'retired' and become 'civilians,' but the result is the same because these civilians don't have a right to military transport home."

It comes as no surprise that these dogs' soldier handlers are devastated when their canine companions have to be left behind overseas. Gerry Proctor, a spokesman for Lackland Air Force base told CNN, "A handler would never speak of their dog as a piece of equipment. The dog is their partner. You can walk away from a damaged tank, but not your dog. Never."

GOLDBERG tells us that attempts have been made to get Congressional involvement. "Legislation pushed by Rep. Walter Jones, R-N.C., that would require military dogs to be retired only upon return to the U.S. has been languishing in Congress for years. No politician wants to be accused of caring more about dogs than people. But that's largely a false choice. The cost of finding room on military transports is negligible. Even if it did come at some additional cost, so what?"

But because of Pentagon policy, "Handlers are sometimes forced to make incredible sacrifices to get their four-legged comrades home on their own."

Lance Cpl. Kent Ferrell, handler of German Shepherd Zora, explains in the Animal Planet documentary *Glory Hounds*, a 2013 production, "There are those who consider our military dogs to be pieces of gear. I, for one, do not believe that at all. To try to remove your heart from the situation is really asking too much of a handler."

He goes on to add, "We can see how vital these animals are [in a combat setting], but also how powerful the bond between the handler and his canine comrade is."

THE GOOD NEWS comes from the private organizations that work (with money and established channels) to ameliorate this morally bankrupt pentagon policy. Three of them are: K9s of the War on Terror, the American Humane Association (not to be confused with the Humane Society of the United States), and the United States War Dog Association.

K9WT's mission statement reads, "To recognize the contributions, accomplishments, and sacrifices made by the K9 teams of the U.S. Military, Department of Homeland Security, and law enforcement in this nation's War on Terror." The organization advocates presenting the K9 Medal for Exceptional Service to deserving K9 teams.

According to the official Web site, "This medal represents the first of its kind to be awarded to animals in the War on Terror. At present the United States is the only major country that does not recognize its war animals with a medal."

The USWDA has created an adoption program for retired military working dogs (MWDs) at Lackland Air Force Base. "Law enforcement, private handlers or private citizens can adopt. Last year about 75 dogs went to law enforcement agencies. Those law enforcement does not accept go to private homes. Approximately 290 dogs ended up in private homes in 2009."

The AHA confirms the Goldberg claim: "A number of dogs are already brought home once their tour of duty ends," says Spokesman Scott Sowers, "however, some are retired overseas," meaning they cannot be brought home on military transports or on the military dime. "[Military] Contractors who also rely on dogs often leave them behind too."

Appalled by the practice, Sowers' organization is looking to Congress to help. According to a July 24 article by Randi Martin, "Members of the organization had a briefing on Capitol Hill Wednesday."

An emotional Kathleen Haybig testified, "He is not a pet, he was my partner. He's not a dog, he's a soldier." Haybig adopted her partner, Bagio, after they both returned from combat and wears a tattoo of him on her arm. "They all need to come home," she said, "because just like us, they are veterans too."

Do I hear an "Amen?"

Another Lost Dog Story

LIKE MANY area readers, I enjoy *Pantagraph* writer Bill Flick's well-crafted, often quirky columns. For my wife Judie and me, his December 6 article about lost dog Rusty, who eventually found his way to a "forever" home went beyond "enjoy."

It brought back poignant memories from some 40 years ago.

According to Flick, Rusty, a young beagle, was one of several Wish Bone Canine Rescue dogs at an adoption event held at O'Brien Mitsubishi in Normal. When he unexpectedly slipped his collar and somehow avoided traffic on Veterans Parkway, he was off on an 8-day adventure.

"By the dozens," Flick writes, "people began posting comments on Facebook." Rusty was spotted at Meijers, the Chateau, the airport, and along Towanda-Barnes Road, among several other places.

Finally, according to Flick, "A homeowner near a far southeast side subdivision, Old Farm Lakes, had heard about Rusty's romp and spotted him. That's also where, wooed by 'a piece of chicken and a friendly hand,' Rusty walked up close enough for the homeowner, 73-year-old Art Wynn, to grab him up into his arms."

"He was shaking and very hungry and he was scared," says Art. "Within two days," Flick informs, "the Wynns—Marsha is Art's wife—had fallen in love, announced Rusty had found a home and filled out adoption papers."

Rusty's rush to freedom no doubt turned lonely and frightening, but the story has the happiest of endings.

NOT SO for our unhappy misadventure with the family dog Nanook back in March of 1974, when I was teaching at Orange County Community College in upstate New York. She wandered away from home in a Catskills blizzard and we never saw her again.

But we have hoped over all the years a family like the Wynns found her and took her in. It was the last, best hope we had at the time and still is on the occasions we recall her disappearance. Forty years turns a lot of calendar pages, but the heart wants what the heart wants.

Nanook (we often called her Nanny) was a Labrador-Malamute mix who, when full grown, reached 70-80 pounds. We raised her from a pup. She was a gentle, affectionate soul, about a year and a half old when that winter storm set in. She was perfectly matched to grow up with our son Jason, who celebrated his first birthday near the same time.

We meant for her to be "his" dog.

At that time, we were renting a quaint country stone house built in 1780, some six miles north of Middletown, where the college campus was located. A dairy farm was on the same property, surrounded by some small meadows and hundreds of acres of woods.

Nanny was accustomed to roaming those wooded areas, but always came home early in the day and sometimes didn't even leave the yard. She wore a collar with a county registration tag.

THE DAY the storm set in, Judie drove to town to pick me up at the college. Before she left the house, she let Nanook out. She didn't want the dog trapped in the house in case we got stranded in the storm.

We got back home (barely) late in the afternoon, but heavy snow was blowing the county road closed.

That night, Nanny didn't come home. It had never happened before. She was built for snow and cold, but that did little to lessen our anxiety. We called for her near the woods, but there was no response. Neither of us got much sleep.

Because the blizzard continued through the night, all the local schools, including the college, were closed the next day. Still no Nanook. We called the police, the local radio station, the dog pound, and the Humane Society to report our missing dog.

We couldn't do much right away to look for her, as the snow was too deep and the county roads were not yet plowed.

WE TRIED—unsuccessfully—to avoid imagining the worst. What if she got lost and disoriented in the storm, without food, and froze to death? What if she got snared in a beaver trap? What if she found her way onto a road that was plowed and got run over?

Unfortunately, these awful outcomes seemed plausible since she was wearing her registration tag; anyone who found her could have confirmed ownership by simply calling the county health department.

Days turned to weeks with no leads or contacts. There were many more restless nights. The stress of *not knowing* was acute. We never gave up hope completely, looking throughout the woods as best we could, taking note of occasional large dogs we spotted near our area, checking our contacts. But there did come a day when we had to face the fact our special four-legged family member would probably never be coming home.

Finally, Judie said to me one day, "I am just going to hope that some loving person has found her and taken her in. Some dog lover just couldn't resist keeping her, tag or no tag. She won't be ours to love, but she will be someone else's to love and care for. She will be healthy and happy."

I latched onto that immediately. And so it was when I read Flick's column about Rusty. Somewhere in those Orange County Catskills, 40 years ago, dwelt an Art Wynn, holding out a piece of chicken and a big heart.

Death of a Family Member

THIS IS a selfish column really, since so many readers have already been here, done this.

I'm only telling you (except for certain details) what you know. You too have suffered the loss of a loving, four-legged family member.

The grief is still so raw I have to work my keyboard through occasional tear-stained glasses. I've been advised to wait a while on this, but for some reason getting through it now seems best. Many of you will understand. For my own good, then:

April 27 was a glorious, sun-splashed spring day but we took no pleasure from it. Instead, there was thick gloom in our house. It was that morning our dog Beau drew his last breath in the vet's office.

There are a few things I'll try to forget. Take the last three days of his life, for instance. He awoke one morning having suffered a stroke sometime during the night. I tried to coax him off the bed to take him outside, but he was unable to stand up straight or walk without falling.

An emergency trip to the vet brought him home with some steroids, but there was no improvement. For three days, he was unable to lift his head or avoid falling. He could only eat by lying on his side and licking up food pellets, one at a time. In the front yard, he circled wildly, often staggering, so disoriented he couldn't find the direction of my voice.

The morning of the fourth day, his condition having worsened, we made another trip to the vet. We hated to discuss the option of euthanasia, but hated more the idea of trying stubbornly to keep him alive so he could suffer longer. His little 14-year-old body had little chance of recovery.

He went peacefully while my wife, Judie, held him in her arms. On our drive home, the grief seemed almost too much to bear; for 12 years he had been our daily loving companion and a source of constant joy and companionship.

On a less traumatic level, I'll try and forget the brutal, dark winter mornings when I took him out on his leash and snow up to his neck made it nearly impossible for him to maneuver to a spot where he could "take care of business."

FAR MORE NUMEROUS are the fondest of memories, the ones I'll hold on to. We adopted Beau, a Bichon Frise, about 13 pounds, from the Humane Society in late spring, 2003. He was two years old, white with brown eyes. He had the Bichon's hypoallergenic coat, so there was no reason to keep him off the furniture.

He was fond of Judie, but for whatever reason, attached himself primarily to me.

Around the house, whatever my destination, it was his too. Bathroom, porch, kitchen, bedroom. When I sat at the computer desk, he curled himself beneath it. If I watched a ball game or movie from the recliner, he jumped up to join me, usually resting on my chest.

In bed, he nudged in beside me, often demanding more than his share of the covers. At times, he liked to crawl beneath the blanket, wedging himself against Judie or me.

It's an amazing thing in life to find somebody who always wants to be with you, no matter what. Good days or bad, good times or bad. To him, I was perfect.

I will always remember how he ran like the wind in an open athletic field when I threw his favorite tennis ball far and high, how he snatched it often on a high bounce and then ran back so we could do it again. He never tired of playing tug of war with his rope toy, or slamming it around on the floor.

MOST OF ALL, I'll treasure the long walks we took together. For years, walking has been my primary form of exercise and Beau was good on a leash from the first day we brought him home. Over the 12 years together we must have logged hundreds—if not thousands—of miles.

When he first became a member of our family, we lived in the Cedar Crest neighborhood in Normal. Our daily jaunts took us near BroMenn hospital, then around the Immanuel Bible Foundation, and along the winding sidewalks among the charming arts and crafts homes in that part of town.

In spring, 2004, we moved to Naples, Florida. The warm climate meant Beau and I could walk nearly every day of the year. And so we did, up and down the neighborhood; he was always alert for the occasional lumbering armadillo. He thought he wanted to catch one, but wouldn't have known what to do with it. When we got back home, I took off his leash in the driveway and watched him scramble along the front of the house searching for geckos.

We moved back to B-N in January, 2007.

Right now Judie and I are going through many disorienting "firsts." No dog to greet us exuberantly when we come home. No need to go outside early in the morning or late in the evening, No need for saving plastic poop bags. No dog underfoot when we are working at the kitchen counter. No little beggar hanging around my chair hoping for a small chunk of my pizza crust (which he usually got).

For the rest of my life I will be grateful for the warm days of April we've had this spring that allowed us to take several walks through our East Bloomington neighborhood. We relished the splendid spring moments delivered by the warm sun, the crocus, the daffodils, and tulips. I had no idea these few special days would be our last chance.

I thumb through the photos of our loyal little guy. We try to take comfort knowing he came to us without a home and we provided a loving, safe, and stable one.

I wish for—make that long for—one last chance to hold him, preferably on my lap, on our porch, with his paws draped over my arm, so he could scan the big world outside. But you already knew that.

Big Duke Makes a Comeback

APRIL 17: Another time, another place, and the youngster's tears might have brought him ridicule. In the locker room, for instance, or on the playground. A bloody nose, or a split lip. What kind of tough guy are you anyway?

But on this occasion, he wept as adults might have done, were they still innocent enough.

His name was Clay, he was 10 or 11 years old, as near as I could estimate, and he was stroking the flank of an at-risk Great Dane named Duke, a recent arrival at the Humane Society of Central Illinois (HSCI) in Normal.

Clay was visiting his Twin City grandparents from the Southwest, and was in the company of his grandmother, volunteering for dog duty at the shelter, which can include watering, walking, cleaning bedding, poop patrol, or merely providing some TLC.

Or all of the above.

Unlikely though it seemed, Duke was able to stand, albeit with a lowered head. He was a living skeleton, so emaciated his ribcage could have passed as a museum display. We had to wonder when he'd had his last meal.

He was infested with fleas.

Somehow, he was alive, but without signs of life. There was no vigor, certainly no sign of any capacity for activity. From time to time, with the large head lowered, he took feeble swipes with his back legs at the pests winning the war along his bones.

Clay and his grandmother gave him pats along the ultra-sharp hip bones, picking at fleas as they went. That's when the tears welled up in a sensitive boy who couldn't help weeping for so much suffering, the part he could see as well as the part he could only imagine. Or the part that might be yet to come.

Duke's neglect was so profound it went beyond physical suffering and took away his dignity. He was degraded. Clay's grandmother and I could only shake our heads; the human capacity to ignore or tolerate the misery of other living creatures seems to have no limits.

BECAUSE I'm a Human Society volunteer, I have had occasion to scratch the big guy behind the ears, or tug at the stuffed animal he often carries in his mouth. Nowadays, he lifts his head higher.

The starving dog arrived at the Humane Society shelter (corner of Kays Drive and Towanda Avenue) on July 16. He came from a small town in our area where a veterinarian had alerted HSCI to his condition.

Once Humane Society investigators got involved, Duke's owners were ordered to relinquish him. He arrived weighing 117 pounds. "We were astonished when we weighed him," says Jennifer Jobe, HSCI animal care coordinator.

Ideal weight for a two-year-old male Great Dane would be about 175 pounds, according to Abby Dirks, an animal specialist at the shelter who has raised three of the biggest breed herself.

Since Duke's stomach was shrunken and nearly dysfunctional, the first challenge was to establish a feeding strategy. According to Jobe, "Our shelter vet examined him and stated the first step we needed to take was to set him up on a specific diet. We needed to monitor his food intake daily and make sure his body was adjusting well.

"We have gradually increased his food each week. He is on a feeding schedule that contains three meals a day. Our shelter vet comes in each week and examines him to see how he is progressing."

In the beginning, progress was slow. Duke could only ingest small amounts of food and even then, digestive difficulties occurred. In the weeks that followed, he gradually gained appetite. Six weeks have seen his weight increase to about 135 pounds, still far from the goal, but a significant improvement.

Dirks recalls the day she burst into the shelter office to declare, "Jenn, he's up to 132 pounds!" Because of her previous experience with the Great Dane breed, she says, "I knew from the day he got here that he would be my baby!"

SOME BABY. 36 inches high at the shoulder, Duke is a little taller than the breed's average adult male. His weight gain has resulted in increased vigor. He carries his head higher, and is able to stroll the grounds on a leash.

His slow but steady progress has been especially gratifying to the organization.

"Everybody wants to walk him," says Jobe. "He's become the office favorite, the staff favorite."

Some days, he gets to stretch out on the office floor while HSCI employees man the phones work their computers, and do business with the public. Like most members of his breed, Duke is quiet, gentle, people loving, and laid back.

It won't be hard finding an adoptive home for Duke. "Last week," says Jobe, "we finally brought him up front to the office, and there were at least three families taking a serious look at him."

But it won't happen immediately. The shelter is following the course of continued caution. "We're taking more time with him, because he is such a special case," says Jobe. "We'll have him for at least a couple more weeks to make sure his weight is stable."

It's unusual for HSCI to house purebred dogs, and especially so for Duke's breed. "We don't get a lot of purebreds," says Jobe, "because they often go to breed-specific rescue organizations. But in Duke's case, we didn't contact any rescue groups; we chose to work with him ourselves."

And work they have done. The final goal will be bittersweet. "Once he is up for adoption, it will be hard to see him go, because he has become such a part of our everyday life here at the shelter," says Jobe. "He is truly our gentle giant.

"But, at the same time, it will be wonderful to see him leave with a family who wants him for who he truly is, a great companion. Duke deserves a second chance at a good life. He has so much to give."

As fortune would have it, Duke will get that second chance. I just hope Clay hears about it.

Mufasa's Journey

THERE'S NO quit in him, even though the trip has been a rocky one. And besides that, the road home may lie just ahead. Everyone associated with his rescue certainly hopes so.

Mufasa is a "real trooper" as Humane Society of Central Illinois (HSCI) staff here in Normal are wont to say. A pure-breed Chow who has resided at the shelter a little more than six months, he had his eyes surgically removed on January 9.

Before that, he was a blind stray wandering the streets and alleys of Streator. Somehow, he survived. Nobody knows if he was abandoned or simply lost, but he found his way to somebody's back yard last summer.

"He could have been dumped," says Stacey Bill, an HSCI animal care specialist, "by somebody who didn't want to pay the veterinarian costs required by his advanced glaucoma. Or he simply could have gotten loose from his owner somehow and wandered off. We don't have any way of knowing for sure."

The Streator home Mufasa "found" rendered a split decision. The son wanted to keep him, but Mom said no. So the son tied him out in the back yard, fed and watered him. At least the lost dog was safe from traffic.

But not safe from pests. When Mufasa arrived at the Normal shelter, he was suffering not just from blindness, but from "fly strike," a condition caused by relentless bug bother. The tips of his ears were bloody, the fur nibbled away. It's one of the few places where a Chow, a.k.a. Chow-Chow, with its dense double coat of fur, is vulnerable.

The dog stayed at the Streator whistle stop for about a month, fighting off flies and other insects.

Mufasa was taken in by the local shelter after the mother in Streator, who had denied the dog entrance to the family circle, made an important phone call. "She knew a woman who no longer lives in town, but who had worked as a shelter volunteer for many years in the past," says Bill. "She made the phone call, and our former volunteer recommended us as a place to care for Mufasa."

So Mufasa took up residence at HSCI (corner of Towanda Avenue and Kays Drive) on September 12.

FROM THE beginning, Mufasa required special attention. Walking a blind dog on a leash can be tricky business. In early January, the care got extra special. His eyes had to be removed.

The surgery was performed by Dr. David Bussan of Town & Country Animal Hospital in Normal. HSCI has a regular working relationship with Town & Country.

Ms. Bill says, "The animal care team and the vet were able to determine there was intense pressure on his eyeballs." Bilateral enucleation (that's what they call it when they take out both your eyes) is a radical procedure, but in this case was deemed necessary.

According to Donna Beltran, a veterinary technician at Town & Country who assisted in Mufasa's surgery, "The procedure is rare, only done if the eyes have no function left and may be causing discomfort."

The dog's blindness, caused by advanced glaucoma, suggested he might have pain. Since animals can't discuss discomfort with medical providers, veterinarians use a device called a tonometer to determine eyeball pressure. After applying numbing eyedrops, vets use the tonometer to take pressure readings from each eye.

"We usually take three readings," says Beltran, "and then average them out." Mufasa's numbers were too high by plenty.

"Once the eye is removed," Beltran explains, "we place a spongy material called gel-foam in the empty eye orbit. It's necessary because when an eye is removed, a lot of blood vessels have to be ligated. Gel-foam helps the clotting. Then the doctor sutures the eyelids closed."

Such surgeries aren't cheap. The Humane Society is grateful to the University High School Earth Club, which donated $250 to help defray the cost. The club has been working with HSCI for the past several years.

Mufasa recovered well back at the shelter, although it took some time. He had to wear one of those clumsy protective cone collars for a while, so he wouldn't paw at the stitched eyelids. He tried to paw his way after balls and other toys but not much luck there either.

During the first couple of weeks after the procedure, he and collar collided with gates and waste baskets and doorjambs, but he was "A real good boy about it all," according to more than one HSCI staff member. There was no behavior to suggest he might be discouraged or frustrated.

HUMANE SOCIETY staff members know—have always known—it won't be easy to find Mufasa a home. A special-needs dog will need a special owner. Ms. Bill reports that several people have shown interest, but in the end, "They are just not sure about taking that jump, involving the particular challenges."

And yet, maybe not so daunting after all. A fenced yard would be on the wish list, says Bill, "So he and the owner could have at least a little liberty. Mufasa adapts well and orients quickly. Stairs probably wouldn't be a problem once he learned his way around. A person with a blind dog would want to avoid moving furniture around because a blind dog is more dependent on routines than others."

At times the Humane Society staff has allowed Mufasa to spend the day, or part of it, in the front office. "He does well in the office," Bill reports. "He manages well."

Mufasa is a basic couch potato, a laid-back canine who takes nearly everything in stride. He enjoys human affection but doesn't demand it. "He's not needy," says Bill.

This temperament is common to the breed. "The Chow is very intelligent," writes Steven Miller of the American Kennel Club, "but like a cat, not as highly motivated to please the master as most other breeds." In fact, the breed has been accused of aloofness. Miller sees it a little differently: "The Chow saves his affection for those he loves most dearly and finds little reason to seek it from strangers."

The Chow breed dates back to ancient China and during some of the emperor dynasties was celebrated on pottery and in sculpture. Its lion-like appearance was regarded as regal.

At 50 pounds, Mufasa is also breed typical. His narrative has been one of hardships, but there are chapters yet to be written. "Since the surgery," Ms. Bill declares, "Mufasa is in a much better place for adoption. He just wants to soak up love and hang out."

Don't Buy that Doggie in the Window.

IF YOU'RE THINKING of buying that cute pup in a pet store window to place 'neath the Christmas tree this year, here's some advice:

Don't do it.

You may have a Christmas morning of children squealing with delight, but you also (most likely) will have a pet whose health is in question and—again most likely—will have contributed to the discouraging and inhumane industry of "puppy mills."

A friend of mine recently recounted for me his unhappy experience with a puppy he bought from a local pet store. The store is no longer in existence, but my friend's memories of the adventure are as fresh as an open wound.

The contract with the purchase required Charlie to have the pup examined by a veterinarian within 24 hours. He couldn't get an appointment with his vet for three days. When he did get in, the little fellow died on the examination table.

When Charlie went back to the store, hoping to get his money back, the owner told him he hadn't met the terms of the contract. 24 hours meant 24 hours. Charlie was out of luck, after being thrust into some untimely grieving.

A DISCUSSION OF the puppy mill industry is not for the squeamish. It brings us face-to-face with unspeakable cruelty practices distinguished by disregard for the emotional and health needs of dependent, sentient beings. All to make a buck. Quite a few bucks, actually.

The National Humane Education Society (NHES) is a leader in the movement to put an end to puppy mills through education, legal action, and legislation. It's a brave but daunting mission, for wherever there's money to be made, the deck is always stacked.

NHES literature reminds us that, "Animals that come from puppy mills can frequently be unhealthy and they can also exhibit behavioral problems. Their lack of contact with people and their early removal from their mother often result in unsocial behaviors which surface as the puppy grows up.

"The U.S. Department of Agriculture is responsible for monitoring and inspecting kennels to make sure they are not violating the housing standards of the Animal Welfare Act. Unfortunately, kennel inspections take low priority at the USDA so kennels are not regularly inspected."

The casual brutality of puppy mills is evident from some of its standard operating procedures. Again, quoting from NHES literature, "Puppy mill kennels usually consist of small wood and wire mesh cages kept outdoors. Female dogs are bred continuously, with no rest between heat cycles. Mothers and their litters often suffer from malnutrition, exposure, and lack of adequate veterinary care. Continuous breeding takes its toll on the females, and they are killed when their bodies give out and can no longer produce enough litters."

The organization urges people to avoid shopping in pet stores that sell puppies. I suppose that would be consumer leverage, if ever so limited.

THERE ARE NO longer any stores in Bloomington-Normal that sell puppies, although there used to be, and there are still plenty of them in nearby communities. Not to worry, though, for our community has a number of far better adoption opportunities for those who want a dog for the holidays and beyond. These pets long for that "forever" home.

These dogs may or may not be that cute puppy, but they for sure are well cared for and have received ongoing veterinarian care. Local shelters like the Humane Society of Central Illinois, Wishbone

Canine Rescue, and McLean County Animal Control have terrific dogs available for adoption every day.

Here's a little contact information: The Humane Society at 423 Kays Drive, Normal, can be reached at 451-1000 to determine visiting hours for pet viewing. They have a very good Web site.

Wishbone has its adoptable dogs in foster care homes around the community. You can find them sometimes at PetCo on Sundays. These pets have been cared for and loved by generous, caring families. Visit their site at: www.wishbonecaninerescue.org.

You can call McLean County Animal Control at 888-5060. Maybe it's just the "pound," but the facility always has terrific dogs waiting for that loving home.

Here are just a few pictures from the Humane Society and Wishbone sites:

"Will Daisy go to Heaven?"

THE FEAST of St. Francis of Assisi, the patron saint of animals, is held on October 4 of the liturgical calendar of the Roman Catholic Church. Often on that day, priests read from the ritual book as they confer blessings on pets of church members and others.

When we lived in Florida, one October 4 we took our dog Beau to a local church to receive such a blessing. A dozen or so dogs and a few cats were under control of their owners among the pews. When we were invited to join the priest at the altar, we stood around him (pretty much in orderly fashion) as he began the blessing.

I have saved the bulletin that included the ritual and the actual blessing. It is too long to quote in full, but here are a few of the salient portions: "The animals of God's creation inhabit the skies, the earth, and the sea. They share in the fortunes of human existence and have a part in human life. God, who confers his gifts on all living things, has often used the service of animals or made them symbolic reminders of the gifts of salvation.

"And animals share in Christ's redemption of all of God's creation. We therefore invoke the divine blessing on these animals through the intercession of St. Francis of Assisi, whose feast day we celebrate today."

The priest then blessed each pet individually by placing his hand on the animal's head, saying the prayer, blessing with the sign of the cross, and then sprinkling with holy water.

I'm not exactly sure why we took Beau to experience this ritual, as knowledge of an afterlife or eternal life (for humans as well as animals) is practically impossible to come by. Even the Bible has little to say about it.

I only know it felt somehow uniquely worthwhile.

NOT SO LONG AGO, our son Jason and his family had to have their ailing dog Daisy, a Border Collie, euthanized. Judie and I were in their home when our 8-year-old granddaughter, Sailor, asked what euthanasia meant.

"It means," Jason explained, "the vet just gave her a shot and she went to sleep so sound she never woke up."

"Will she go to heaven?" Sailor asked.

What answer was forthcoming I can't remember. The adults in the room probably stumbled to some sort of an equivocal yes.

Sailor's question was the same as mine some 65 years ago when we had to have our lovable shepherd mix Shep put to sleep.

Adults who answer "yes" to this question are generally thought to be romancing the magical thinking on file for Santa Claus or tooth fairies. Not to be taken seriously by those who have come of age, but just to try and mollify the tender psyche of a child.

BUT NOT SO fast perhaps. Although a discussion of the after-life is a highly confusing proposition with little Biblical guidance or consensus, some significant theologians have found potential room for members of the animal kingdom. Two of them are John Wesley (founder of the Methodist Church) and C. S. Lewis.

Wesley, a profoundly thoughtful 18th century Anglican Priest and bullish advocate for social justice, also had a streak of the animal rights advocate. He deplored animal cruelty and/or neglect.

According to an installment of the *Conversation in Faith Weblog*, in his Sermon 60, "The General Deliverance," "Wesley gives reasons why we should spend time considering the condition and fate of animals. When we see how much God cares for creatures, we can rest assured God cares more for us. And because God cares for animals, we also should care for them."

Like Lewis, he maintained the suffering of animals as well as humans began with the Fall in the garden. It was only then that humans began to slaughter beasts for food or fear attack from them. Prior to Original Sin, God's vision (Genesis 1:29–30) was that green plants and fruit were to be the diet for all creatures. Carnivorous activity necessitates death and suffering.

Again, quoting from the *Weblog*, "Wesley makes the case that animals will be part of the New Creation. He claims they will be restored 'to a far higher degree . . . than they ever enjoyed' before the Fall."

This view brings to mind Isaiah 11:6–11, "The wolf will live with the lamb, the leopard will lie down with the goat, the calf and the lion and the yearling together . . . and the lion will eat straw like the ox . . ."

Lewis, like Wesley, held that Christ's death on the cross not only redeemed mankind, but all of creation as well. In a passage from his book *The Great Divorce*, he writes of a woman arriving in heaven with a collection of animals in tow: "Every beast and bird that came near her had its place in her love. In her they became themselves. And now the abundance of life she has in Christ from the Father flows over into them."

BACK TO WESLEY. The *Weblog* also states, "Wesley notes [in Sermon 60] that since animals are not moral agents they cannot sin, but yet they suffer. The problem of animal suffering may cause us to question God's justice. Wesley writes that 'something better remains after death for these poor creatures also; that these, likewise, shall one day be delivered from this bondage of corruption and shall then receive an ample amends for all their present sufferings.'"

So yes, Sailor, there may well be a place for Daisy in heaven after all.

About the Author

James W. Bennett has written several critically acclaimed books for teens and adults. He has been a community college English teacher, special education program assistant, church youth minister, resident camp manager, photographer, basketball coach, night janitor, and a newspaper columnist. He currently resides in Bloomington, Illinois, with his wife, Judith. He has a son, Jason, who is married to Dayna. James and Judith relish their two grandchildren, Sailor and Finnegan.

CPSIA information can be obtained
at www.ICGtesting.com
Printed in the USA
BVHW03s1859120318
510379BV00001B/64/P